DISCARD

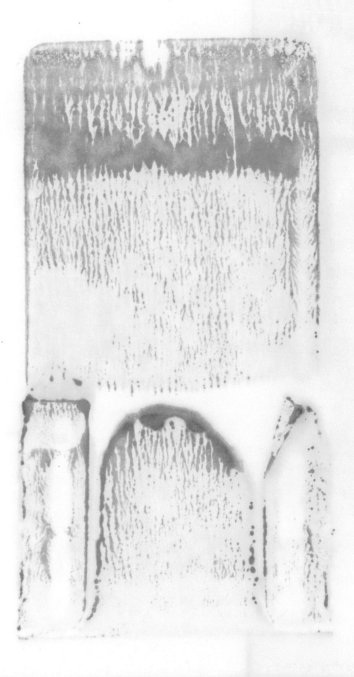

BOOKMEN'S BEDLAM

An Olio

BOOKMEN'S BEDLAM

of Literary Oddities

By WALTER HART BLUMENTHAL

Essay Index Reprint Series

BOOKS FOR LIBRARIES PRESS
FREEPORT, NEW YORK

Reprinted from a copy in the Rutgers University Library

STANDARD BOOK NUMBER:
8369-1022-2

LIBRARY OF CONGRESS CATALOG CARD NUMBER:
77-80383

PRINTED IN THE UNITED STATES OF AMERICA

TO A QUARTET OF DEPARTED CRONIES
WHO WERE CHRONIC BOOKMEN:

Dr. A. S. W. Rosenbach

Alwin Scheuer

Arthur Pforzheimer

Wilbur Macey Stone

FOREWORD

You may have heard about the man who lent his neighbor a dictionary he had received as a present. When the neighbor—who soon returned it—was asked if he liked it, he replied: "Yes, but I would have liked it better if it hadn't changed the subject so often." We may chuckle over the story, but the truth is there are, in fact, too many subjects!

The New York Public Library has eighty miles of bookshelves. As of June 30, 1954, the Library of Congress had 10,155,307 books and pamphlets, and 14,282,594 manuscripts, letters, and written documents. By way of contrast there is a library that holds only one book! Built at Amritsar, India, of costly marble, copper, and gold leaf, it enshrines the holy book of the Sikhs.

Some folks read books, some collect them, some do both. But few amass huge garners like Robert Hoe, whose private library brought $1,932,056.60 at seventy-nine sessions of auction dispersal in 1911–1912; or like Jerome Kern whose collection sold for $1,729,462.50 in 1929. Not many mortals can read more than a score or two volumes a year, nor find time to do more than keep apace of the literature in their respective vocations. And likes and leanings incline them willy-nilly to limit the choice of their reading.

There is a pertinent fable recounted by Anatole France. When young Prince Zemire succeeded his father on the throne of Persia, he summoned all the wise men of his kingdom. Telling them he wished to benefit by learning about the mistakes of the past, he commanded: "Write me a history of the world, and make certain that it be complete."

After a lapse of twenty years the learned men reappeared before the king, followed by a caravan of camels, each bearing a hundred volumes. The king, engrossed in affairs of state, expressed his gratitude, but pointed out: "I am now middle-aged, and even if I live to be old I shall not have time to read such a long history. Abridge it!"

After laboring fifteen more years the learned men returned, followed by three camels bearing each a hundred volumes, and reported: "Here is our new work; we believe that nothing essential is omitted." But the king, grown older and ailing, demurred and demanded further abridgement.

Ten years later they came back again, followed by a young elephant bearing only a hundred volumes. "This time," they said, "we have been exceedingly brief." "But not sufficiently so," replied the king, "condense and make haste."

Then, five years later, the sole surviving wise man appeared, walking with crutches and leading a small ass bearing one large book.

"Hurry!" called an officer. "The king is at the point of death."

"I die," grieved the king, "without knowing the history of mankind."

"Not so, Sire," answered the aged man of learning: "I can compress it for you into three words—'They were born, suffered, and died.'"

That bulk is not synonymous with merit is pointed in that satire of Daniel Defoe, *The Compleat English Gentleman,* wherein he relates how a grown-wealthy squire who, having acquired a fine house, desired to fill quickly the shelves of his newly appointed library. Entering the shop of a bookseller he looked about and then inquired: "Pray, Sir, what shall I give you for all the books upon that side of your shop?" When after a bit of haggling the deal was consummated, books did, indeed, fill the squire's shelves. But his possessions formed no library, for the result of all he had acquired was but its outer semblance.

Though there be all manner of books, yet must the discriminating devise his or her own selection of them. Taking for our own text Shakespeare's query in *Timon of Athens*, "What particular rarity? What strange?" in the pages which follow we shall meander among those volumes that attract by reason of their peculiarities. Long ago the author of the *Ship of Fools* concerned himself with a parcel of strange books; and through the centuries such curiosities of the shelves continue to reflect the foibles, frailties, and follies of humankind. Almost every large library has a little group of books that provoke the "Oh, my!" of visitors, aghast or agape at the odd or the ornate, the singular or the sumptuous.

To seek to encompass all the many varieties of queer volumes within the covers of this book were like spreading a net to catch the wind. Here is a mélange, a parade of pages for those who, like Hamlet, bring to the rehearsal an "antic disposition." Behold the droll, the deranged, the depraved among books—all the bizarre, the bazaar of lore and annals of the beaux arts. There are all manner of strange books in the tragicomedy of the shelves. Men have been immolated for their books and men have been immortalized. But it is the uncommon rather than the classic, the obscure as well as the renowned, which one seeks to find in the sideshows of the literary circus. And when one puts a second book beside a first, 'tis then that one becomes a collector!

There are many aspects to the unusual; volumes in nowise eccentric may capture a collector interest by their odd or fresh approach to a particular subject. A Philadelphia collector of Lincolniana finds zest, apart from his range of volumes about that president, in trying to secure copies of the books Lincoln is known to have read. Aside from the fact that *Pilgrim's Progress* is one of many classics of English literature, the prison provenance of its writing might inspire a quest for other instances of authorship behind the bars. Books written by the blind—sightless authors of inner vision—might stimulate another collection, as might also books illustrated by their authors, from Lear, DuMaurier, Thackeray, Kipling, to Pyle, Remington, Van Loon, and Cowboy Russell. Unfinished

novels such as Dickens' *Drood* or Hawthorne's *Dolliver* may appeal to
one, suppressed books to another, cryptography to a third. One might
apply that plush word concinnity to such purpose and pursuit. As most
mortals seek escape from the humdrum treadmill of everyday existence
by occasional roaming, so here we shall seek recreation along the many
curious bypaths of bookdom, ramblings which lead to strange encounters.
Indeed—borrowing from *The Tempest*—they lead "from strange to
stranger."

This strangeness is as diverse among books as among mortals. It
may concern the physical volume—the typography, paper, binding, or
ink; or the contents; or the circumstances of authorship; or perhaps the
effects produced by the volume in the world at large. But occasionally
there are items which refuse to fall into any one of these convenient
categories; just as queerness itself tends to defy definition in a strict
sense, so the written projections of men's minds often baffle pigeonhole
(or Dewey-system) grouping. Yet in this very fact lies a clue to the
fascination of the pursuit; a hint that there is more than meets the eye
suggests the banal may become the baroque.

Examples of unusual attributes of the physical properties of a book
abound and are comparatively easy to classify. The Houghton Library
at Harvard possesses several fourteenth-century manuscript rolls
measuring when unwound thirty to forty feet in length. One of the
earliest forms in which books were made, these manuscripts are usually
classified as Roll Books.

An example of contents unusual in conception is that wise and
amusing little book, now perhaps out of print, called *Lincoln's Doctor's
Dog*. No one would suspect from the title that it treats of best-sellers and
how to write and publish them. But the author, George Stevens, points
out that all books about Lincoln sell well, as do books by doctors or
about doctors, likewise about dogs. Obviously, we conclude, the world's
best-seller of all time should have been *Lincoln's Doctor's Dog!*

An instance of strangeness in the circumstances of authorship may
be found in Paul Green's *Mr. Mac's History* of a decade ago. Combining

fact and fiction, this is an informal, affectionate chronicle of the Little
Bethel region of North Carolina as seen through the eyes and wisdom
of Mr. Mac, the local historian, who wrote his history on strips of
wallpaper torn from the side of his cabin.

How a volume may become extraordinary by reason of the abnormal
effects it produced can be envisioned by harking back to that forgotten
incendiary essay of 1857, *The Impending Crisis of the South* by Hinton
Rowan Helper, who advocated shipping Negroes back to Africa. Helper
argued that the South was economically prostrate because of slave labor.
His book caused more of an uproar below the Mason and Dixon line than
did Stowe's *Uncle Tom's Cabin*—and in Arkansas three men were hanged
by mobs for possessing copies of it.

Every volume having the habiliments of strangeness, for this or that
reason, serves as a peepshow to the past. It is the intent of the pages
which follow to open up a little vista off the beaten track of routine
reading for those who find the strange convolutions of the mind
intriguing, who share the opinion that even heaven would be monotonous
if all souls were alike.

CONTENTS

BOOKMEN'S BEDLAM

CAVE, CRYPT AND COFFIN

IT IS PASSING STRANGE that the attachment for books should not have led more men to insist their cherished volumes be interred with them. In ancient Egypt it was the embalmer's custom to encase with the mummy of an author whatever manuscripts of his there were at hand. Indeed, the earliest recorded bookseller was an embalmer of Nile gentry who traded in papyri during his spare time. What with the sentimental customs to which humans are addicted, it could be rather a nice ritual. Eugene Field was one author who did express the desire that certain of his books should be buried with him, and if this be egotism it is of the pardonable variety.

Collectors, too, could find it unacceptable to be parted forever from a favorite volume, though few would feel the excessive devotion of Frederic R. Marvin's "book-lover in the wild West who," he tells us in his delectable *Excursions of a Book-lover*, "wished that after his death his body might be opened, and that under his ribs, close to his heart, there might be stowed away a certain little book that he had treasured through many long years."

Of course this is a bit excessive in the way of post-mortem devotion; most of us would be content with a tomb-tome apart from personal excavation by the mortician! And while our too brief bodies need not be cloven to embrace a book, it would be a usage comportable with culture if every true lover of literature were put away with a chosen volume or two to comfort the ultimate boredom of his bones. But such is the pettiness of man, that we regret our words "or two" the instant they are inadvertently added; for we foresee those whose vanity would not stop at two, but swagger graveward with two hundred.

Rossetti's consignment of his unpublished poems to the coffin of his wife, and the exhumation seven years later to recover the manuscript parcel, forms a macabre incident in literary annals. In an article in the October, 1933, issue of *The Colophon*, Janet Camp Buck relates that the wife died in 1862 at the age of twenty-nine "in circumstances indicating suicide"; and that in 1869 resurrection of the gray calf-bound holograph volume was entrusted to a friend named Howell to whom Rossetti wrote: "The book in question is bound in rough gray calf and has, I am almost sure, red edges to the leaves. This will distinguish it from the Bible also there as I told you."

Gabriel describes the recovery of the bound manuscript in a letter to his brother dated October 13, 1869: "All in the coffin was found quite perfect; but the book, though not in any way destroyed, is soaked through and through and had to be still further saturated with disinfectants. It is now in the hands of the medical man who was associated with Howell in the disinterment and who is carefully drying it leaf by leaf." The proceedings were cloaked in secrecy, but were later disclosed through a probable breach of confidence on the part of one of the participants.

From another source comes the report of eight sheets which were interred in a little oilskin case, containing a group of sonnets which Rossetti wrote while his wife lay dying. These sheets, subsequently in the possession of a noted bookdealer, appear to have been additional to, if not part of, the gray calf-bound volume that was exhumed—another relic of the mortuary library Rossetti regretted when he fell in love seven years after the interment.

Before books became a drug on the market in cheap reprint form or remainders, vended like grocery supplies and commercialized out of all countenance, the regard in which they were held was naturally less casual. Not that the caliber of the contents was more enlightening or sustaining, but a plethora of printing has the effect of rendering commonplace what once was distinctive. As with synthetic pearls or reproduced paintings, the access of mechanized craftsmanship in publishing has led to the dissemination of books like so many bricks. The glut of books has vastly increased since Job lamented that there was no end of them. These rather oblique reflections were stimulated by coming upon a passage in Professor Charles R. Morey's "Introduction" in a volume devoted to the Morgan illuminated manuscripts, wherein he says: "It is a fact often noticed by classical archeologists that, while in the earlier periods of antiquity the deceased is commonly represented on his tombstone as a warrior or in some physical function, it was the custom on late Roman tombs to depict the dead as reading, or holding a book."

The late Holbrook Jackson in his precious garner of booklore devotes several pages to bibliotaphs, among whom he includes those who bury themselves among books, or who cram their homes to the rafters with unread volumes merely out of possessive mania. But among those who designated books to be put underground, or stipulated other funerary deposit, he overlooks one or two pertinent instances.

Before citing these, however, we chronicle with delight the touching and unique proviso of that bookseller and bibliographer, James Edwards, who bought and dispersed many noted collections in England and on the Continent, and whose careful catalogues were commended by Dibdin. His own private library, accumulated at his country seat and sold in 1815, included the famous Bedford Missal. Dying at Harrow the following year, he left written instructions that his coffin should be made out of some of the stout shelves of his library; and it was done as he desired.

Sir Thomas Browne expressly willed in his last testament that his Elzevir *Horace*, "worn out with and by me," should go into the grave with him to solace oblivion. In the will of Sir Thomas Ormond, dated 1515, that devout Earl directed: "I will my Sawter boke covered with whyte lether and my name written with myne owne hands in th' ende of same shall be fixed with a cheyne of Iron at my Tombe ther to remayne for the Service of God." The chained *Psalter* long kept its vigil where the body was buried in the church of St. Thomas Acon, upon the north side of the "high aulter."

Still earlier, William Lyndewood, Bishop of St. David's and author of the *Provinciale*, by his will bearing a date in 1443 directed that a copy of his book should be kept chained in the upper part of St. Stephen's Chapel at Westminster, where he was buried, to serve as a standard text to which any and all future editions should be referred. This practice, while not so frequent as to be called a custom, had not lapsed in more modern days, for as late as the seventies there was a Bible chained to a tomb in the church of St. Michael-at-Palace, Norwich, England.

One of the most celebrated of early English bindings—dating from the seventh century according to G. D. Hobson, or from the tenth century according to Gordon Duff—is of decorated red goatskin over thin boards of limewood (5¼″ by 3¾″) and encases a manuscript of the Gospel of St. John which came from the coffin of St. Cuthbert in 1104. It is now at Stonyhurst College, Blackburn, England. As tradition has it, this relic was buried with the body of the saint at Lindisfarne in the seventh century. Soon thereafter the friars set forth with the coffin and other relics to find a new monastic site. When they came to Durham, "they could not draw his coffin all of them which formerly was lightly drawn," so they remained there and built the Cathedral. When the tomb was opened St. Cuthbert's Gospel was removed to the muniment casket of the Cathedral. Thence, after the dissolution of the monasteries, it passed through other hands until brought from Liège to Stonyhurst by one of the Jesuit fathers about 1770.

The centuries afford other instances. It is said that when Charlemagne died in 814 he was buried with an engrossed copy of the Four Gospels, in gold characters on purple vellum, in his hand. According to one tradition, this manuscript was taken out "when the tomb was broken open by Pope Otho III," and came into possession of a library at Aix-la-Chapelle, where in the palace the imperial library and atelier of Charlemagne had been located. Or as Goldschmidt describes it: "The Vienna Gospels on which the German kings used to take their coronation oath is supposed to have been discovered by Otto III on the knees of Charlemagne when the former had the Emperor's sepulchre opened. A second Gospel manuscript is an old possession of the treasury-chamber of the cathedral at Aix-la-Chapelle, a third preserved in the library at Brussels. . . ." At the present day one of these Gospels of Charlemagne in jeweled binding is in the Victoria and Albert Museum, London, but the provenance is uncertain. This may be the exhumed exemplar. Or it may be the Gospels in the Schatzkammer in Vienna.

The ways of ancient Egypt were wondrous strange, and it must have been a nuisance for the influential to mollify such a clutter of gods. Even though a concept of monotheism arose in the Eighteenth Dynasty, the old theogony lingered on. The literature of the pharaohs, such as it was, is mostly gone. But there is a mortuary aspect that must not be missed. Though not a bookish people in our sense, the builders of the pyramids were literate in a cumbersome way, and relished having texts in their last resting-places. Maspero writes that one of the tombs of the Fourth Dynasty designates its once mortal contents "Scribe of the House of Books." But these were not books ranged on library shelves; they were tiers of jars, each vessel containing one or more papyri rolls in upright stance.

Closer to our topic were the funerary inscriptions, known as "Coffin Texts," which were found upon the inner linings of caskets in which the nobles and elect had been interred. These marginalia of death which have been collected and edited by Breasted and others, show that the mortician and the scribe were cronies. The fragments of "Antiope" found by Flinders Petrie were used as inner wrappers for a coffin of about 100 C.E.

Linen mummy cloth was used by the priesthood of the Nile to receive writing; and linen was similarly inscribed in certain rituals of ancient Rome, as mentioned by Pliny and Livy. The material was of a texture unequalled today.

Osiris, according to Egyptian belief, questioned the dead, and

weighed their merits. Those who met with rejection were forever confined
to their tombs, famishing and athirst. Hence, to fortify for either
contingency, to placate the gods or nourish the dead, burials included
talismans and gifts, food and drink.

But chief reliance was upon portions of the *Book of the Dead*—
priestly prayer formulas and exorcisms intended to appease, or
hoodwink, Osiris. The laity believed that these texts had been composed
by Thoth, god of wisdom, for the benefit of the pilgrim soul. Concocted at
various periods, copies of this compilation, or portions, were buried with
the mummy; and of the thousands of papyri still extant, a large
proportion are fragments of the *Book of the Dead* in numerous differing
texts. This collective title was given by Lipsius, for the Egyptian
appellation to these safe-conduct papyrus rolls found in various tombs
was "Coming Forth [from Death] by Day." To the ancient Egyptians it
was the alpha and omega of the death trip—a celestial guidebook.
"Selections from it were painted upon the mummy-cases," we are told,
"chapters from it were often enclosed with the corpse; sentences from it
were engraved upon the walls of the tomb; the living, if they were wise,
painfully learned large portions of it word by word." Through a span of
centuries its 166 chapters were compiled; and from a thousand tombs and
mummy wrappings its text has been rescued and pieced together.

Lost books have been rescued from the bosom of the earth to which
chance or intention had consigned them. The extra-canonical *Book of
Enoch* was for a long time known only through versions in the Ethiopic
and Slavonic languages, although it was first written in Greek. In 1886 a
papyrus was discovered in an early Christian grave at Akhmin, Egypt,
containing thirty-two chapters of the original text.

Of the sixty-three Coptic manuscripts in the Pierpont Morgan
Library, fifty large parchment volumes in ancient bindings, dating
between 823 and 914 c.e., were found in 1910 by a group of Arab
workmen in sand dunes skirting the southern edge of the Fayoum Oasis
in Egypt, where once stood the monastery of St. Michael of the Desert.
In digging for garden soil close by the ruins of a former building site

these Arabs discovered a brick vault in which the volumes had been buried
a thousand years ago when a general destruction of monasteries and
Coptic churches occurred. The Scriptures had been rendered into several
Egyptian idioms during those early centuries when Coptic (the Arabic
term for Egyptian) holy orders dwelt along the fringe of the desert. A
remnant of the Egyptian people had resisted absorption through eight
centuries of Graeco-Roman rule as well as the subsequent Moslem
conquest, and the Coptic language survived as a spoken tongue into the
sixteenth century. The finding of those fifty volumes was a landmark in
the annals of unearthed literary treasures.

One of the Coptic bindings in the Morgan Library is a seventh-
century specimen in which the upper and lower boards are formed of
sheets of papyrus covered with brown goatskin which is adorned with
plaques of cutout red sheepskin. It is believed to have once encased an
Egyptian version of the Gospels on papyrus. Though not one of the relics
dug from the sand dunes in 1910, it belongs in the same category.

Remarkable in all its details is the story of the discovery by Sir
Aurel Stein of a sealed and hidden library of precious Oriental
manuscripts in a spur of the ancient Wall of China. That scientist headed
expeditions in 1907 and 1911 into Chinese Turkestan and adjacent parts
of innermost Asia. There, in a walled-up cell or chapel in the "Caves of
the Thousand Buddhas" at Tun-Huang were piled 1130 bundles, each
neatly sewed up in fabric, and each containing ten or more manuscript
rolls.

The cave colony was founded in 366 and the cell was walled up in
1035. Sir Aurel Stein learned of the repository from a Taoist priest. The
bundled manuscript rolls were piled about ten feet high in a nine-foot-
square chamber. The finds, dating from the beginning of the fifth century
to the end of the tenth, after having been sealed up for nearly nine
hundred years, were in sound condition and included the world's oldest
printed book, a copy of the Diamond Sutra (*Chin Kang Ching*), a
section of the Buddhist scriptures. Dated 868 and well preserved, it is
now in the British Museum. Its text was one of the most widely read

works in Buddhist literature. It is so called because as the diamond transcends all other gems in brilliance so does this in wisdom. Precious beyond price, Carter states: "This is the oldest printed book known that is dated, or of which the date can be ascertained. Some undated book from Turfan or elsewhere may conceivably be older, but it seems unlikely."

The Diamond Sutra shows a technical proficiency superior to the block printing that preceded the era of Gutenberg in Europe. The book has six sheets of text and one shorter strip bearing a pictorial woodcut, the whole pasted in sequence and forming a sixteen-foot roll. From the size of the sheets (2½' long and almost a foot wide) the size of the blocks from which the sheets were impressed can be visualized. Concluding the text is the colophon: "The ninth year of the Haien-t'ung reign, fourth moon, fifth day [May 11, 868] by Wang Chieh, for free general distribution, in order in deep reverence to perpetuate the memory of his parents." Other than this brief epilogue, nothing is known of him, but he, too, is or should be enshrined in the world's memory as the first known printer of books.

Also among the mass of manuscripts in this Buddhist cache were some dated more than a century later than the printed Diamond Sutra, indicating that here, as in Europe, printing did not immediately supersede calligraphy. Among the thousands of manuscript rolls were only three other printed bookrolls and one small folded specimen. This latter folded sutra, dated 949, consists of eight pages, printed on one side only in the manner of block books. In one lengthy strip of paper, it was folded to form pages in the manner of a present-day timetable, except that the folds at one edge were pasted together. Thus it is truly a book, this concertina-style (as it has been called) marking here as elsewhere the transition stage between the ancient roll and the later stitched method.

Among the various other rescued papyrus relics of Egypt is the Edwin Smith Papyrus now in the Library of the New York Academy of Medicine. This onetime roll, measuring 15' 4½" by 13" bears twenty-two columns of medical text. It was acquired at Luxor in 1862 by the Egyptologist whose name it bears, and by whom it was cut into sections

and framed between glass. Translated by James Breasted, it is the oldest
extant specimen of surgical and therapeutic knowledge. The assumption
is that it was preserved in a tomb.

Literary papyri from the Nile region and cuneiform clay tablets
from dune-buried cities of Assyria and Babylonia still come to light, but
scroll records on animal skin and parchment were more disposed to
decomposition than laminated fiber or baked bricket. In Egypt thirty-five
hundred years ago, the vizier Rekhmire was not only the keeper of arcana
in the Temple of Amon, but also the high judge having custody of the
forty books of the law, the forty skins or leather rolls of the *corpus juris*
which were required to be on hand when court was convened. Rekhmire is
depicted on his tomb with the forty rolls before him—a memorial of a
book collection of the fifteenth century B.C.

A strange echo of the American past harks back to the Pharoah era
when linen mummy swathes bore hieratic symbols. During the Revolution
and into the early nineteenth century, rag linen for paper conversion was
scarce in the stripling Republic, as it had also been in the colonies, and
papermakers besought Yankee shipmasters sailing overseas to bring back
bales of paper potential. Shortly after the War of 1812 one enterprising
captain brought from Alexandria a partial cargo of linen wrappings
which had been removed from thousands of Egyptian mummies. Quite
possibly more than one edition of an American book of the time was
printed on paper from this source, and the noted contemporary printer,
Joel Munsell, mentions its use for one of the issues of a newspaper.

Darius the Great sought to defeat time by causing to be carved on
the face of the cliff of Moung Behistun in Iran the record of his victories.
High above the ancient caravan route from Persia to Babylonia an
enormous petroglyph is hewn on the huge surface of native stone. Carved
in three languages in three columns, it measures fifty-two feet long and
more than twenty feet tall. So, too, Rameses III flouted oblivion on the
massy pylon at Thebes.

Tomb texts of the pyramids have but recently come to light, and it
was in 1953 that Biblical scrolls were found by Arab shepherds in a cave

on the shore of the Dead Sea. And men still seek to perpetuate their story. An eight-foot, torpedo-shaped tube of copper alloy was exhibited at the New York World's Fair in 1939–1940. Containing a Bible on India all-rag paper, and an eleven-million word microfilm account of twentieth-century civilization, this Time Capsule was sunk in a fifty-foot well and sealed with concrete in September, 1940, to await inspection by the earth-dwellers of A.D. 6939.

Sometimes eccentric individuals employ queer methods in striving to perpetuate themselves. William Hope Harvey, for example, author of the little paper-covered *Coin's Financial School*, which sold half a million copies despite its monetary fallacies. Harvey ran for President on the Liberty Party ticket in 1932, and he erected a concrete pyramid at Mena, Arkansas, sixty feet square at its base and towering 130 feet. Therein was immured a "history of our civilization and the cause of its downfall."

Sometimes authors have no forewarning of the demise of their works. A biography of Peter Cooper by Thomas Hughes, who wrote *Tom Brown's School Days*, is an instance. The entire edition with the exception of six author's copies was suppressed by the Cooper family and reportedly buried in Cooper Union, then under construction.

De Quincey tells of John Stewart, whose return-to-nature cult was to be imparted to posterity by prevailing on disciples to bury copies of his works, so that the enmity of opponents might not consign his views to oblivion. These books were to be "properly secured from damp, at a depth of seven or eight feet below the surface of the earth," and the secret of their interment confided to one of the new generation by each possessor on his deathbed.

Other instances are recounted by Holbrook Jackson, including the garden burial by Augustine Birrell of a nineteen-volume set of Hannah More because it bored him and took up needed shelf-room.

In the days of the alchemists Basil Valentine, searcher for the Philosopher's Stone, hid all the manuscripts of his pseudo-scientific delvings under a marble slab behind the altar in the Abbey Church at

Erfurt; and there they might have remained for an indefinite time had not a storm dislodged them.

Not unlike this is the story of the memoirs of General de Caulaincourt, published in 1935 under the title *With Napoleon in Russia*. An intimate of the emperor and close to him in the historic retreat from Moscow, Armand de Caulaincourt died in 1827, leaving two copies of his memoirs. One of these was sent to Paris uncorrected; the other, corrected, was walled up in the family château in Picardy. The family refused to permit publication, until Caulaincourt's grandson, the third Duke of Vicenza, began the preparation of an edition at the outset of World War I. The German Army mined the château, and in 1933 an architect investigating the ruins discovered the corrected manuscript in a battered tin chest.

A score of years ago an American dealer in Chinese art came into possession of a fifteenth-century bronze cross-legged Buddha eight feet high, which had formerly belonged to the actor Richard Mansfield. The seated figure was on a drumlike pedestal covered with hundreds of small engraved Buddhas. A concealed panel was detected in the back, and the hollow chest of the Oriental god was found to be stuffed with manuscripts, coins, and other objects. There were seven Chinese prayer books, the binding of one in silk worked with endless knots—a Buddhist symbol. In addition to these there were a number of rolls containing invocations, inscribed on rice paper and rolled into tight cylinders resembling large Chinese firecrackers. All these tokens of worshippers were revealed by chance in moving the figure to the dealer's premises.

According to doubtful tradition, the so-called Laws of Numa, legendary second king of Rome, were buried with his remains. Livy and Plutarch relate that two stone chests were found in 181 B.C., one alleged by the inscription it bore to have held the corpse and the other his book rolls. The first when opened was empty. The second is said to have contained fourteen scrolls treating of laws, priestly and civil, and other matters. These volumes were publicly burnt as subversive of the current trend. Skeptical authorities on early Roman history, however, declare the supposed lawbooks were forgeries, planted and exhumed for politi:al purposes.

It is a long story. The sacred books of Thoth or Hermes are lost. Diocletian destroyed Egyptian manuscripts "lest her magicians blast his empire with their incantations." Severus collected all writings on the mysteries and buried them in the tomb of Alexander the Great. It is a long leap from then to the story of Khuda Baksh, gatherer of Oriental books and manuscripts, who, dying in 1908, was buried as he ordered in the inner open court within the walls of his library at Patna on the Ganges. His was the finest collection of Moslem literature in private hands, and the British Museum had sought in vain to acquire it.

In Philadelphia, Dr. James Rush and his wife were interred in the extant Ridgway Library that was then his home. They were buried in a vault in the building, the bodies by the prescription of the testator being imbedded in concrete. His large collection of books was made available to the public after his death, with the designation Ridgway, the maiden name of his wife. And a few years ago, a copy of the writings of René Descartes was buried in the French Pantheon with appropriate ceremonies, although his heart had been left in Sweden, where the philosopher died, when his remains were brought to France long ago.

Little known, but remarkable, was the practice in Ceylon of burying or immuring sacred *ola* manuscripts in Buddhist shrines (*Dagobas*), together with precious objects of gold and silver, as well as gems. One such incomplete list is cited in the administration reports of Ceylon for 1889, together with "a rough memorandum of their cost as given in the records kept in the temple." This extraordinary inventory includes:

> *Five prakarma* [*books*] *of the* Vinaya Pitaka, *written on silver plates* ....*7,500 rupees*
> *Seven prakarma of the* Abhidharma Pitaka, *on silver plates* ....*9,480 rupees*
> Digha-Nikaya, *and a number of other books of the* Suttra Pitaka, *on silver plates* ....*2,200 rupees*
> *Several titles of works on* ola *leaves* .... *345 rupees*

> *Two covers for a book, silver and gold, studded with*
> *gems* ....*2,525 rupees*
> Satipatthana, Pratimokôha, *and other religious books,*
> *written on 37 plates of gold, each weighing five*
> *sovereigns* .'..........................*1,980 rupees*
> Tataka Atuwawa, *written on 900 copper plates, each three*
> *spans long* ....*2,250 rupees*

There were in addition hundreds of gold, silver, and bronze relics, ornaments, gems, including "603 precious stones, 2,000 uncut stones, ten crowns, and many other things." Needless to say, no such buried literary treasure is known elsewhere in the modern world; for buried it virtually is, in the particular shrine in which the assortment of propitiatory tributes is immured.

It was an ancient Hebraic custom for worn and blemished scrolls of the Law to be placed in an earthen vessel and buried in the grave of a scholar. The earliest reference thereto is Talmudic (Megillah 26b). Authorities cited for this practice lived about 300 C.E., but the custom was much older. It may have arisen out of the ancient usage of burying with a man the objects he had most used in life or which he most prized. There was also the purpose of avoiding desecration of the written name of God through burning or inadvertent casting away, a motive that later led to the establishment of a "genizah," literally hiding or hiding-place, in each locality.

The burial of Hebrew books, present-day instances of which occur from time to time in orthodox communities, is in accordance with this venerable practice. It is observed in Bagdad and in Brooklyn, N. Y. The Hebrew term *genizah* is better known generally since the discoveries half a century ago by the revered Dr. Solomon Schechter, who restricted the use of the word chiefly to the hoard found in the old synagogue near Cairo.

In medieval times and since, worn scrolls or scraps of parchment and leaves of paper containing the names of God, known as *shemoth*, were not thrown away, but relegated to a hiding- or burial-place because

of the sanctity they received from such inscriptions, and to avoid
profanation. Most ancient synagogues had literary morgues (*genizoth*)
that included broken ceremonial objects, fragments, and, latterly,
defective or desecrated scrolls. In course of time mere secular writings, if
in Hebrew characters, were accorded a like treatment.

In some Eastern countries today burials of *shemoth* take place every
decade, when a memorial is pronounced, followed by a feast, and on these
occasions the right of burying each sack is sold as a *mitzvah*
(blessing). One month later a stone is laid over the place of burial and
inscribed as the genizah of that year. Elkan Nathan Adler states:

> In the Orient generally, "shemoth" are from time to time
> deposited temporarily in some corner or cupboard of the
> synagogue, often below the ark or "almemar." When the
> collecton grows too big, or when some special occasion arises,
> such as a drought, the papers are solemnly gathered up and
> carried off to the "bet hayyim" and buried there with some
> ceremony. With this custom is associated the far older
> practise of burying a great or good man with a "sefer"
> (scroll) which has become "pasul" (unfit for use).

This, in gist, comprehends an unusual custom in what might be
termed mortuary booklore. "In Morocco, in Algiers, in Turkey, and even
in Egypt, such paper-interments continually occur," we are told, "and
not the least important part of the Taylor-Schechter collection has come
from the graveyard."

In Prague the genizah is between the roofbeams of the old
synagogue, and according to legend this secret storeroom is protected
from unfriendly intrusion. At Bokhara also the roof conceals a chamber,
but, curiously, "disused scrolls of the Law are walled up by stucco in
arched alcoves surrounding the interior of the building."

When accessible and recovered, the jetsam of genizahs constitute
valuable material for research, and their contents are pored over by
scholars in the field of Semitics and history. The Cairo genizah is the

most famous site where such manuscripts were consigned to intended
oblivion. For more than thirteen hundred years this synagogue at Fostet,
near Cairo, was frequented. The secret cache, above one end of the
gallery, lacked an entrance, but, through a hole in the wall, reached
only by a ladder, books and manuscripts were dumped for more than a
thousand years! It was only in modern times when the synagogue
underwent repairs that the depository was disclosed.

A mass of these parchment and paper relics was found in the
synagogue receptacle and in the Jewish cemetery outside the modern
city. Local dealers in antiquities soon became aware of this treasure
trove, procured specimens by clandestine methods, and sold them where
they could. Adler writes: "When Sayce visited the synagogue many of
the contents of the genizah had been thrown out and buried in the
ground, through a part of which a road was subsequently cut. This
would account for the evident exposure to dampness which some of the
oldest fragments have undergone and for their earthy odor. Sayce
acquired many fragments from the caretakers of the synagogue, which
are now in the Bodleian Library. Other libraries and collectors made
similar acquisitions."

It was the identification of a part of the Hebrew original of the
long lost book of Ben Sira among the Bodleian fragments, in 1896, that
induced Schechter to proceed to Cairo and bring back virtually all that
remained of the written *disjecta* of the genizah there. The bulk of this
recovered material is preserved at Cambridge University. Some specimens
which Schechter had retained in his own collection came into the
possession of the Jewish Theological Seminary of America, including an
autograph signature of Maimonides of about the year 1173.

In recent years Biblical manuscript scrolls have been recovered near
the Dead Sea. One such in a cave near Jericho was found by a Bedouin
shepherd when an estray goat led the way through a small circular
opening in a rock-face and down the aperture to a cave. In 1954, McGill
University secured for fifteen thousand dollars from the Jordanian
Government a substantial part of these Old Testament scrolls in ancient

script. One, twenty-two feet long, is in an almost perfect state of preservation. The dry climate and their concealment in jars kept these relics from decay.

Poignant episodes sometimes occur with respect to literary works. One such is the story of a splendid Hebrew scroll of the Torah long treasured by the revived Jewish community in Madrid, whence Jews had suffered expulsion in 1492. This manuscript of the Pentateuch was taken from Spain in the year of exile. During the French Revolution it was buried at Bayonne and forgotten for seventy years. Now it is back in the land of its origin, revered by the congregation there into whose possession it came.

There are quaint oddities, too, in this rambling field of interred literature. Although spurious in its alleged derivation, there is Raphael's *Royal Book of Dreams, from an Ancient Curious Manuscript, Buried in the Earth during several Centuries, containing 1,024 Oracles,* which was published in 1830.

The American Indians must not be overlooked in this sepulchral chapter. When Sequoyah died in 1843 all his books and possessions were buried with this Cherokee Cadmus after the manner of the older Cherokees. Sequoyah it was who invented a written syllabary for his tribe.

The Indian tribe known as the Lenni Lênapé, or Delawares, as also the Chippewa, buried their sacred birchbark tribal chronicle, the shamans being said to have unearthed it and renewed decayed parts at intervals of seven years. This pictographic record, spanning centuries from mythic days to the coming of the whites in a genesis and migration chant, was called *Walam Olum,* (painted score) among the Delawares, and its terse annals were memorized by the *medawiwin* or shamans. No specimen has survived, but the text is given, and transliterated, by Brinton from a copy procured by Rafinesque in 1820.

In Yucatan where a high culture plane was achieved, none of the *Anhaltes,* or ancient books of the Maya dealing with their history, calendar system, and religion, have come down to us. Landa, first Bishop of Yucatan, burnt all that he could discover, regarding them as the work of the devil; but observations of contemporary chroniclers indicate that such books, made from agave fiber, coated with a solution of lime upon which the hieroglyphs could be lastingly painted, were buried in graves of their priests.

In cave, crypt, and coffin mankind has sought to preserve literary vestiges of himself, to enshrine his books of devotion, to afford the passing soul guidance or celestial passport. The motives were threefold: to conceal, to preserve, to comfort.

He who shares Hamlet's "antic disposition," and gazes at his bookshelves with unstaled delight knows the unending variety of circumstance and chitchat that pertain to volumes in themselves, sometimes tedious and profitless. The papyri taken from mummycases of ancient Egypt may have no urgent message for most of us, but time endows all things with a patina of veneration, and above all hallows the written word, that direct bridge of the generations.

Hence it is not for its intrinsic value that one keeps *The Religion of Protestants: A Safe Way to Salvation*, which William Chillingworth had published in 1638 to voice his rational views; but rather because pastor Francis Cheynell, whose Calvinist heart was full of hate for the author and the book, refused to bury the body of dead Chillingworth and vented his detestation by burying the book instead! Chillingworth had turned Catholic, but recanted; whereat Cheynell distrusted the former's Protestant professions. Whether the book burial was symbolical or actual is uncertain, but in a tract written by Cheynell in 1644, *The Sickness, Heresy, Death and Burial of William Chillingworth . . . and a Short Oration at the Buriall of his Hereticall Book*, we read:

> I shall undertake to bury his errours, which are published in this so much admired, yet unworthy booke; and happy would it be for this Kingdome, if this booke and all its fellows could be so buried, that they might never rise more, unless it were to a confutation. . . . Get thee gone then, thou cursed booke, which hath seduced so many

precious soules; get thee gone, thou corrupt, rotten booke, earth to earth, and dust to dust; get thee gone into the place of rottennesse, that thou maiest rot with thy Author, and see corruption.

A hearty malediction this!

ECCENTRICA

AS ECCENTRICITY in persons is a flexible term and one more easily applied to others than to oneself, so oddity in books will vary in manner and degree of interpretation. Gradually, over a score of years, however, specimens and data on such oddities accumulated sufficiently to allow various facets of the subject to be considered under specific classification. There still remains, nevertheless, a congeries of the unusual that seems to fit in nowhere, to insist on remaining in splendid isolation. Ranging from the downright aberrant or freakish to the peculiar or merely uncommon, one scarcely knows where to start and when to call a halt.

A singular product of one mind which appears to be eccentric enough bears the title *The Song of Songs Which Is Solomon's* (Boston, 1904). It is perhaps the only book in the world in which one line is printed on a page. This rendition consists of more than four hundred pages, "versified, monogrammed, and designed" by the author, George Winslow Pierce, who declares himself "an algebraist." The solitary lines midway on each page, with an expanse of white above and below, constitute a unique typographical aberration.

Some writers of the past, and no doubt of the present, can compose only in utmost seclusion, even in sound-proof retreats, others only out-of-doors. Many a pundit, if we are to believe the annalists, could pen his cogitations only in bed, or while reasonably drunk, or in green ink, or while striding to and fro in the presence of a comely stenographer. These may be dismissed with amusement, but the numerous authors who have labored despite physical handicap command our admiration. One need only cite *A Memoir of John Carter* by William Dampier (London, 1850), who was paralyzed in all his limbs. His writings and drawings were made with pen or pencil held in his mouth. Then there was the young editor, Franticek Filip of Czechoslovakia, who wrote his copy with his feet. Filip, who had no hands, edited an organ in Prague, and not only wielded a pedal pencil, but used a typewriter with a measure of dexterity.

Frequently the extraneous circumstances pertaining to the publication of a book are strange, although its contents may be quite commonplace. For instance, there is the author on whom was bestowed a vast territory for writing one book. He might have preferred cash, but Joao de Barrosh, the Portuguese who wrote a sixteenth-century work entitled *Cronica do Clarimundo* and dedicated it to King Joao III of Portugal, received in royal payment the entire province of Maranha, 177,000 square miles or about the size of France. What the poor chronicler did with this considerable estate, now part of Brazil, is not known, but His Majesty was doubtless glad to be rid of it at that time.

Now and then one finds works otherwise conventional that disclose an odd bit of trivia. *Lady Gough's Book of Etiquette*, written in the Victorian era, forbade the placing of books by male authors alongside books by female authors—unless they were married. Segregation of the sexes is no longer an amenity of the shelves; but the color line is still drawn between some covers, for more than one Southern city directory maintains its "White Department" and "Colored Department" in a sort of printed Jim Crowism.

Perhaps the enticement of this search for *eccentrica* is that it permits the quester to roam so far afield. Singularity may crop up in the oddest and most unexpected corners; and by their very miscellaneous nature these oddities defy orderly presentation. Let us take three instances pertaining to piety and peace, and a trio having the background of war or the martial provenance.

On the side of sanctity—with the modern note—is the zipper Bible, an American binding feature introduced in 1933, in which the sliding fastener completely encloses the "divinity circuit" edges of the volume when not in use. And harking back to the days of Black Letter text there is that somewhat forbidding small quarto of devotion which has the distinction of being the earliest book in which the use of the comma has been observed—a handy mark which deserves a note of its typographical birth. The work in which it is said to have been first used is *A Devout Treatyse called the tree and xii frutes of the holy goost* (*Enprynted at London in the Fletestrete, 1534*), and of the three copies extant the only perfect one is in Trinity College, Cambridge.

The third of this righteous group has a millennial slant. Unlike Franklin's famous facetious hoax of the Brussels Academy of savants in which he considers how excrement may be relieved of its unpleasant atmosphere by a modicum of spices in the diet, this is a sober pamphlet by a Swabian shoemaker, wherein he sought to prove that man owed his moral sickness to the fact that he satisfied his alimentary needs in closed rooms and with the aid of artificial paper. If, instead, opined this sage of the bench and bodkin, man spent these daily moments out in the woods and availed himself of the natural moss, all spiritual poisons would be dissipated in the surrounding air, and he would be at the same time bodily and soulfully purified, returning to his work with a strengthened social conscience and a diminished egoism. Then and thereby, declared the shoemaker, true love of humanity would be awakened, and the Kingdom of God on Earth would be at hand.

The other trio starts with a tall and imposing imprint that started a war, which cannot be said of many items. It is the first edition of "The Stamp Act," taking some thirty pages of a volume of various enactments decreed by Parliament and George III in 1765. The "British Colonies and Plantations in America," which this Act assesses, melted their pewter into bullets as a postscript to this levy.

The second is a queer little publication of a few pages which was printed at Sebastopol in the Crimea by the Imperial French Army Press in 1856, and which consists of didactic verses in French incorporating twenty precepts for the game of whist. Bearing the Imperial arms on the title and produced to relieve the tedium of the siege, this extravagance of a portable press devoted to proclamations and army orders would be difficult to surpass.

Another martial volume is an extraordinary binding acquired by the Library of Congress from the Winter Palace Library of the last Czar. It is tersely described by the rare book custodian of our national collections as a large book containing "a history of the Czar's own regiment, bound in the actual uniform of the soldiers, with an astrakhan hat for the front panel, together with the insignia worn on the cap. The clasps are made of the regimental gold buttons, and the book is decorated with two ribbons representing the orders of St. Andrew and St. George, presented to the regiment for heroism during campaigns."

It will be seen what a gallimaufry these strange volumes comprise. Were *facetiæ* included, this would be the place to cite *Oddest of All Oddities: an entire new Odd Collection, intended for the use of every Odd Subject in this Oddest of all Odd Ages, by Obadiah Ollapod, Odd Fish,*" which Londoners of 1820 read with relish. Or the volume entitled "*!!!*" (New York, 1881), by George Hepworth, a work of fantasy fiction.

Books have been bound in all manner of shoddy and rich fabrics, from bandana cotton and burlap sacking to silk brocade and Venice velvet, from homespun to satin, from crash to moiré silk, from canvas to tapestry. There have been volumes clothed in common calico, others garbed in paisley or fine textures out of the East, a cookbook in suitable oilcloth, a novel in chintz. Or the eye may caress an exotic creation of Japanese hand-lettered poems bound in pale blue silk crepe, hand-painted in dreamy watercolors. From durable buckram to embroidered cloth-of-gold the range is wide.

But in the matter of the varied stuffs that have been used for bindings it is not of the exquisite that we speak here. Not of jewelled bindings or inlaid ivory covers, not of enameled beauties or filigree silver, not of mosaic leathers nor yet of painted vellum, but only of a few queer specimens of a more bizarre nature.

During prohibition days a publisher issued a volume of ancient and modern brewing recipes for amateur home brewers "bound in red-checked liquid-proof *tablecloth* reminiscent of other days." Which is a reminder that one of the dry commentaries on the Eighteenth Amendment was issued in the parched era by the Commission of Internal Revenue in a 250-page volume of regulations consisting of 2,403 sections interpreting the manufacture, sale, or transportation of intoxicating liquors which in the Amendment itself was set forth in only forty-four words!

The very habiliments of fame sometimes descend to us in the investure of books. General Sir George Napier had a life of the dwarf court jester bound in a piece of silk waistcoat from Charles the First's wardrobe. Jeffrey Hudson, this midget who, until his thirtieth year when he began to grow, measured but eighteen inches, is accorded a chapter in Morris Bishop's *A Gallery of Eccentrics* (New York, 1928).

But Charles had other waistcoats, and at the Perry sale seventy years ago in London a copy of *The New-Yeres Gift*, dated 1636, similarly garbed sold for £8 8s. Moreover it was tied with the blue ribbon of the Garter. When this particular volume, which was from the Heber Library, turned up at a New York auction sale in 1934, it brought four hundred dollars. Enclosed in a protective French levant solander case, the binding itself is embroidered with flowers in silver wire, and must once have appeared quite decorative on the regal paunch.

The wife of the poet Wordsworth covered her books in pieces of her own discarded dresses, and she was something of a pioneer among feminine bookbinders in England. The British Museum has one specimen of her handicraft clad in green material with small white sprays. In fact figured textile has a pleasing effect and it is surprising that it is not more often used. Many years ago the British publisher Richard Bentley put out one of Miss Rhoda Broughton's novels in this style.

Indeed, this particular kind of personal touch did not cease with

Mrs. Wordsworth. When Carl Van Vechten wished to add a volume to his permanent possessions, "he had it bound in a flower print from one of his wife's summer dresses." The best case in point, gleaned from one of Goodspeed's discursive little monthly catalogues, concerns a copy of *A New England Nun and Other Stories* (London, 1891), by Mary E. Wilkins Freeman. The binding is half calf, with flowered cloth sides, and accompanying the book is this autograph presentation note from the author in explanation of the binding:

> My Dear Mr. French,
>   *I take great pleasure in sending you my New England Nun attired in a remnant of one of my worldly gowns, and I send with her my hearty thanks for your kindness.*
>   *Very sincerely yours,*
>   Mary E. Wilkins.

The bookseller's price for these cloistered tales in worldly garb was none too much for so quaint and delightful an item. Yet there is another volume still more fetching by reason of its odd covering. It is *Mary, Wife of Lincoln* (New York, 1928). The author, Mrs. Kate Helm, was a grand-niece of Mrs. Lincoln, and the tapestry inserted on the outside cover of a few copies was taken from a curtain in the home of the future wife of Lincoln in Lexington, Kentucky.

Macray, who has such a wealth of curious *libraria* tattle in his *Annals of the Bodleian,* mentions a copy of John Jonston's *Thaumatographia naturalis* as bound in a piece of coarse tapestry, "with the figures of a man and a woman." During the seventeenth-century vogue of embroidered bindings, canvas was often the foundation for the needlework; figured tapestry was also in favor. Those who covered old Armenian Bibles were likewise partial to oddments of material, from a piece of shawl to a faded remnant of coverlet or hanging, with bangles.

One recalls a sheaf of plantation songs entitled *Lyrics from Cotton-Land,* which was appropriately bound in a bandana handkerchief;

likewise a collection of Romany stories called *The Gipsy Patteran*. Some years ago an English textile manufacturer wrote a book on his craft and bound the edition in calico of his own making. Desirable simplicity was achieved in the outward guise of Mahatma Gandhi's story of his life as issued a few years ago by an American publisher in a binding of *khaddar*, the native homespun of India ; and the Roycroft Press issued an edition of Elbert Hubbard's *Abe Lincoln and Nancy Hanks* in brown homespun. Burlap is a somewhat similar stuff that has been used once or twice for its homely appearance. But really charming are such appropriate bindings as the edition of the novel, *Java Girl*, strikingly invested in native Javan batik with a design of fantastic birds and exotic flowers, the lettering on the backbone being executed in copper to harmonize with the fabric ; or Herman Melville's *Typee* in native tapa cloth from the South Seas ; or Don Blanding's verses published in Honolulu and bound in Hawaiian hula hula grass.

It was in 1822 that Archibald Leighton is said to have substituted cloth for boards, thus effecting a decided change for the better in ordinary bookbinding. He used calico which he had dyed and calendered, and the books bore paper or leather labels. Between 1860 and 1880 the cloth was sometimes inlaid or overlaid with colored paper panels, ornamentally designed, or cut out in fretwork, and even grained to suggest wood.

The Bentley novels experimented in diversified innovations. A glimpse of the scope of treatment is afforded by the following passage from Michael Sadleir's *The Evolution of Publishers' Binding Styles* (London, 1930) :

> One of Marie Corelli's books had a bow of actual silk ribbon let in on each volume. In another case tartan ribbons were ingeniously allowed to adorn a history of a Scottish regiment. Another novel had a visiting card inlaid diagonally across the fronts. Imitation half-bindings (carried out in cloth, but suggesting morocco spines and corners) ; overprints of silver or iridescent inks ; side panels deeply

impressed—these were frequent experiments. Material in blind
relief—a sort of lincrusta—was occasionally used. An effect
of china tiles was obtained by a specially stout glazed paper,
suitably patterned. One book at least had panels of thin
wood on front and back; another incorporated thin sheets of
cork with cloth; several were bound in tapestry, in unglazed
chintz, even in rough homespun canvas.

The long series of Bentley novels were a virtual institution in
England, and we are told: "The queer thing is that these freakish
elaborations were not merely the eccentricities of a decadence, but had an
element of hard practical justification. Obviously they caught the eye.
But also they served as torches in the dark. The big circulating libraries
kept their thousands of three-volume novels in dark storerooms. Assistants
groped after subscribers' choice, or—even more frequently—for something
to offer to the vague ladies who wandered in asking for 'a nice novel.' It
was much easier to identify a book by feel than by sight, and Messrs.
Bentley found that their novels circulated more readily because—thanks
to the nobs, rugosities and other crenellations of their peculiar get-up—
the library assistants could recognize the identity of their several titles
merely by fingering and, to save time and trouble, would select one of
those titles for immediate supply."

Not until 1841 had a binding cloth been made exclusively for books.
Although Archibald Leighton used calico in 1822, it cannot be said with
certainty that he was the first to substitute cloth for boards. According to
a writer in *Notes and Queries,* the invention that now seems so
commonplace was resorted to by "Mr. R. E. Lawson, of Stanhope
Street, Blackfriars, formerly in the employ of Mr. Charles Sully, and
the first book bound in cloth was a manuscript volume of music, which
was subsequently purchased by Mr. Alfred Herbert, the marine artist.
On this volume being shown to the late Mr. Pickering, who was at that
time, 1823, printing a diamond edition of the classics, he thought the
material would be admirably adapted for the covers of the work. The
cloth was purchased at the corner of Wilderness Row, St. John Street,

and 500 copies of the diamond classics were covered by Mr. Lawson with glue."

This seems quite circumstantial, but the solution of who was the first binder to use cloth and which was the first book so bound is not rendered easier by the existence of one of the Pickering classics in "diamond" type—a copy of the petite edition of Cicero in original cloth, unopened—*dated 1821*, and sold by the bookseller as "the first volume ever issued in a cloth binding." Perhaps the sheets were printed in 1821 and remained unbound for a year or two. It seems strange that cloth was not thought of long before as suitable for books.

Which leads to a paragraph on something quite different, wallpaper. Of course one knows of the famous wallpaper issue of the Vicksburg *Daily Citizen* for July 4th, 1863, which was printed on the white side of a batch of fine English stock of that nature, and that a number of Confederate books of that period had wallpaper covers. There was even an edition of one of Victor Hugo's works put out in wallpaper binding by a Richmond printer while the guns were thundering. But it remained for Gelett Burgess to give us that venture called *The Lark* on wallpaper throughout its few pages, and the trifle of eight leaves, *Le Petit Journal des Refusees*, which, to make it more unusual, was sent forth with one corner lopped off in odd format. And in Australia in 1927 appeared Charles Bertie's *Story of the Royal Hotel and the Theatre Royal, Sydney*, with covers that were once on the dining room wall of that hostelry.

The "strange covertures" of books, as Holbrook Jackson phrased it, range from sandalwood to shagreen, from pelts to felts, from oxhide to ostrichskin, from unborn kid to tanned human epidermis. Metals and damasks, ivory and feathers, cork and enamels, in artistic, exotic, or eccentric binding regale the quester. Lace from the boudoir, python from the jungle, shark from the sea, contribute to the array, if the search be patient and the searcher content to scrutinize rather than possess. Holbrook Jackson who, above all others since Dibdin, canvassed these matters, well said that "to achieve these allurements men have ranged the earth and trawled the seas." Yet his province was the whole of bibliophily, and in the more confined labyrinth of *eccentrica* there were strange bypaths beyond his purview, and amazing ambush turns that eluded him.

Certainly to a limited degree there is scope for the use of sympathetic material in the garbing of books, as well as in their design and embellishment, whether by way of memento or in pictorial effects through inlaid leatherwork. But such symbolism when overdone verges on the curious or downright bizarre. Binding the logbook of a clipper in sailcloth may strike our sea-going fancy; but if, let us say, it also sports a glass-covered sunken inlay of an embalmed hypogriff, it would exceed the casually unusual and become quarry for the chase. There are repellent works that deserve to be bound in the hide of the hyena and ghoulish volumes that call for vampire covers. Octave Uzanne, on the pretty side, suggests dainty vestments with a sentimental touch, a bit of old velvet or heirloom brocade; and many a cherished volume has been garbed in such appealing stuff, reminiscent of romance or token of bygone days and the texture of rich memories. Horne comments on the pleasant foppery that prevailed in the adornment of some books, and Holbrook Jackson devoted several pages to the "bibliopegic dandyism" to which certain kings and courtiers were addicted.

Singularly appropriate is the binding of bed-ticking for the sheets of De Maupassant's *A Coquette's Love*—singular also in that only one copy was so covered and since bestowed on us by Wilbur Macey Stone, with his 1897 bookplate showing Psyche thumbing a snub nose at a doddering aspirant to her favors.

From the same source came information concerning Louise Imogen Guiney's *Monsieur Henri: a Footnote to French History*, of which an author's edition of fifty copies in 1892 had a binding of the plaid pattern worn by Henri de La Rochejaqueline, brought from Chollet in 1891.

Following the lead of Octave Uzanne, Andrew Lang and Brander Matthews dwell briefly on the exercise of the collector's taste in the

selection of unorthodox materials to relieve the monotony of most
bindings. Uzanne in his *Les Caprices d'un Bibliophile*, which is rather
hard to come upon, suggests that the light and engaging tales of the
eighteenth century might well be clad in a damask or brocade of the
period; and in his *La Reliure Moderne* he pictures one which he
designates *Cartonnage à la Pompadour.*

Uzanne suggests old scraps of brocade, Venice velvet, embroidery, or
the like; and Lang opines that a romance of Crebillon might be fittingly
decked in a now dead but once fair lady's train. "The leathers of China
and Japan," says Lang, "with their strange tints and gilded devices may
be used for books of fantasy, like *Gaspard de la Nuit*, or the *Opium
Eater*, or Poe's poems, or the verses of Gérard de Nerval."

There have been bindings in which miniatures, or enameled panels, or
tiles have been inlaid; others in which medallions, medals, or coins have
been let into the boards. But what could be a more ironic embellishment
than the huge embroidered bee taken in 1870 from the throne of
Napoleon III and embedded in the cover of a copy of Hugo's *Napoleon
le Petit?*

Brander Matthews recalls appropriate book coverings. There was
the novel, *Princess of Java*, clad in the cotton print worn by the
Javanese; and Lafcadio Hearn's slave story, *Youma*, covered with the
simple West Indian fabric suitable to the character. To quote him
directly: "A London publisher sent forth a tiny little tome of old-time
fashions, *Our Grandmothers' Gowns*, bound with the chintzes and calicoes
of bygone days. The American edition of Charles Lamb's *Poetry for
Children* was issued in a half-binding of some woven material such as is
used in the nursery for the pinafores of childhood; and the same
publisher covered Jacob Riis's stimulating account of *How the Other
Half Lives* with a stuff very like that from which the laborer's overalls
are made." Others are cited, from the Persian silk in which Browning's
Asolando was clad to the sturdy canvas cover of *A Girl's Life 80 Years
Ago*, cleverly dieprinted to imitate a sampler of the olden days.

The range of covers taken from the animal kingdom is wide, from limp Persian Yapp to ostrichskin tanned dark brown and with darker nodules; from kangaroo to crocodile; from white unborn kid to shark shagreen. Among the varieties of deluxe bookbinding leathers shown at an exhibition in 1954 were snakeskin (python), raw cape goatskin, calf (sumac-tanned and dyed), pigskin, fishskin (tanned dogfish), oxhide, natural Niger, levant (finished cape goat), walrus (1¼″ thick), tanned elephant ear, java lizard, deerskin, red Niger, and sealskin. Oriental shagreen, as it is called, is usually asses' skin, noduled by pressing seeds in the hide and soaking, which causes the pits to swell outward.

Longfellow's *Hiawatha* in buckskin, with Frederic Remington illustrations, delighted an older generation. Copies of *Cache la Poudre: the Romance of a Tenderfoot* (1905) were garbed in fringed buckskin. One hundred copies of J. Frank Dobie's *The Mustangs* (1952) were bound in a glossy, brown, long-haired horsehide, complete with white spots, and known as the Pinto edition. His earlier volume, *The Longhorns* (1941), had a limited edition covered in rawhide.

Many of the books of Iceland are to this day covered in sealskin. In the British Museum there is a copy of Governor Phillip's *Voyage to Botany Bay* (London, 1789) bound in kangaroo. Several copies of *History of the Reign of James the Second*, by Charles James Fox, were encased in foxskin by Jeffrey the bookseller. Mary Tofts, who two centuries ago was a mental case (claiming a confinement in which she had given birth to rabbits!), provoked several controversial pamphlets, copies of which in the Duke of Roxburghe's library (sold in 1812) were bound in rabbitskin.

The lowly ass has given his hide to more than one book. And not only for the outward protection of volumes have descendants of Balaam's mount had their exteriors consigned. In at least one instance the actual text of a work was inscribed on this medium, if tradition is to be trusted, so that, aping *Much Ado About Nothing*, the donkeys who went to the making of said work might well have cited "O, that he were here to write me down an ass!"

The instance alluded to concerns that huge illuminated manuscript tome in the Royal Library of Stockholm known as the "Devil's Bible," so-called because legend tells that it was written down and colored in a single night by a monk who was doomed to die, but who with satanic assistance succeeded in his earthly task. In acknowledgment of this aid the medieval copyist made a full-page portrait of the Prince of Darkness squatting on the last page, horns, cloven hoofs, and all. Long kept hidden, this curious volume was brought out a few years ago, following a request for a photostat copy from the city of Prague, whence it had been taken at the Swedish conquest of that place in 1648, during the Thirty Years' War. Written eight hundred years ago, it is one of the largest Bibles in the world, the pages a yard tall by half that width. To make its 309 "parchment" sheets one hundred donkeys' hides were required.

In 1903 the Samuel Putnam Avery Collection was exhibited at Columbia University, and among the items shown was a notebook with leaves made from the skin of an ass. It was bound in embroidered canvas in the time of Charles I, the needlework being in fine tent or tapestry stitch with groundwork in silver thread, while the edges of the covers were bound with silver guimp.

There are Hindu sects of Central India at the present time whose ritual requires that their meager religious literature be bound only with donkeyskins. To complete the data on this long-eared theme it must be noted that there is record of a Latin copy of the *Golden Ass* of Apuleius, dated 1501, so bound; and in recent years the Limited Editions Club issued a new translation of this classic similarly assignated.

But there were other literary adventures of the ass besides that of the patient beast who ambled behind Rosinante, the creature whom Sancho bestrode in Cervantes' chronicle. Or of the ass in Aesop's fables or in Stevenson's *Travels with a Donkey*. A far older and less celebrated work, in fact a crabbed Latin treatise virtually unknown, composed by Christian Paullini and printed at Frankfort in 1695, bears the title *Onographia Curiosa: de Asino, Liber Historico-Physico-Medicus*, with further specifications in the manner of that day. The author, after enlarging upon the odd books which in his time or before had been written about strange and curious subjects—books on rats and mice, fleas and flies, lice, beetles, blindness, lies, shadows, wool, nothing, nobody, drunkenness, gout, stupidity, and praise of the devil—decided to devote a volume to the ass. And so, in addition to quoting descriptions and allusions to famous asses in history, he attacked his theme under five heads: philological and physical, political, theological, medical, and economical! The use of the donkey on coins, paintings, statuary, epitaphs, and in military affairs is not overlooked; and in conclusion the thorough author treats the ass from a mechanical, alimentary, superstituous and magical point of view. For good measure this engaging disquisition has an appropriate frontispiece and an engraving of a louse.

Several years ago was published a revealing book, *Rats, Lice and History*, written by Hans Zinsser, treating of the havoc these pests wrought through typhus in the decimation of armies and as a factor in history.

A German bookseller once wrote about a small binding sprinkled with golden fleas, the title *Tractatule de Pulcibus* (Little Tractate on Fleas) being itself lettered in these dubious adornments. Concerning this there is no additional information; nor is there any need to dwell on John Southall's *A Treatise of Buggs, shewing when and how they were first brought into England*. This pamphlet of 1730 was by a "Maker of Nonpareil Liquor for Destroying Buggs and Nits."

Older and more elaborate was a jocose Latin dissertation on fleas, in which their legal status is debated. The sprightly forgotten author, O. Zaunschliffer, under the pseudonym Opizius Jocoserius, perpetrated this somewhat ponderous jape at Marburg in 1688, and among the numerous questions debated with heavy humor are the following: Does a noblewoman's flea enjoy higher rank than a commoner's flea? Is an ex-communicate's flea also to be regarded as excommunicated? Is it an offense to call a female "Sack of Fleas" or "Flea-Zoo"? Can a commoner's flea contract matrimony with a Senator's flea?

Before forsaking the topic mention must be made of one of the most curious trifles encountered. Published anonymously in 1739 (the author,

THE ONLY ROUND BOOK IN THE WORLD

Executed by Caspar Meuser, late sixteenth-century binder to the Court of Saxony. The richly gold-tooled covers fold back at the middle; edges (below) are decorated in colors over gilt. (From the collection of Olga Hirsch, Frankfurt, Germany.)

HEART-SHAPED BOOK

Reminiscent of the lily-shaped missal made for Diana of Poitiers in 1555, this volume was executed ca. 1590 by Caspar Meuser, binder to the Court of Saxony, and bound for the Kurfürstin Anna Von Sachsen. Measuring eight inches in width and containing two little works—a book of prayers and hints on domestic economy—it is bound in calf and hand-tooled in gold.

A "TRIPITAKA" OR PALI MANUSCRIPT

*Written in Burmese on ninety-seven palm leaves enclosed in
a papier-mâché bottle; leaves (8" x 2") are perforated and
held together by a cord; the bottle, about the size of a one-
quart thermos bottle, is oxblood red with black and gold
ornaments; a cord around bottle extends upward to form a
handle. (In New York Public Library, Manuscript Division,
Box 4, No. 21.)*

F. E. Bruckmann), this work describes a newly invented flea trap. Its
ninety-four-page account of "the newly invented curious flea-trap for the
complete extinction of fleas" (*Die neu-erfundene curieuse Floh-Falle, zu
gänzlicher Ausrottung der Flöhe*) includes a survey of all the literature
on fleadom. The device itself consists of a small hollow cylinder with a
lengthwise row of holes, the contraption to be worn as a pendant around
the neck. Within the cylinder is a tiny rod which when baited with a dab
of honey or syrup would lure the varmints to sticky captivity, whereupon
the rod is withdrawn. The quarry, suggests the author, should be
"dispatched in some way, by murder, drowning, beheading, hanging, or
some similar end." To make sure that his text is comprehended, the
inventor includes an engraved plate of the flea-trap mechanism.

Both the ass and the flea may well have their place in this vexing
cosmos, where the nit and the nightingale take their fling of life. Between
the whys and the wherefores we stand nonplussed, like Buridan's ass
which, midway between two utterly equal measures of oats and unable to
choose, starved to death. Not so Shakespeare's "valiant flea that dare
eat his breakfast on the lip of a lion."

But before burning our *pons asinorum* we should remember that
revealing study, *The Criminal Prosecution and Capital Punishment of
Animals* (New York, 1906), by E. P. Evans, the only book in English
on this subject of medieval and modern legal processes against offending
bugs and beasts.

Books have been written on nothing, and, as an Irish wag might say,
on less. Belloc in his essays *On Nothing and Kindred Topics* gives us
spritely stimulation; but Mathelá, a French author, published a book
entitled *Nothing* which consisted of two hundred blank pages, many
copies of which were sold for ten francs each. Collectors of literary curios
may have on their shelves that cynical volume entitled *Wisdom of the
Ages*, which is also blank from cover to cover. Elbert Hubbard's *Silence*
was devoid of text, and, in answer to a query as to which of his writings
was most popular, the sage of Roycroft whimsically replied: "Probably
that one on 'Silence.' " Another example untouched by type, save for the

outward title, was *What I Know About Wall Street After Fourteen Years' Experience*, appearing appropriately in 1929.

Scarcely more verbose than these vacuous works was the book Mark Lemon issued through Punch, *Advice to Those Intending to Marry*, with one word, *Dont*. Less laconic was the French author, A. Breteuil, who wrote the words "I Love You" a million and one times in token of his passion for the actress Clarisse Tarrant; but she spurned his suit, and two years' work and twenty thousand sheets of paper went for naught.

The downfall of Horatio Bottomley in England came about in 1922 when he was tried on the charge of misappropriation in the War and Victory loan lotteries. This onetime owner of the paper *John Bull* incurred the ire of an associate in the lotteries, a dour printer named Reuben Bigland, who printed and circulated a pamphlet, *What Horatio Bottomley Has Done for His Country*, of twenty-four blank pages.

Another peculiar British item, relying on the symbolical use of color, is the so-called Wordless Book, which except for the title page contains not one syllable, but was devised by a person of piety who thought to convey an allegory in the color scheme of its leaves. Two are black, the unredeemed heart of the sinner; two crimson, the divine redemption; two white, the purified soul ripe for salvation; and two gold, signet of heavenly felicity. Was it not Byron's dictum that "a book's a book although there's nothing in it"?

A singular example of literary piety was the *Dévote salutation aux membres sacrés du corps da la glorieuse Vierge mère de Dieu* (Paris, 1678). It evinces the enthusiasm of the author, "le R. P. I. H. Capucin," for the corporeal beauties of the Virgin Mary. A copy of this monkish sextodecimo was in the library of the noted bibliophile Charles Nodier. In its sixteen pages it specified nineteen bodily parts to which are dedicated devout paragraphs of adoration—not forgetting the soul, which is the twentieth and last. Nodier a century ago reprinted the odd list in his curious *Mélanges tirés d'une petite bibliothèque*. Peignot, who cites it, mentions an earlier devout catechism on the life of the Virgin Mary, likewise exalting the eroginous area.

Such is the catholicity of a true bookman that without
embarrassment his shelves may embrace both a penetrating homily over
the virgin zone, as the Cromwellian poets were wont to call it, and a little
brochure unlocking the legacy of the chastity belt. The trouble with those
iron girdles of old was that love was always a better locksmith than
virtue. And as for that little treatise on the immaculate physique, were its
approach to the topic less temperate we should suspect the tonsured
author of having kindled a fire he could not quench.

Recalling Disraeli's aphorism, that all women should marry, but no
men, one might venture that being married by the clergyman's book is all
too common, but being wedded to a volume has happened only once.
Sabbatai Zevi (1626–1676) was a religious zealot and messianic
pretender who won a widespread following among the Jews of his time.
Many of his acts were designed to enhance his authority among his
supporters. One of these was his marriage to the Scroll of the Law, which
was performed at Salonica, then in Turkey, between 1653 and 1658. The
ceremony was connected with the mystic view whereby the Scroll of the
Law (Torah) was considered representative of the divine spirit of
revelation. With the holy code arrayed in bridal vestments, the ceremony
was performed in the presence of witnesses exactly in the manner of a
Jewish wedding, Sabbatai Zevi placing the ring upon the top of one of
the wooden rollers around which the Scroll is always wound.

An instance where the marks of mourning were extended even to
one's books is found in the curious practice of Henri III of France, who
is said to have suffered from recurrent morbid melancholia. At the death
of the Princesse de Condé, Marie de Clèves, whom he passionately loved,
this King showed himself in public with his apparel laden with funereal
emblems—black skulls on his shoulders, black edgings on his robes, and
black ribbons in his shoes. Moreover, he had skulls stamped on the covers
of his books, as Desportes has described. One such volume which a New
York bookseller not long ago offered for sale has five black skulls
adorning the back cover of the canary-colored calf in which it was bound,
or rebound, for the melancholy monarch in **1575.**

It was Henry, Prince of Wales, the eldest son of James I, who brought together those precious old royal libraries of the realm now housed in the British Museum. His death in 1612 inspired curious tributes in somber token of mourning. Calling him "Prince Panaretus," one Joshua Sylvester wrote an elegy published that year entitled: *Lachrimae Lachrimarum, or The Distillation of Teares Shede for the untimely Death of the incomparable Prince Panaretus.* The title is printed in white on a black ground, with the Royal Arms at the top. The text is printed on the recto of each leaf, black-bordered at top and bottom, and with side supports of skeletons. The reverse of each leaf is black, with the Arms in white, except the last leaf which has the Feathers, Crown and Motto of the Prince of Wales.

But there were other such tributes, one commemorating Charles I having white printing on a black background. The death of a sovereign led to effusions entitled *Teares Distilled* or the like. These elegies resorted to the typographical somberness of black title pages lettered in white, sometimes with one or more wholly black pages interspersed in the text. Such sable trappings occur in the 1613 edition of *Two elegies, consecrated to the never-dying memorie of the most worthily admyred, most hartily loved, and generally bewayled Prince, Henry,* by Christopher Brooke and William Browne, whose names do not appear on the title page. The first leaf is black, relieved by a rectangle of white within which are the princely Arms in black. The dedication leaf bears a symbolical white-on-black woodcut of tears, and there are six other pages entirely in black.

It will be recalled by lovers of the jocular Laurence Sterne that in the first edition of *Tristram Shandy,* at the point in the narrative where the death of Yorick occurs, a black page is inserted. Being a Doctor of Divinity and to offset the avalanche of criticism that descended upon him as a result of the appearance of the first two volumes of *Tristram,* Sterne began the publication of *The Sermons of Mr. Yorick* as an antidote. It is said his wife helped him with them, and they are so decorous and unlike Sterne that they must have been an irksome chore.

Apart from mourning but in keeping with the gloomy mien of religion towards the close of the seventeenth century and into the eighteenth, there was a vogue for devout books in black morocco bindings, soberly tooled without gold, with the edges of the paper stained black. The suggestion of Davenport seems unlikely that these black bindings may have been "a national sign of sympathy with the Princess Anne, the younger daughter of James II," who had seventeen children none of whom survived childhood. "It is quite possible," says Davenport, "that these continual deaths in one family may have suggested the idea that suitable books should be bound in a mourning way, and it is just possible this may be the true explanation."

While on this nigrescent theme it may be said that there are but two complete black manuscripts known, both illuminated, one in the Morgan Collection and the Sforza *Book of Hours* in the National Library at Vienna. They are for this reason alone among the most curious in the annals of queer books. The Morgan *Hours of the Virgin* is a fifteenth-century Flemish manuscript in Latin, and the entire text is written in silver on vellum dyed black. There are rich purples and gold throughout, with some green initials—a gorgeous little book.

That abused Muse who presides over the poetic faculties has had some curious effusions hurled at her at book length. Medicine's most famous poem, in Latin hexameter and of ample proportions, was put forth in 1530 by its learned author, Girolamo Fracastoro of Verona. On the unedifying subject of "syphilis or the French disease" the Temple of Fame was assaulted. Yet Scaliger calls it a divine poem and its author the most distinguished poet since Virgil. Indeed, this physician and philosopher was among the most brilliant minds of the Renaissance, and the scholarly, from Bacon to Humboldt, have praised him and his works. When it is realized that 127 editions of his metrical *Syphilis Sive Morbus Gallicus* appeared between the Editio Princeps of 1530 and the latest English text of 1934, its influence is apparent. Of these there have been 45 Latin editions (the latest in 1907), 30 Italian (the latest 1930), 14 English, 9 French, 5 German, 1 Spanish, 1 Portuguese, and 22 bilingual

—quite a record for a piece of medical poetry. How many of the translations were versified renditions we cannot say, but most were in prose.

What may well be termed the most curious product of American poetry is *Dentologia: A Poem on the Diseases of the Teeth. In Five Cantos. By Solyman Brown* (New York, 1840). The author's real name was Eleazar Parmly, and he aids brave readers "with Notes, Practical, Historical, Illustrative and Explanatory." For good measure he appends a list of about three hundred fellow dentists throughout the United States who were original susbscribers to this molaresque work. As Zangwill wittily wrote to a budding but mediocre poet who sent a volume of his verses, "We shall lose no time in reading it."

One of the works illustrated by George Cruikshank in 1815 was *The Life of Napoleon, A Hudibrastic Poem*. But far more singular was the work which put Napoleon's Law Code into French verse, appearing at Paris in 1810. The *avocat au conseil* who remained anonymous in his *Code Napoleon, en vers français* was M. Rochelle, and in a preliminary poetic flight he dedicates the effort to the Empress Marie-Louise, second wife of the Corsican. In a prose preface that follows he declares his poetic purpose to have been to render the laws more easily memorized, especially by women who have responsibilities as mothers, guardians, or administrators of property, and also in matters of inheritance, making contracts or drafting wills. For French rhymed verse to achieve the literal legal intent of these Napoleonic provisions was a task at which the author did not balk. The extent of his poetaster opus may be appreciated when one considers that he versified the 2,281 Articles of the Code, fashioning in all more than sixteen thousand lines. What rhymester's feat can excel this *corpus juris* in meter?

Over here in 1882, Major Frederick Howe put forth his *History of America in Rhyme*, the eighty pages of which rehearse "all the leading events associated with dates," as the title page exults. The Major may have been a good soldier, but as a versifier his spurs were on his tongue. It is rank doggerel, which can be forgiven when the author struggles loyally, as in that 381-page screed by Adrian Hitt entitled *The Grant Poem, Containing Grant's Public Career and Private Life from the Cradle to the Grave* (New York, 1886), with illustrations by the author. Relieved by spriteliness is a slender volume by Earl H. Emmons, *Odeography of Benjamin Franklin* (New York, 1929), a rollicking versified biography, limited to a hundred copies and produced by a private press. To round out the record, in 1934 was published *The United States History in Rhyme*, by Caroline E. Logan, a pamphlet from Dillsburg, Pennsylvania. That this kind of verse vice was old is shown by the fourteenth-century Bavarian manuscript of a world-chronicle in German rhyme, compiled by an unknown author and now the property of the Morgan Library.

The versatility of renowned linguists in days gone by is a matter of astonishment. Men who had mastered thirty or more languages vied with pundits who explored little-known idioms, translated the Scriptures into Fiji, Micmac, Rarotongan, or what not, whereas, a century or so before, treatises were written on the probable tongue spoken by Adam and Eve in the paradisal triangle with the serpent.

However, it is not the prodigious linguists, nor the 1077-odd languages and dialects into which the Bible or parts thereof have been rendered, including the African Kololo and Indian Mikir, that is of immediate concern, but rather a few of the unexpected translations encountered by one with an eye for the queer among books. Biographies of Lincoln in Greek, Arabic, Chinese, Czech, Danish, Dutch, Finnish, Hungarian, Japanese, Korean, Polish, Portuguese, Welsh, or assorted other tongues are available in the McLellan Lincoln Collection at Brown University; and lives of Lincoln have been rendered into unfamiliar languages as diverse as Icelandic Norse and Hawaiian, Eskimo and Hebrew, Siouan and Slovak.

The deeds of the Father of his Country were enshrined in Latin prose by an Ohio classicist, named Francis Glass, a century ago under the title *Washingtoni Vita* (New York, 1835). Glass taught in a one-man, one-class frontier schoolhouse. For "bullets" in his text this Erasmus of the West contrived *glandes plumbeae,* or leaden missiles, and for the Quakers he devised *Tremebundi.* The book, posthumously published, saw three editions and was popular in classrooms.

Another Westerner, Roy C. Flickinger of the University of Iowa, published a Latin volume of songs in 1925, including renditions of "The Star-Spangled Banner," "America," and "Lead Kindly Light."

A Latin version of *Robinson Crusoe,* made by F. J. Goffaux and published at London in 1823, was recently had for six shillings; and a century later appeared Shakespeare's *Sonnets* in the Ciceronian lingo at the hands of A. T. Barton. Similarly Keats was rendered by Charles Merivale in a Latinized *Hyperion* published at Cambridge in 1862 and noted in a dealer's catalogue at twelve shillings. A *Treasure Island* in Latin was launched in New York in 1922, with colored plates by N. C. Wyeth. Of the Defoe classic there have been, by the way, at least four renditions in Hebrew, and it may be found in Japanese and other languages "including the Scandinavian."

The seeker after such specimens of well-known themes or figures in little-known guise will find their acquisition no cloying pursuit. It may be a horny-souled seventeenth-century text that attracts because it is printed in alternate pages of Greek and Latin, and comes from one of the fountainheads of the art, such as Leyden; it may be the only Latin Washington funeral address, such as that of Joseph Willard, delivered and published in 1800; or such a work as *Theodore Roosevelt the American,* which appeared in 1926, addressed to both English and Italian readers, with the narrative carried on opposite pages in both languages. As long ago as 1797 an interlinear *Robinson Crusoe* appeared in France as a tool in learning English.

Queen Christina of Sweden was conversant in Hebrew, and in her time there were other Christian Hebraists. The corporate seal of Yale has Hebrew symbols and that tongue was so mastered by Ezra Stiles, early president of that college, that in 1781 he delivered an oration therein which is still preserved among his papers. Goethe studied the Bible in the Hebrew original, and as his first romance he devised six brothers, each of whom "wrote" chapters in a different language, Goethe thereby perfecting himself in German, English, French, Italian, Latin, and Judæo-German (Yiddish), the last through a teacher of the Frankfurt ghetto of his day.

Collecting must now be specialized to give real satisfaction. Few with a bent for languages have as yet garnered in this field. They may get much zest from a pursuit that can give them many unexpected items from *Uncle Tom's Cabin* in Ukrainian to *Hamlet* in Hindustani. Hebrew, even before its recent renaissance as a living language, has given versions of surprising range, from *Pilgrim's Progress, Paradise Lost,* and *The Vicar of Wakefield,* to *Ben Hur, Huckleberry Finn,* and *Treasure Island.* There is, indeed, a little bibliography of some two hundred such Hebraica, compiled in 1929 by Israel Schapiro.

Queer methods or motives cling to several of these translations. Thus Marianne Nevill in 1829 prepared a Hebrew rendition of the Book of Common Prayer, intended for Jews who were supposed to have embraced Christianity. A copy of this curious volume is in the New York Public Library. It was published in a lithographic edition and the colophon reads: "Written in Lithographic Ink by Marianne Nevill in One Month for the use of the Christian Israelites at Smyrna." The text represents the Hebrew version made by Abraham bar Jacob, a convert, about 1717, whose original manuscript is preserved in the Library of Trinity College, Dublin. The reverse of the title page bears this attestation:

CERTIFICATE: I CERTIFY THAT DURING THE TIME I WAS TRANSLATING AND TRANSCRIBING THIS PRAYER BOOK FOR THE USE OF THE CHRISTIAN ISRAELITES THAT LEST THEY SHOULD DEEM IT AN OFFENCE TO USE A BOOK OF PRAYER WRITTEN BY A GENTILE, I ABSTAINED FROM EATING ANYTHING FORBIDDEN BY THE LAW OF MOSES, NOR DID I USE ANY PENS BUT NEW ONES, THAT HAD NOT BEEN USED IN ANY OTHER WRITING.

—MARIANNE NEVILL,
DUBLIN, 1829.

Dr. Joshua Bloch, who describes this oddity, states: "As to the use of the new pen, she seems to have been imitating the Jewish scribes, who when making the Scripture Rolls, are wont at certain passages to consecrate their pens (calamus) to sacred use."

One of the most whimsical of literary curiosities was fashioned by the artist, W. J. Linton, who in 1886 took Catullus' epigram, *"Nulli se dicit mulier mea nubere malle"* (My wife says that she prefers to marry no man), and gave it thirty-two different renderings in as many English quatrains. There are three quatrains to the page, and the impression of "In Dispraise of a Woman: Catullus with Variations" was limited to twenty-five copies in choice italic.

On polyglot Bibles—with as many as nine languages to the page in parallel columns—there is no need to linger, nor do more than mention the volume containing the Lord's Prayer in 155 tongues, or that of a century later comprising five hundred idioms. Edmund Fry, the most learned typefounder of his day, in 1799 published his *Pantographia: Containing All the known Alphabets in the World.* And at Venice in 1837 appeared a work printed in twenty-four languages, European and Oriental, by the monks at the Armenian Monastery on the Island of St. Lazare, as a specimen of their printing types.

One despairs of encompassing all the strange volumes that properly belong in the literary bedlam. *The Natural History of Humbugs* contends with similar works on bores, and on tuft-hunters. From themes such as these one may wander to the Dutch work on fortune-telling by the letters of the name Jesus Christ, which a Dominican professor of theology published at Delft in 1698.

Let it not be thought that eccentric circumstances of authorship are a thing of the past. Witness Jesse Stuart's volume of sonnets entitled *Man With a Bull-tongue Plow* (1950). They were excellent sonnets, but noted here only because of their author's insistence that he wrote them on *leaves* when he reached the end of a furrow in plowing.

Still stranger in its writing was *Peter Moen's Diary* (1951), which was composed during the Norwegian author's solitary confinement in a

Nazi prison. As writing equipment he used a pin from a blackout curtain and pricked his story on coarse toilet paper. The book was a best seller in Scandinavia and was issued also in America in English.

Finally there is the only unwritten book, yet one that makes good reading! By James Lordan, and entitled *Colloquies*, this volume was composed directly out of the printer-author's head, at the type case in old Romsey, England, where he had a small shop, and did this work in intervals of leisure. Dated 1844, it treats of poets and poetry in essay style.

There can be no better words with which to conclude this chapter on Eccentrica than those of J. H. Slater who, commenting in one of his works on certain early editions and strange books, says: "To form a collection of books of this class, or having such peculiarities, would be no light task, while the knowledge necessary for the purpose would be of a most varied and unusual character. There are many, no doubt, who will think that it might be employed to better advantage, but that is not a question either for them or for us. The collector of books who prefers to stray from the ordinary and beaten tracks and to wander where he will, led by his own fancy and unfettered by rule, must of necessity be possessed of originality and self-confidence not likely to desert him in whatever direction his steps may turn."

THE BOOKMAN SETS SAIL

THE LURE AND THE LORE of the sea may entice the inveterate booklover, even though it is his preference to remain safe ashore in his cozy library. He may be content with sea yarns and the annals of strange voyages; but if so inclined, there is possible an even closer association, for many a volume is linked to the restless brine in ways other than contents. The range is wide, from one which smacks of the sea in its binding to another that recalls the curious history of a strange Bible now treasured in the New York Public Library.

The binding of the *Story of Bermuda* (1932)—a volume which brought the word "pearlescence" into the bookmaker's vocabulary—is a cloth of nacre finish, this coating being made from the scales of certain fish and containing some of the same substance that gives an opalescent sheen to real pearls. It is used in producing synthetic pearls and was applied to the binding material by a special chemical process developed after long experiment. This appropriate touch is enhanced by the green-stained edges of the book and a hippogriff stamped on the cover.

Another seafaring volume tells anew the facts about the mutiny on the *Bounty* with its extraordinary train of consequences, but it fails to include that which is most pertinent to our theme: the story of the Pitcairn Bibles. Here it is, as concisely as does justice to the strange circumstances.

In 1787 the *Bounty* left England for the South Seas with a crew of forty-six, reaching Tahiti after ten months at sea. The vessel was sailing homeward when a quarrel arose three days out, and part of the crew mutinied. After the mutineers set adrift the commander with eighteen loyal men in small boats, they sailed the *Bounty* back to Tahiti where some of the sailors remained. Taking aboard ten native women, ten native men, and a girl, the rest of the mutineers set sail for the uninhabited island which came to be called Pitcairn. The bloodshed which soon followed diminished the colony until in 1800 only one of the original crew of the *Bounty*, John Adams, and five native women and nineteen children survived.

Sobered by his experiences, Adams turned to the small Edinburgh Bible which had been brought ashore from the scuttled ship and lain forgotten. From the Bible he formulated a code of laws for his little marooned community, and from it also he taught them to read and write. For eight years the patriarch ruled his queer colony, with the Bible the source of his primitive laws and precepts. Then came the first ship, the American vessel *Topaz*, which lay to in order to get fresh water. Years later another ship put in and reports of the strange settlement filtered back to England. Adams died in 1829 but the colony continued to prosper. Stray ships came and occasional sailors settled on the island.

When in 1839 the American whaler *Cyrus* of Nantucket touched the island the mate, Levi Hayden, found two of the native widows of the mutineers still alive at an extremely old age. One of these, Mrs. Mary Christian, gave him a little Bible, saying the type was too small for her failing eyesight, Hayden giving her in exchange his own with larger print. Mrs. Christian's Bible, which, except for a prayerbook, may have been for many years the only book on the island, was acquired by the New York Public Library in 1924. Hayden brought back two Bibles, the second having been given to him by a youth, John Adams, grandson of the patriarch of the island. It had been rebound in what appeared to be fishskin and was acquired in 1896 by the Connecticut Historical Society. One of the two volumes was the original Pitcairn Bible; the other may have been left by a ship prior to the coming of the *Cyrus*.

With our own bookman's cruise launched, it is time to start
gathering the cargo of *curiosa*, for instance a copy of Charles Kingsley's
The Water-Babies, which elegantly bound, with the doublures inlaid with
seashells, appeared at the sale of the Achelis private library in New York.
And this oddity brings to mind the purported facsimile of Columbus'
diary published about 1880. It is entitled *Ye Secrete Log Book of ye
Spanish Admiral, noted and written by himself in the year 1492–93*, and
is bound in water-stained parchment encrusted with shells. Lovely
tortoise-shell bindings were the vogue in Holland a century or two ago
when silversmithing was at its height there; such books were ornamented
with clasps and bosses in exquisitely chased metal, or overlaid in filigree.
And inlaid mother-of-pearl has been used, occasionally, to beautify
sumptuous book bindings. It is rumored that there is also a book with an
oyster-shell binding but details are lacking.

Iceland with its venerable literature occasionally clothed its classics
in sealskin and, in imitation of that style, copies of *An Iceland Fisherman*
by Pierre Loti have been so garbed. But the skin of both the seal and the
sea lion are too oily and soft to find favor. The Grolier Club, at an
exhibition in 1903, included two volumes in sealskin binding, one with
repoussé and pierced silver framework, the other with silver borders and
clasps.

Fishskin has been used for bindings now and then, but it is inelastic
and inclined to crack at the joints. Ten or more Dutch and German
eighteenth-century books bound in the skins of sharks and other fish, all
ornamented with silver were included in the Grolier exhibition of unusual
books. An American example exhibited was *The Grolier Club Handlist of
Editions of the Complete Angler* (New York, 1893), bound in Javanese
sharkskin bordered with the skin of a Florida garpike; a silver monogram
and the seal of the Grolier Club are fastened on the front cover, and the
volume has a jade bookmark in the form of a fish. The skins of sharks
caught in the Caribbean or the China Sea are now tanned into shagreen,
being then converted into workable leather on a commercial scale. Captain
William E. Young's *Shark! Shark!* (1933) was so clad; the trade edition

had a sharkskin back, with a limited edition wholly bound in this sea leather.

A unique departure from the fish bindings is "the book-fish"—the cod, which, when cut open by the fishmonger of Cambridge Market in 1626, revealed in its belly a small parchment-bound volume, scarcely recognizable from the jelly-like mass into which it was clotted. Washed and the leaves pried apart, it was found to contain three religious tracts by Richard Tracy (and possibly John Frith), dedicated to Lord Cromwell; published in 1540, it was entitled *A Preparation for Death; The Treasure of Knowledge; A Mirror, or Looking Glass, to Know Thyself By.* The find occasioned much excitement and foreboding. Benjamin Prime, the Bachelor's Beadle, had it conveyed to the Vice-Chancellor who "made inquisition into the truth of the matter." Satisfied, he deemed it "a special admonition to us at Cambridge," and recounted the discovery in an epistle to Archbishop Usher. A new edition was published the next year with the title *Vox Piscis, or the Book of the Fish, containing Three Treatises which were found in the belly of a Cod-Fish, in Cambridge market, on Midsummer Eve last, 1626.* In this reprint the authorship is ascribed to John Frith alone, erroneously so according to Holbrook Jackson (the dual names come from *Notes and Queries* (1858)). A frontispiece shows the fish with a book in its mouth.

D'Israeli in his *Curiosities of Literature* tells a tale about Bishop Barbosa of Ugento, who in 1649 had printed a treatise, *De Officio Episcopi,* the manuscript of which he rescued from the fish market after one of his servants had brought home a purchase wrapped in a sheet of the Latin script.

In addition to its sealskin bindings, which were not uncommon, Iceland yields a piscatorial angle strange indeed. For among the books acquired by Harvard in 1931 from the collection of Kristján Kristjánsson of Reykjavik were seventeenth- and eighteenth-century volumes revealing that the natives of the island a century or so ago used a pertinent medium of exchange. On the title page of a work by Stefán Halldórsson is the statement: *"Selst inbunden aa Skrif Pappyr 12*

Fiskum; En aa Prent Pappyr 10 Fiskum" (Sold bound, printed on writing paper, for 12 fish; but on print paper, 10 fish). Another book, printed at Hólar in 1797, Jon Jonsson's *Sigurhroos Hugvekiur,* gives the price with even more intimate detail: "Sold bound for 16 fish; unbound, 13 fish; whereby it may be seen that there is no profit, since the sheet comes to less than 2 'skildings.' Our only concern is the glory of God and to lighten the people's burden."

Many a ship has gone to the bottom with not only its human freight but also precious cargo of art treasure. And those who avidly read of the piratical exploits of Morgan and Kidd may plot dotted charts of vessels that sank during the centuries with rich prize of gold bullion or ingots in the strong-room. From those picaresque days, there are tales of rich laden craft that are now phantom hulks on the sunless floors of the seven seas—and some of these tales have to do with books. Indeed, William Blades in his volume on *The Enemies of Books* should have included a chapter on the maw of the ocean and the sunken literature that from the early argosies to the present has paid tribute to the wrack of the devouring sea. D'Israeli in his above-mentioned work writes: "The republic of letters has suffered irreparable losses by shipwrecks. National libraries have often perished at sea, from the circumstances of conquerors transporting them into their own kingdoms."

When the illustrious Gian-Vincenzio Pinelli died in 1601 at Padua, he left a noble library to his heirs. Fourteen chests of manuscripts and one hundred and sixteen chests of printed books were placed on three vessels bound for Naples, where the family resided. One of the ships was captured by corsairs who, enraged at finding nothing on board but books, threw them overboard. Some of the chests which are said to have drifted to the beach at Fermo, or volumes which were scattered on the strand there, were salvaged by the Bishop of that place. Other shiploads were ultimately acquired by Cardinal Borromeo and later came into the possession of the great Ambrosian Library at Milan.

Many times precious books of learned travelers have been lost at sea. Guarino Veronese recovered many manuscripts in Greece, but on his

*Silver-filigree hornbook for titled
English children.*

*Hebrew hornbook—a
great rarity; five inches
tall (with handle).*

CUT-HYMNBOOK

*These products of
Yankee ingenuity
were split to the
spine in binding; the
upper leaves bore the
hymns, the lower
sections, the musical
notation, permitting
various hymns and
music to be
juxtaposed, as
announced to the
worshippers.*

CHAINED LIBRARIES FOR UNCHAINED MINDS

Fig. 69. The interior of the Library of the University of Leyden.
From a print by Jan Cornelis Woudanus, dated 1610.

return to Italy was shipwrecked and his treasures were engulfed. So, too, the Dutch scholar Hudde who, when returning to Europe after thirty years in China, lost all his collection in the sea. And Rafinesque, that little-known American savant of a century ago, on a voyage homeward suffered the loss by shipwreck of all his books and manuscripts on natural history.

Prior relates that Dennis Daly, an early collector of Elizabethan works, notably of Shakespeariana, lost all his library, including many first editions, when the ship on which he was voyaging "foundered off Beachy Head." And from Rosenbach comes the information that the young American Harry Elkins Widener, after the Huth Sale at London in 1912, tucked a second edition of Bacon's *Essays* into his coat, observing: "I think I'll take this little Bacon with me in my pocket, and if I am shipwrecked it will go down with me." He sailed on the *Titanic.*

One wonders if the superbly jewelled copy of Omar's *Rubáiyát* that also went down with the *Titanic* was "wolfed up by a shark" for its morsel of levant—the gems spewed out into the watery waste. It was one of the world's most sumptuous books. Two years went into its making at the hands of those master craftsmen, Sangorski and Sutcliffe, and it was on its way to a wealthy American collector. Rubies, turquoises, amethysts, topazes and garnets studded its covers and enshrined those questioning quatrains:

> *One moment in Annihilation's waste,*
> *One moment of the Well of Life to taste —*
> *The stars are setting . . .*

The Italian salvage ship *Artiglio* in June, 1932, reached the bullion room of the sunken liner *Egypt,* which had gone down a decade before off the coast of Brest with five million dollars in gold and silver aboard. Previously, amid the débris brought up by the iron baskets were several Bibles, for Lord Inchcape had insisted that there must be a Bible for each passenger's cabin. One slimy black mass when dropped to the deck contained Bibles, catalogues, a *Paradise Lost,* a dictionary, and a history of England, as well as clotted bundles of rupee notes printed in London for a native state of India.

The toll of the sea was greater in days gone by when the hazards of literature were also great. The loss of an entire edition of most contemporary works would be no matter for lamentation, but in earlier times many a manuscript and hundreds of volumes that were ocean casualties could never be replaced. Of no great moment was the fact that most of the first edition of J. M. Keynes's *Economic Consequences of the Peace* was lost in 1919 during transportation from Edinburgh to London by coastal steamer. More momentous was the mishap back in 1731 which nearly caused the total loss of what was destined to be one of the Bodleian Library's chief collections of English historical manuscripts and early printed books. Bishop Thomas Tanner, changing his residence from Norwich to Oxford, arranged to send his books thither. The latter part of the transportation being by barge on the Thames, the carelessness of a waterman as he passed through a lock caused the whole load to be tumbled into the Thames. When after twenty hours they were salvaged, seven wagonloads were so damaged each volume had to be taken apart and the contents dried on lines; most of these were later rebound but many still show signs of their soaking.

An instance is recounted by Reginald S. Faber in *The Library* (1889) of a baker in a village on Lake Maggiore who, having somehow come into possession of a mass of old folios and other works, was using them for fuel and otherwise in his little bakery. Hearing of this, and appreciating the sacrilege, Faber and a companion made a trip to the shop in a small boat from a nearby town. They purchased most of the remaining volumes—all worthy of preservation and many to be prized— and placed them in their tiny craft. On the return one of the two made a sudden lunge at a fish and capsized the cockle. Faber saved only one little Venetian *Petrarca* which chanced to be in his pocket and which, he says, "tattered and stained, lies on the table beside me as I write these lines."

In the circumstances of its making, one of the strangest books in the world is surely the *Aurora Australis*, produced at the frigid headquarters of the British Antarctic Expedition during the winter months in the frozen south, April to July, 1908. This first book to be written, printed, and bound in polar regions, was edited by E. H. Shackleton (later Sir Ernest), and consists of sprightly contributions of boreal literary flavor by members of the party. The covers of the volume were deftly made from the wood of packing cases that had contained provisions. One English collector has a copy with the word "KIDNEYS" stamped in capital letters on the ration-box boards in which his specimen is encased. Of the ninety copies printed and so bound, the majority were kept by members of the expedition. On the leather backstrip is blind-stamped the lettering of the title and a penguin device. The bevelled wooden boards, measuring 7⅞″ by 10¾″, seem to be laminated, although the thickness is only ¼″. The deckle-edge folded sheets are perforated near the inner edge and laced with green cord through a strengthening inside strip of leather along the joints.

Not content with an ordinary feat, the makers of this book illustrated it under the adverse conditions of the Antarctic. The engraved title page of the copy in the Spencer Collection of the New York Public Library has a vignette in blue, and the half titles scattered between contributions are in sanguine and black. The volume consists of ninety-nine unnumbered leaves and ten plates, of which three are etchings and seven lithographs. The artwork, typography, and hand-platen presswork reveal little or no indication of the trying circumstances under which the books were produced; but the imprint reads: "Printed at the sign of the Penguins, by Joyce and Wild. Latitude 77 32′ south, longitude 166 12′ east, Antarctica, 1908."

How all this was achieved is told by the explorer Shackleton in his preface. He recalls that his first Antarctic editorial job, six years before, had been a single typewritten copy of the South Polar *Times*. But the later expedition had come prepared for the winter immurement by bringing a printing and lithographic outfit as well as the paper necessary for the making of this memento during the months of darkness. Moreover, in anticipation of the project, several of the members before sailing sought instruction at an English printing plant, serving apprenticeships of three weeks. "During the sunless months which are now our portion," the preface reads, "months lit only by vagrant moon and elusive aurora, we have found in this work an interest and a relaxation, and hope eventually it will prove the same to our friends in the distant Northland."

An additional preface explains:

> Since writing the Preface for this book I have again looked over its pages, and though I can see but little not up to the usual standard in bookmaking, the printers are not satisfied that it is everything it ought to be. But the reader will understand better the difficulty of producing such a book quite up to the mark, when he is told that, owing to the low temperature in the hut, the only way to keep the printing ink in a fit state to use was to have a candle burning under the inking plate; and so, if some pages are printed more lightly than others, it is due to the difficulty of regulating the heat, and consequently the thinning or thickening of the ink. Again the printing office was only six feet by seven and had to accommodate a large sewing machine and bunks for two men, so the lack of room was a disadvantage; but I feel sure that those who see this book will not be captious critics.

In conclusion, Shackleton points out that the printing of *Aurora Australis* was done by Joyce and Wild, the artwork by Marston, and the wooden covers by Day. The ingenuity and success with which this odd work was written and fabricated in the depth of an Antarctic winter are remarkable.

Though this amazing performance has no rival, there is another item that calls for chronicle here. Commanded by Horatio T. Austin, a British Arctic expedition sailed from the Thames in May, 1850, in search of Sir John Franklin and his missing companions. The ships were *H.M.S. Resolute*, the *Assistance*, and two smaller craft. The squadron was locked in the Polar ice from September 24th until the following August 11th, including the three-months' Arctic night. To while away the tedium a

little newspaper was concocted in manuscript on the fifteenth of each
month and was called the *Aurora Borealis*. The contents first appeared
in print in *Arctic Miscellanies* (London, 1852), dedicated to "the lords
of the Admiralty," and setting forth in the preface: "The pages of the
'Arctic Miscellanies' were never intended for the press, and accident alone
has brought them before the public. It was not supposed that the
circulation of the 'Aurora Borealis' would have extended beyond the little
squadron under Captain Austin, when it first appeared in the Frozen
Ocean."

Some of the articles in this little newspaper were written by officers,
including the venerable Sir John Ross, and others by the weatherbeaten
tars before the mast. Each issue was arranged, and the contributions
legibly copied into it by the editor, who was one of the officers of the
Assistance. The result was the 347-page volume published after the
return of the expedition. A note states thanks are due "to Sir Edward
Parry and to Colonel Sabine, the institutors of papers in the Arctic
regions, to whom we are indebted for the idea of establishing our own."

Strangely enough in view of this manuscript newspaper, there was a
printing press aboard one of the vessels. It was intended for printing
balloon papers, but the stock of paper sufficed to print songs and
playbills for amateur theatricals. The preface tells us that: "So great a
passion did printing become amongst them, that when at length their
stock of paper was run out, they printed on chamois-leather, on shirts,
and in one instance on a blanket." One of the articles further tells of silk
pocket-handkerchiefs sent to press, and of calico, but the blanket is truly
unique and we wonder where it now is, and whether it was folded
bookwise. The contributions of the *Aurora Borealis* as collected in *Arctic
Miscellanies* are dated Baffin's Bay, June, 1850, to September, 1851.
Also stemming from the same expedition is a lithographed folio album
published in London in 1852 and entitled *Facsimile of the Illustrated
Arctic News, published on board* H.M.S. Resolute . . . *in search of the
expedition under Sir John Franklin. (Edited by T. Osborne and
G. F. M'Dougall).*

Some other curious little items worth mentioning—and there are doubtless more—are the *Polar Almanack for 1854*, printed aboard *H.M.S. Enterprise* in Camden Bay (lat. 70 N., long. 145 W.) ; volumes or diaries bound in flour-sacking by members of the party of Rear-Admiral Richard E. Byrd while in the Antarctic; and volumes of sea annals bound in wood from the hulks of famous ships, such as *True Stories of* H.M.S. Royal George (1841), which was wrecked off Spithead.

Beside these veritable curiosities belongs a mock book labelled on the backstrip *Isaak Walton's Complete Angler*, which is a leather-covered wooden receptacle containing artificial flies for fishing tackle.

Nelson relics always fetch high prices. The logbook of the flagship *Victory*, kept by Nelson's sailing master, Thomas Atkinson, was for many years in the collection of Thomas Barrett of Pears' Soap fame, but in 1919 was purchased by Lord Wollavington for the huge sum of twenty-five thousand dollars and presented to the British nation.

In legendary lore there are at least two stories that merit mention. Madan in his *Books in Manuscript* tells of the recovery of the eleventh-century illuminated *Gospel Book of St. Margaret, Queen of Scotland* which—not who—according to tradition was "rescued from drowning," salvaged unmarred from the bottom of a stream. After centuries of obscurity as to its whereabouts, it was found in 1887 in a small Suffolk parish library, was seemingly identified as the fabulous tome, and is now in the Bodleian Library at Oxford.

Then there is the *Gospels of St. Cuthbert* which, lacking its golden, gem-studded covers, now reposes in the British Museum as part of the collection presented by Sir Robert Cotton. This *Textus Sancti Cuthberti* preserved from early Saxon times by the monks of St. Cuthbert was miraculously saved from the sea. There are two versions that have come down a thousand years. One tells us that when the Danes invaded the vicinity and burned the Lindisfarne monastery, the monks set out on a voyage to Ireland but were driven back by a storm, the precious book, in a chest, being washed overboard. So far the accounts tally. But one declares that "owing to the merits of St. Cuthbert, the sea ebbed much farther than usual, and the holy volume was found at least three miles from the shore." The other, which this writer prefers, states that "some time after, whilst sailing up the Solway Firth, they espied the lost work shining in its golden cover on the sandy beach." Then, for the second time, it was placed in the coffin of St. Cuthbert which was in the church at Durham, and here it remained for more than a century until the restoration of Lindisfarne Abbey. With the dissolution of the English monasteries, thousands of volumes were destroyed or despoiled, and this ancient tome was shorn of its covers. It finally came into the Cottonian collection, and thence reached safe harbor in the British Museum.

But of all the tales of books lost in the sea or recovered from the deep, perhaps the most touching is that which relates how Leigh Hunt cast into the funeral pyre of Shelley a copy of *Lamia* which Hunt had lent him in mutual admiration of Keats, and which had been found tucked in the bosom of the drowned poet. Incidentally, the Pierpont Morgan Library has the watersoaked manuscript of the "Indian Serenade" in the autograph of Shelley, which had also been retrieved from the body or found in the boat *Don Juan* at the time of the poet's death.

In this bookman's voyage a net has been cast hither and yon, seine-hauling the lore concerning books swallowed by the sea, and by the fishes thereof, or recovered from the depths; of books dressed in the skin of sharks and other finny fellows; of other odd literary flotsam. But this little book adventure would not be complete without mention of Dame Juliana Berners, the earliest woman author in the English language. For of truth she is said to have written *A treatyse of fysshynge wyth an angle* which Wynkyn de Worde printed in 1496 and which is also said to be the first piscatorial essay in our mother tongue.

But our annals hark back much further; indeed, almost to the very beginning, earlier than in the tract by a mediæval saint who by virtue of his powers revealed what passed in Jonah's mind during the time that worthy meditated in the belly of the whale. Joachimus Maderus, a

German savant, in 1666 published his *De scriptis et bibliothecis antediluvianis* in which he held that men were familiar with all the arts before the Flood, concluding from passages in the Books of the Saints (interpreted to his need) that there were libraries in those days, and actually giving titles of works that *might* have dated earlier than the deluge! Further than this can no man go.

There is fascination in all that concerns the sea. Something of its spell is imparted by a Conrad or woven into verse by a Masefield. Those booklovers who have an addiction to unusual sea lore will be intrigued by books printed aboard ship. The volumes which fall under the head of sea-imprints are quite few, perhaps half a dozen; although the three or four articles at most that have been written about one or another of these products of floating presses go into detail as to this or that item, in no instance do they include all such titles.

Leaflets and proclamations of sea-presses, such as the two folio leaves issued on the flagship of the French fleet in Boston Harbor in 1778, are in a class with ephemera of perambulating presses on dry land. A printing press once operated from the shelter of a covered wagon in the pioneering days of the West; as early as 1870 a few issues of a small newssheet were printed aboard a transcontinental train; and from that year to 1883 atop Mount Washington appeared a small gazette called *Among the Clouds.*

A British Admiral of the time of Queen Elizabeth is said to have ordered printed aboard his flagship a maritime dictionary listing mariners' terms and all the parts and accoutrements of a vessel, with definitions, but no copy of this has come down to us. The printing of a Dutch Bible on board a ship cruising in the Baltic as early as 1564 is vaguely cited by Cotton.

The *Odi di Labindo* consists, strangely enough, of Italian poems written and printed in 1782 on Admiral Rodney's flagship *Formidable.* The only known original copy has the autograph of Lord Rodney, though a photostatic reproduction of ten copies was made in 1928 for distribution to leading libraries. Labindo was the pseudonym of the poet Giovanni Fantoni.

The first legitimate book printed at sea, however, is perhaps the one entitled *The Bloody Journal kept by William Davidson on board a Russian Pirate in the year 1789. Mediterranean: Printed on board H.M. Ship* Caledonia. *1812.* Sir Walter Scott heard of the existence of this manuscript journal, and thinking from its title that it would form a suitable subject for a poem, secured a certified copy. Sir Walter found the material far too revolting to form the basis of a poem, so he inserted it in *The Edinburgh Annual Register* for 1810, under the title "Journal of a Levant Pirate," and prefixed a short sketch containing particulars of the author Davidson's life. A copy of the *Register* was sent to the *Caledonia* and the "Journal" was reprinted by the cadets on board—for whose amusement a printing press had been supplied by Admiral Pellew —while blockading the French fleet shut up in Toulouse.

Davidson was a Scotch sailor and was drowned. The ship of which he wrote was a Russian privateer called the *Saint Dinnan*, commissioned to act against the Turks and Greeks. He was on board from December 1, 1788, until September 6, 1789, and butchery of their victims by the lawless crew was almost a daily occurrence.

In 1811 (or 1812) the officers of the *Caledonia* printed a much larger book of nearly a hundred pages, containing translations of Ruiz de Padron's celebrated speech on the Inquisition, and the oration entitled "Bread and Bulls," attributed to one Jovellanos. The translations were made on board at the admiral's request, and the enthusiasm of the translators runs riot over the abolition of the Inquisition and the novelty of literary freedom in Spain.

F. J. de Chastellux' French volume of travels in America, entitled *Voyage de Newport à Philadelphie, Albany, &c* was printed in 1781 aboard Rochambeau's French fleet ("de l'imprimerie Royale de l'Escadre"), during the occupancy of Newport, Rhode Island, by the French in the course of the American Revolution. Chastellux later reported his American travels in 1780–1782 in *Voyages dans l'Amérique septentrionale*, which appeared in Paris in 1786 and in an English version soon thereafter. Howard M. Chapin, librarian of the Rhode Island Historical Society, who has written a pamphlet (*Contributions to Rhode Island Bibliography, No. 2*) concerning the press which was aboard one of the ships, tells us that an almanac called *Calendrier français pour l'année 1781* was also printed in Newport harbor at the time. Chapin's data first appeared in the *Providence Magazine,* and one hundred fifty copies of his pamphlet were reprinted.

Twelve of the twenty-four copies of the volume printed aboard the French fleet were presented by Chastellux to friends in America, and twelve to friends in France. One copy was owned by Roderick Terry, former doyen of the Newport Historical Society; a second is in the New York Public Library; and a third is at Harvard, bequeathed by Charles Sumner. The New York Library copy was the property of Eliza Moore Marbois, wife of M. de Marbois, secretary of the French Embassy, near whom, M. de Chastellux explains, he was lodged during his stay in Philadelphia. The daughter of Mme Marbois—a lady with a romantic career—married a prime minister of Louis Bonaparte.

This naval printing office of Rochambeau's squadron, temporarily established on land, also issued a newspaper in French, *La Gazette Française de Newport;* the fact of this newspaper's existence was based on advertisements soliciting subscriptions that appeared in two contemporary Providence newspapers, but for a long time no copies were believed to be extant. In 1925, however, a series of seven numbers and one supplement were discovered.

Some seventy years later in another harbor across the continent the *Henry Lee* dropped anchor. During her long voyage around the Horn on her way to the California gold rush, a book had been printed on shipboard by J. L. Hall. Only one copy of this *Journal of the Hartford Union Mining and Trading Company* is extant, prized by the Society of California Pioneers in its library in San Francisco. A reprint, augmented by experiences ashore, appeared in 1898 as *Around the Horn in '49.*

To Charles Grandpierre's penchant for sea-printing must be credited four items—two books, and two previous pamphlet pieces embodied in one of these books. One of the shorter pieces has this title: *Temperance in Argentina, or results of Personal Liberty and of Prohibition, by Chas. Grandpierre, A.B., LL.B. Printed as Manuscript aboard* S.S. Verdi, *Lamport & Holt Line. Copyright 1912.* The Preface of this twenty-eight-page pamphlet informs us: "The following pages are a reproduction of some of my notes and of fragments of the manuscript of lectures given in various places. Its revised contents will form part of a book 'What we may learn from other Americans.' " In the text he opines that the drinking habits in Argentina are superior to ours and that our attitude toward alcohol is "nonsensical." Another pamphlet of sixty-four pages in gray wrappers was printed by Grandpierre aboard the *S.S. Verdi,* the title reading: *Five South American Cities; Ports of Call of the* S.S. Verdi, *Lamport & Holt Line* (undated, but about 1912). When the promised volume, of which these two endeavors form a part was published, the title had been revised to read *What We Learn from The Other Americans.* Consisting of two hundred fifty-eight pages, it notes: "Printed as Manuscript while at Sea, aboard *S.S. Verdi.* Copies are not for Sale." This curious mimeographed note is pasted on the fly-leaf:

> In Lieu of Preface. This book is the first ever written and printed on board of ship while at sea. This explains, and excuses, its defects. Only 200 copies were printed and numbered. No attempt has been made to appear impartial. The aim has been to state just what the title implies, and to present the "other side" of Latin American civilization, avoiding a repetition of all the bad that may be mentioned about "Other Americans," as well as all the good that may be said about us, both of which have been told often enough.

But this is not all. Tipped in between title and first page of text is a folded mimeographed sheet whereon the author tells, among other things, that he has in his day "run away from a guardian at sixteen, become stowaway on a steamship, risen to the rank of officer; worked his way through the University of Missouri and through the University of Leipzig; written several books in three different languages."

Grandpierre also has to his credit *A Systematic Dictionary of Sea Terms, Printed at Sea, aboard* American Legion, *Munson Line.* This pleasant little work of ninety-six pages, with a copyright date of 1928, informs in a preface headed "The Language of the Sea," that "One of the changes brought about by specialization of the work in large steamers, is the passing of many terms and expressive forms of speech, and the changing meaning of others." The contents define all manner of maritime terms common to the lingo of the tar or to admiralty parlance. The listing ranges from *doldrums* and *Red Wagon* (a steamship man's term of contempt for sailing vessels) to *athwart* and *Covered with Monkeys* (a vessel upon which libels or liens have been pasted); from *gunwales* and *rogues yarn* (a colored strand through lengths of cordage for identification and discouragement of theft) to *beachcomber* and *strike-me-dead* (white bread, a surprise); from *lubber* and *To Bleed a Buoy* (to let out the water which has leaked into a can or nun) to *derelict* and *Iron Sick* (an iron or steel hull whose plates often get loose). Grandpierre did a good job and was no doubt proud of it. He seems to have had a snug harbor at a spot called Valley Cottage, New York, for the *Dictionary of Sea Terms* cites that retreat also on the title page. In fact this Valley Cottage was the place from which he issued in 1924 his *Oasis Epigrams; some original, some copied, some rehashed, some just stolen,* or at least the third edition in 1928, newly titled *Some Musings of a Seafaring Man.*

The next to latest sea-imprint known to this chronicler is *Nine Months On a Cruise, and Experiences in Nicaragua,* by William E. Richmond, chief yeoman, U.S.N. On the title page of this 115-page book bound in yellow cloth with stapled pages, is printed: "San Diego, Published on Board the U.S.S. California, 1912." Whether the printing was done at sea or in harbor is not clear; San Diego may refer to the binding and distribution. A headnote to Chapter One reads: "Being a history of the cruise of the U.S.S. California from November 15, 1911, to August 15, 1912, to the Hawaiian Islands, Philipine [*sic*] Islands, China and Japan." It includes halftone illustrations and the binding is lettered and stamped with an ornamental border; there is no information on how large an edition was printed.

Finally, mention should be made of a pamphlet entitled *The Missourian,* dated Tokio Bay, September 10, 1945. Written by men aboard the U. S. *Missouri* and printed on the ship's press, the narrative describes what took place on the memorable day when the Japanese surrender was signed.

Conrad calls *The Brassbounder,* written by a teller of sea yarns, the Scottish shipmaster Captain David Bone, the finest saltwater story of its kind since *Two Years Before the Mast.* In his ship, the *Tuscania,* Captain Bone installed the first known seafaring bookshop. And for this "High Seas Bookshop" an edition of his *The Lookout Man* was especially imprinted in 1923, with a title page bearing the *Tuscania* designation. On the publication date copies were duly displayed and sold in mid-ocean. Christopher Morley points out that, in writing and sponsoring the first book ever *published* on the briny deep, Bone established a precedent for bibliographers. "As you know," Morley comments, "printing is not publication. The publishing of a book means the actual vending of it to customers, and the first copies of that book that were ever sold were sold in mid-Atlantic on the ship Tuscania." It is interesting to note that it was William McFee, the novelist and marine engineer, who for several voyages presided over this seagoing bookshop as its first careening bookseller.

A BLOCKHEAD'S BOOKSHELF

A RECENT BOOK-AUCTION CATALOGUE included a volume on clipper ships, each side of which was paneled in an oblong fragment of the hull of a famed and bygone vessel. And occasionally volumes here and abroad have been found which were encased in wood cut from the timber of historic and dismantled ships, or from celebrated trees. Most bookmen have heard of one or another of these, but no one, it seems, has attempted to collect a shelfful, for good reason—prohibitive search and scant results. Here are a few, however, which might well find places on the complete listing which, it seems, has yet to be attempted for the first time.

Several copies of *True Stories of* H.M.S. Royal George, by Henry Slight, Esq., were put in covers of quarter-inch thickness made from the wood of the wreck of that ship which was blown up in 1840 after several futile attempts to float her. This 120-page book, published at Ryde, Isle of Wight, in 1841, is almost miniature in size, measuring 3½″ by 2½″. It contains survivors' versions of the foundering of the vessel at Spithead in 1782, an account of attempted salvage operations, and verses to the warship and its crew. There were also a few slightly larger copies similarly bound with the imprint Portsea, 1843.

One of the most unusual items in this category is an edition of ninety copies of *Aurora Australis*, written, set, printed and wood-bound in the

Antarctic winter quarters of the Shackleton Expedition of 1908. As
more fully noted in another chapter, the volumes were bound in wood
from packing cases that had contained provisions and are sightly
specimens that would do credit to the makers even if produced under
circumstances less adverse.

In the Baroness Burdett-Coutts 1922 sale at Sotheby's, there was a
carved casket for Shakespeare's works, made of a portion of "Herne's
oak" and presented to the Baroness by Queen Victoria. On a silver plate
inside the lid is the following inscription: "This casket, carved out of
Herne's oak, the tree mentioned in 'The Merry Wives of Windsor,'
contains the First Quarto Edition of Shakespeare's poems, published
anno 1640, and the still more rare first edition of the dramatic works,
published in 1623. The old tree fell down in 1863."

The latter volume, the famous First Folio known as the "Daniel
copy," was purchased by the Baroness in 1864 for the then
unprecedented sum of £816 to prevent its being taken out of England by
an overseas bidder. This delighted Queen Victoria so much that she gave
the Baroness some wood from Herne's oak, which was long a landmark
in Windsor Great Park and the trysting-place in one of the most
effective scenes of *The Merry Wives of Windsor*. The Baroness had the
wood made into the case in which the folio and poems have ever since
been kept. At the 1922 sale the precious little chest and its contents—
which included an account of the casket written by the Baroness—was
bought by an American who paid £8,600 for it; it is now on display in
the Folger Library, Washington.

Uncommon but now and then procurable is *The Little Shakespeare*,
a diminutive bijou, the covers of which are made of oak from the Holy
Trinity Church, Stratford, where Shakespeare was baptized and buried.

While an example of it may be acquired for a comparative song,
$17,500 was needed to win the first edition of *Paradise Lost* sold at
auction in New York in 1935. It fetched this sum not only because it
was believed to be the finest copy in existence, having a provenance of
noted collections, but because its original brown sheep binding is

preserved in protecting covers made from the wood of a rafter from the house in Westminster in which Milton began writing this landmark of literature. Pasted on the inside front protecting cover is a printed account of the demolition of this house. The volume was discovered in 1867 at Lamport Hall, the seat of the Isham family.

Odd, indeed, in the way of binding, is still another book whose covers felt the tramp of Caesar's legions two thousand years ago. The facts are these: H. Klemm, whose collection of rare books is now part of the Buchgewerbe-Museum at Leipsic, was the author of a bibliographical work published in 1884. He had some copies of it bound in wood taken from the foundations of the old Roman bridge at Mainz, birthplace of printing with movable types. These covers were cut from an oak beam used by the Roman army to support a bridge across the Rhine. Though the beam had been under water for over nineteen hundred years, the lengthy submersion did not deteriorate the wood in any marked degree. One of these specimens of bookbinding curiosa was shown at a Grolier Club Exhibition, and a copy was owned by Otto W. Fuhrmann, graphic arts expert of New York. He stated that the remains of the bridge were discovered about 1880, and that the oak beams were so well preserved that one of the piers was set up in the courtyard of the Historical Museum for permanent display. That the bridge was built soon after Caesar's first crossing of the Rhine, toward the beginning of the Christian era, was proven by the finding of a bronze log-stamping implement in the piling bearing the symbol of the 22nd Legion, anciently stationed at Mainz.

The American collector Paul Jordan-Smith tells how he picked up from the "Shilling Box" of a London shop a facsimile of Sir Thomas Browne's *Religio Medici* which was one of a few copies that had been bound up in thin oak boards taken from that seventeenth-century author's old house at Norwich. And there are two or three copies of Goldsmith bound in wood preserved from the old timbers of "Dolly's Chop House," where he was wont to consort with his cronies.

A volume of Burns's poems is bound in wooden covers reportedly made of a fragment of the bed in which he died. And, as one Britisher wrote, "the forests of Scotland must have been partially denuded by the one-time demand for copies of Scott or Burns suitably strait-waistcoated in wood having a real (or alleged) connection with the haunts of these sons of Caledonia." Though this is an exaggeration—as anyone who tries to find a copy will discover—the idea is not so strange, for many religious works a generation ago were clad in wood from the Holy Land, and sentiment cherished these tokens made from the cedars of Lebanon or the olive trees on the slopes above Jerusalem. A new crop which has come of late, usually has pressed flowers between its pages.

At a display of modern Italian bookbinders' art held at the Casa Italiana, New York, several volumes were bound in olive wood, with hand-wrought iron clasps. That such production is not obsolete nor restricted to isolated volumes is seen in the Random House one-hundred-dollar Whitman's *Leaves of Grass*, produced in 1930 from the 1892 edition by the Grabhorn Press of San Francisco in four hundred folio copies, with sides of seven-ply walnut and a red morocco backbone. In January, 1892, Whitman, nearing death, was anxious to see the last edition of the work by which he is best known, so Horace Traubel had some fifty copies made up for him on cheap paper and roughly bound. Most of these copies, which came to be known as the Death-Bed Edition, were sent to the poet's intimates and admirers.

There are doubtless other books bound in fragments of ships, houses, trees or furniture associated with great names. Kindred relics now and then crop up in art auction-rooms. In 1936 in connection with the dispersal of a library, the British firm of Sotheby & Co. disposed of an important Shakespeare relic—a goblet made from the mulberry tree planted by the poet in his garden at New Place, Stratford-on-Avon. Carved with a portrait of Shakespeare and his coat-of-arms (executed by Thomas Sharp in 1799), adorned with silver mounts and lining, it stands eight inches high. Letters from E. C. Wellstood, Librarian of Shakespeare's birthplace, accompany the goblet, vouching for its authenticity.

But the association seems closer when it is a book that links an illustrious name with a token of onetime proximity to that personage. Who would not wish to possess a *Life of Nelson* bound in wood from the cask of rum in which his body was sent home? Or the *Memoirs of Jeff Davis* in beveled boards made from the flagpole at Fort Sumter? Or Mark Twain's *Life on the Mississippi* in part of the paddlewheel of a steamboat he once piloted?

Should the blockhead bibliophile be lucky enough to acquire one of those few copies of Bunyan's *Pilgrim's Progress* having generous polished panels of eloquent oak procured from Elstow Church when it was restored in 1880, he will be indeed rewarded. Elstow Church was that seven-hundred-year-old edifice where the tinker rang the belfry chimes as a boy and preached as a man, where Bunyan, his parents, and his children were baptized. For centuries before Bunyan's birth and for centuries after his death the wood now preserved as inlays of these few volumes saw the procession of generations that dwelt in old Elstow when it was a nunnery, and outlasted those other generations that worshipped there when it became a Protestant church after the dissolution. Some copies of another edition of this same classic, called the "Elstow Edition," with outline drawings by Gunston and others, is said to have been bound in oak boards taken from the old timber of the church when the remaining building was renovated in 1880.

A volume sold at the dispersal of W. S. Simpson's St. Paul's Cathedral Library in London has appropriate wooden sides made of fragments taken from the belfry of St. Paul's when that church underwent repair in 1893.

It represents no great feat to have a *Hiawatha* clothed with inlays of birchbark. On birchbark, too, printed and bound in wrappers thereof in 1882–1883, was the *Birch Bark Poems* of Charles F. Lummis. To make these miniature volumes of twelve pages, the author cut the bark, split and trimmed it, set the type, and did the printing during college vacations to help earn his way. In 1936 a collection of poems by Roy Carlson Colman appeared in California covered with redwood; and in

A BLOCKHEAD'S BOOKSHELF

1890 a German anthology on tobacco by G. Lewinstein, *Für und Wider den Tabak*, was bound in cigar-box boards, with cedar paper fly-leaves and yellow bookmarker such as was used to bundle cheroots. Similar in appearance is *The Soverane Herbe: A History of Tobacco* by W. A. Penn in 1901. Chance and patience will reveal other worthwhile finds; and though some may raise an eyebrow at this peculiar collecting hobby, others will keep an eye open for those relics of lumber that in proper hands could be fashioned to adorn a book associated with an historic site or subject.

Mention might also be made of such spurious books as the not uncommon table "volume,"—in reality a little Swiss musicbox, with wooden covers carved in the style of the cuckoo clocks of yore, which plays a tune when the lid is lifted—or the leather-covered box, resembling a book and duly titled Izaak Walton's *Angler*, which is a kit of fishing accessories.

Frank Sullivan in a facetious foreword to his *Innocent Bystanding* remarked: "A word concerning the paper and typography of the book might not be amiss. It is printed on paper the pulp for which was specially chewed by the author from special spruce trees grown in the Canadian forests. This 'labor of love' occupied three full years or two years, eleven months and twenty odd days longer than the day in which Rome was not built by Romulus and Remus, 752 B.C."

It is appropriate to include a few words about *The Wooden Works of Thomas Anonymous*, published by The Backwoods Bindery, Sumter, S. C., in 1904. Its thirty pliant pages are of plywood as thin as bristol board. These are perforated, and together with the heavier covers, which resemble the cedar of a cigar box, are held together by nickel rings and an ornamental brass chain. With several pyrographic illustrations, this curious volume is estimable only by reason of oddity. In a facetious preface the author writes that, overcome by a desire to commune with Nature, he "took to the woods."

But this is nothing novel. An old tome, possibly dating from the fourteenth century, was found some years ago by the Norwegian Society for the Conservation of Historic Monuments. This relic was discovered during the restoration of a church in the village of Hopperstad and taken to the University of Christiania where a museum of antiquities is maintained. Made up of thin beechboards, the rarity is bound together at the back, and covered with wax. The boards are slightly raised on the edges to avoid sticking and to preserve the characters. Inscriptions appear to have been traced on the wax with a fine needle. Portions of the lettering may have been incised in less remote times, but most are several centuries old.

Toward the close of the eighteenth century, there existed at Warstein, Westphalia, a singular "wooden library" belonging to one Schildbach. According to Fitzgerald, the imitation books composing it were made of wood, each a specimen of a different tree. The spines were made of bark with the scientific and common name of the variety on red leather labels. One side was constructed of a polished cross-section of the same stock; the other side showed the natural grain of the wood. The whole formed a box inside which were preserved the leaves, seed, blossoms, or dried fruit pertaining to the tree, a small piece of the root together with the moss that grows on the trunk, and mounted specimens of the insects that infest the wood or foliage. These sylvan volumes were alike in size and several score in number. A somewhat similar "wooden library" is said to have been in a monastery at Prague; another of seventy-nine volumes in the Hungarian National Museum. Oldtime naturalists, too, sometimes had such arboreal sets. According to Lawrence S. Thompson, the Bavarian forester Kandid Huler, who died in 1813, was reputed to have owned such a set of fifty-one volumes.

Notable, if not analogous, is the shelf of volumes entitled *The American Woods, Exhibited by Actual Specimens* (1888–1928), prepared by Romeyn B. Hough. Hough, who died in 1924 and was the author of several scientific books on trees, conceived the idea of issuing information on our native trees in cross-sections of wood. His achievement consists of fourteen green, cloth-covered boxes resembling ordinary volumes, each with a clasp and each containing an inner portfolio of twenty-five loose card-mounts. In each card-mount three transparent samples of a particular variety of tree are inserted, showing the grain in transverse, radial, and tangential sections. The black bristolboard holding the specimens of each page bears the name of the variety in Latin, English, German, French, and Spanish. The threefold cutting enables one to see how sections of the same tree vary in appearance, as the angle of the cut meets the grain. The card-mounts measure about six by eight inches, and each of the three wood specimens inserted on a card is about four inches wide by two high. Of *carte de visite* thickness, they are visible from both sides. The printing qualities of these small wooden sheets are praised by Hough, but, save for exceptional purposes, their tenderness precludes much handling. He mastered the technique of cutting such sections and opened a commercial industry in cross-section business cards and the like.

Thirteen fascicles of *The American Woods* had been issued at the time of Hough's death: Part I, with appendix on American trees, was published in 1888, and Part XIII in 1913. In 1928 his daughter, Marjorie G. Hough, issued Part XIV, containing specimens which had been identified, collected, and sectioned before her father's death. Presumably there were few sets made of this remarkable work—a rare contribution to the literature of American forestry. The beauty of grain and diversity of pattern seen in these sylvan specimens defy description.

Primitive recordings on wood, such as tally-sticks, are surprising survivals. Though extant specimens are uncommon, tally-sticks, notched to record financial transactions, were not unknown in nineteenth-century England. Names and dates were carved or inked. After being notched, they were cut in two; one half was kept in the Exchequer, the other half circulated. In use until 1826, the Exchequer halves were stored in the old Star Chamber until 1834, when, the space being needed for other purposes, they were disposed of as fuel for heating the Houses of Parliament; indeed it appears so many were used the stoves became overheated and the Houses of Parliament burned down!

A masterpiece of intarsia was created by George A. Simonds for the National Geographic Society a decade ago in *Wild Animals of North America*, with a moose salient on the cover. The sky is tulip wood from Brazil; the moose's body, mottled walnut butt from Australia. The bushes in the foreground are bubinga from Africa, and the mountains, amaranth from Dutch Guiana, American cherry, and walnut. The water pads are poplar burl, and the water, maple crotch. The moose's eye is made of two woods, American holly and gaboon ebony from Africa. The water glimpsed through the rosewood trees is gray harewood from England.

Dard Hunter, versatile searcher after the secrets of papermaking, printed various books which, with the exception of the binding and the first two written by others, consisted entirely of his own handiwork and brainwork. He made the paper by hand, designed the type, cast it, set it, and for the several books written by himself did his own presswork.

The productions of this esteemed bookmaster were naturally printed in small output. His *Primitive Papermaking* is an account of a Mexican sojourn and of a voyage to the Pacific Islands in search of information relating to the making and use of bark paper. The volume is notable for the reason that it contains thirty-four original specimens of the barks of the Pacific Islands used in papermaking. This was the fifth book from his private press in Chillicothe, Ohio, and was published in two hundred copies in 1927. The romantic interest of this work, as well as the high authority of its contents, make it a much-sought collector's item. Another of his works is that on *Old Papermaking in China and Japan* with actual specimens, centuries old, of Chinese paper from bamboo and mulberry bark, Japanese paper from mitsumata bark, Persian paper from china grass, Tibetan and other papers from these botanical substances as well as gampi and other growths.

The fancy of Dard Hunter to hie to the South Seas and fashion a book there from the natural resources which an island and his ingenuity might provide, brings to mind the curious literary problem posed by Arthur Machen. If a man of literary inclinations were marooned on a desert island and hopeless of rescue, would he write? Or, assuming he was without materials, would he feel the necessity of devising some means of writing? Would he write though convinced no eye but his own would ever see the product of his pen? Machen contended that he would. As reported in the press, he reasoned: "The hypothetical Crusoe might have no better implements available than quills of parrots' feathers, paper made out of the bark of the guru tree, and ink obtained by macerating the root of a certain plant. But, granted his possession of the literary faculty, he would possess also the literary impulse. He would write because he liked writing, apart from whatever fate might be in store for the thing written."

It is rather pleasant to think that trees have been associated with literature, that they, on occasion, have given of their bark and body to the making of books. The use of cork has naturally not been excluded, though only four instances of printing on cork are known. A volume prepared by A. J. Mayer for the exhibition of the world's industries at London in 1851 was one of these. It consisted of sixty-four plates after Rembrandt, Murillo, and other artists, but the number of sheets which had to be rejected made it a costly project.

Three editions of *Don Quixote*, each in two volumes, were also prepared entirely on pages of cork. The first was published by Eudaldo Canibell in 1905, and was printed at San Felix de Guixola, Catalonia, each volume containing something less than two hundred folios. In 1906 the printing house of Don Octavio Viader, located at the same place, issued an edition of fifty-two copies; and other editions appeared at Barcelona in 1907, and again in 1933. Bound in cork boards, these curious works are outwardly ornamented by what may have been the pressure of a heated plate. The typography is admirable, though the pages, which are of silken thinness, are filled with countless tiny perforations.

One hundred copies of a bi-lingual edition of *Hamlet* were printed at Barcelona in 1930, on leaves of cork measuring 10½″ by 8¼″. With illustrations in color, the English version on ninety-five leaves is followed by the Spanish rendition on seventy-eight leaves. The sheets are printed on one side only, within tinted ornamental borders, and each opening chapter is heightened with gold.

In an experimental effort to find substitutes for rags in paper manufacture, an extraordinary volume of one hundred twenty-six pages of prose and verse, *Œuvres du Marquis de Villette* was published in London in 1786. The papermaker, M. Léorier Delisle, in a dedicatory epistle explains that since usual paper material was becoming increasingly scarce, substitute materials, otherwise more or less useless, should be put to use. As proof of his point, he printed the writings of the Marquis Charles de Villette on a species of marshmallow paper (*papier de guimauve*) in one edition, and on paper made from the bark of the lime tree in another. Following the writings are twenty-one specimen leaves, each made of a different substance, to wit: moss, thistles, nettles, hops, reeds, seaweed (algae) and two other specimens of water plants; bark of the willow, the osier, and the sallow; bark of the poplar, elm, lime, and oak; the roots of foxtail grass, spindle-tree, hazel wood, burdock leaves; and the botanical horsefoot—oddly enough straw is not included in this unprecedented collection. One copy of this strangely fabricated book, it has been said, was printed on rose-colored paper.

In the Stevens Collection at the University of Vermont is a copy of Jacob Christian Schaeffer's six-volume *Neue Versucht das Pflanzenreich zum Papier-Machen* (1765–1771), with eighty-two specimen leaves of paper made without rags from wood and vegetable fiber, a work celebrated in the history of papermaking. This was a pioneer treatise, published at Regensburg, and its Amsterdam edition of 1770 contained, in addition to the text, eighteen sample sheets made from straw, nettles, earthmoss, cattails, and aloes leaves.

The classic example of the use of straw is the work of Matthias Koops in 1800 entitled *An Historical Account of the Substances which have been used to describe Events and to convey Ideas from the earliest Date to the Invention of Paper*. This volume, and a second edition in 1801, the author "lays at His Majesty's feet" as the first instance of a useful paper made from straw without rags or other admixture (the appendix, however, is printed on paper made from wood alone). An

A BLOCKHEAD'S BOOKSHELF

infrequent use of colored straw in the sixteenth to eighteenth centuries has been noted by Hodgkins. Filaments usually of wheat or oats, dyed or enamelled with delicate tints, were occasionally used for ornamenting bookbindings, but more often for plaques, étuis, mirror-frames, and the like.

Cornstalk fiber has also been used in the making of a book. In London, William Cobbett had the title page and contents leaf of his nineteenth-century *A Treatise on Corn* printed on paper made of the husks of corn which he had grown. Although a process for preparing paper from cornstalks has been known since 1765, the first book printed on a stock made with the object of utilizing farm waste products, appears to have been George M. Rommell's *Farm Products in Industry* which was printed on paper made largely of cornstalk pulp, with a proportion of sulphite and flax fiber. Some copies were bound in a material fabricated from cottonseed hulls. The same substance furnished the antique-finish paper for the text and the coated stock on which the illustrations appear. In the course of chemical experiments that preceded the making of this book, cornstalks were ennobled into paper in eight hours.

And there are others who have gone to plants and trees for materials on which to record their stories. Book paper containing elements of esparto grass were first introduced into England by Routledge in 1861. The Huntington Library has a two-hundred-year-old Arabic manuscript *Koran* written on bombycine paper made from the wool of the cotton plant. Bark pictographs of the Delaware (Lenni Lênapé) Indians record centuries of their past, and Brinton's account of this Walam Olum, as it was called, merits mention. A new rendition was issued by the Indiana Historical Society in 1954. Wordless novels of Frans Masareel and Lynd Ward tell their tales in sequences of woodcuts.

Thus, borrowing Pope's couplet, we have:

> *The bookful blockhead, ignorantly read,*
> *With loads of learned lumber in his head.*

NOT FOR THE THIN-SKINNED

JAMES ALLEN, better known in his day as George Walton, was a notorious scoundrel of numerous aliases who a century ago terrorized New England. With the bravado of his kind, on one of his several escapes from jail he left a note in which he gave notice to the public that he was the "master of his own skin." And so it proved in the end. His last act of banditry, executed on a prominent Springfield gentleman, John Fenno, netted him a twenty-year prison term. He had served but two years of his term when in 1837 he died of consumption. Shortly before his death he made the extraordinary request that his own skin be used to bind his autobiography and that a copy so bound should be presented to John Fenno as a token of esteem for Fenno's stout resistance when held up by Allen.

A year later, this scoundrel's account of his exploits and repentance was published under the title: *Narrative of the Life of James Allen, alias George Walton, alias Jonas Pierce, alias James H. York, alias Burley Grove, the Highwayman. Being his deathbed confession to the Warden of the Massachusetts State Prison.* Bound by a Boston craftsman named Peter Low, the binding, putty color with yellowish tinge, bears the label: *"Hic Liber Waltonis Cute Compactus Est."* The volume is now in the possession of the Boston Athenaeum.

The omniscient compiler of *The Anatomy of Bibliomania* alludes to several instances of British culprits flayed after execution and their hides used for literary leather. In concluding his brief allusion to this macabre theme, he relates that in 1891 a physician instructed the noted English craftsman Zaehnsdorf to bind a copy of Hans Holbein's *Dance of Death* in the skin of a woman. The tanning had been done by Sweeting of Shaftsbury Avenue, with human hair replacing the usual silk of the headbands. Though Jackson was then uncertain as to the whereabouts of the volume, it is now known to have been acquired by the Grolier Club of New York, which secured it from Beverly Chew. In 1903 this volume and two other volumes of *Dance of Death* also bound in human skin were a part of the Grolier Club's exhibit of curious books. The binding of the two other volumes were respectively a black human skin binding, and a white inlaid with black morocco, tooled with death's heads and knucklebones by an American binder.

It would seem that several other copies of the Holbein title, deemed appropriate for such treatment, were so garbed here and abroad. One, sold at the William D. Breaker sale in 1935, had a skull medallion modelled in leather which was centered on the front cover with two tiny rows of ivory chip teeth; on the back flyleaf was a voucher of the British binders, Sangorski and Sutcliffe, that the binding was human skin.

An American collector, W. E. Louttit, Jr., in 1944 possessed three of these "personal" volumes: a Holbein, bound by Cox, a Chicago binder about 1898; *De Humani Corporis Fabrica*, by Andreas Vesalius; and Adolphe Belot's *Mademoiselle Giraud, My Wife*, which may be the copy in "three-quarters human skin, tooled and gilt" offered in a 1936 catalogue of the Bodley Book Shop.

In the Lane Medical Library at Stanford University is an extraordinary volume, being one of a scattered trio of quarto size bound in the negroid skin of the same corpus. Adorning the front cover of each is a small silver plaque showing side by side a Negro head and a skull in *repoussé* profile. At the top of the design is lettered the name of the early artist (Jan) Ladmirál, and the base of the plate bears the stencil: Ex Libris, Hans Friedenthal. The original skin measured 25″ by 29″

but shrank in tanning. A description stated the texture was remarkable, intermediate in appearance between coarse African goat and pigskin. The rear part had a distinct grain, but breast and belly were more finely marked. The thickness was that of a morocco goatskin, thinning on the flank, the whole quite pinguid. The Stanford volume contains two Latin medical dissertations by Bernhard Albinus, dated Leyden, 1636–1637, one being on the causes of racial pigmentation among blacks and others. As an added touch the binding doublures are of the pelt of "graveyard" mole.

The second of the mentioned trio, printed between 1736 and 1741, contains six Latin Theses by Albinus on anatomy and was at last report in the possession of a well-known London bookseller. The third, entitled *Das Rätsel des Menschen* (The Riddle of Mankind), was retained by the bibliophile Friedenthal. All three are embellished with fine copperplates printed in color by Ladmiral, being the earliest such anatomical engravings in color with the exception of a single print by Le Blon. All three were bound of the same skin by Paul Kersten of Berlin in 1910.

Some years ago a well-known rare-book dealer stated that he had sent a Negro skin, salted, to Zaehnsdorf to bind Phillis Wheatley's *Poems* and other books by Negroes and that he had difficulty in getting it out of this country. Refused as human skin and as an anatomical specimen, the roll was finally sent as animal skin. At a New York book sale in 1935, the catalogue noted that a first edition of Phillis Wheatley's *Poems on Various Subjects* (London, 1773), the earliest published work by a Negro dwelling in North America, was "Said to be bound in human Negro skin."

It is mere hearsay that one or more Southern planters of slavery days regarded the possession of books bound in the skin of deceased colored favorites a token of their affection. Alfred de Sauty relates how his facetious remark in a Chicago lecture on bindings—that *Uncle Tom's Cabin* might be suitably clad in Negro skin—led a mortician in the audience soon thereafter to send to him at the Lakeside Press a still moist rectangular roll removed at the local morgue. Despite rumor that it was used as desired, the binder declares the grisly segment was promptly consigned to the boiler room furnace.

The Newberry Library, Chicago, acquired in 1919 a bound Arabic manuscript as part of the bequest of John M. Wing of that city who died in 1917. According to the late George B. Utley, librarian, little is known of its previous history. A flyleaf inscription, however, informs us that it was "Found in the Palace of the King of Delhi, Sept. 21st 1857, seven days after the assault. [signed] James Wise, M.D. Bound in human skin." In a letter to Dr. Wise, tipped in at the back, the sender, whose name cannot be deciphered, reports that the manuscript is a "narrative of events connected with the Dekkan, comprising biographies, deeds, genealogies, &c. of sundry notables by a Nawab Wurzeer of Hyderabad," a great military commander. Apparently the work was written by an amanuensis, the "Humble and most insignificant of men, Mir Baki 'Ali, who completed it in the year of the Hegira 1226 [about 1848 c.e.]." The binding has been stained a dark maroon and has gilt medallions inlaid in the corners and center in Levantine style. Competent examination has confirmed its nature.

A Koran in Arabic, also bound in human skin stained dark red and highly polished so that it resembles levant morocco, was offered some years ago in a catalogue of W. Heffer & Sons. Published at Bombay in 1867, it was an authenticated specimen, formerly the property of the East African chief, Bushiri ibn Salim, who revolted against the German authorities in 1888 but was subdued by a combined force of English, German, and Portuguese troops. In 1941 the volume was acquired by the Cleveland Public Library as part of the John Griswold White Collection of folklore and oriental literature.

Similarly in the Watkinson Library at Hartford is a volume, *Le Traicté de Peyne* (Paris, 1868), believed to be so invested in its light tan leather, with gold and brown decoration. It was among the fine bindings bequeathed by Samuel P. Avery, noted bibliophile, to nieces in West Hartford, and is now on indefinite loan to the Library. Whether or not the binding actually is of human skin is uncertain.

Acquired in 1930 by the Library of Congress in the Vollbehr Collection of early printed books was one volume by Paulus de Sancta Maria, known as Paul of Burgos, entitled *Scrutinium Scripturarum* (Strassburg, 1470). The author was a Jewish apostate who became Bishop of Cartagena, and this scrutiny of the scriptures, anti-Semitic in nature, is hidebound in a double sense. It is perhaps the largest of these skin bindings, measuring 8½″ by 11½″. The skin was left in its natural color and is entirely without tooling or other ornamentation except for the four heavy bands on the spine. There is no indication as to when the present binding was put on, but it does not appear to be contemporary with the printing of the book.

Harvard Law Library a few years ago purchased from a New Orleans bookdealer a Latin work on the laws of the Spanish kings, by Johann Gutierrez, printed at Madrid in 1606, with a manuscript note at the end stating the binding was in the skin of one John Wright. Who John Wright was is not known, and whether or not the covers are anthropodermic is uncertain.

At an Odd Book Exhibit of Harvard's Houghton Library in 1948 a copy of Arsène Houssaye's *Des Destinées de l'Ame* was exhibited. It came from the Stetson collection and is bound in skin taken from the back of an insane woman who died in one of the French hospitals. Its authenticity is unquestioned.

The Library of the University of California at Los Angeles, according to librarian Robert Vosper, acquired in the James Westfall Thompson Collection a volume entitled *Relations des Mouvemens de la Ville de Messine*, published in Paris in 1676. Inside the cover is noted in a contemporary hand that the book is from the library of Armand Jerome Bignon and that it is bound in human skin.

A Los Angeles bookseller in a 1934 catalogue included a copy of *Les Soliloques du Pauvre*, by Jehan Rictus, "in three-quarter human skin, from the library of Lawrence Maynard with his autograph signed account of the binding," which is dated Paris, 1903.

Another queer specimen owned by an American collector of midget books is a tiny putty-gray volume entitled *Little Poems for Little Folks*, published at Philadelphia in 1847, and bound in integument taken from the arm of a bibliophile—or so it is attested.

An unconfirmed story of the late nineteenth century concerns several such volumes believed to have been then owned by a Dr. Matthew Wood of Philadelphia, all allegedly from the post-mortem exterior of one Allemand Kauffmann, who was a law student in Germany in 1813. Despondent as to his career but seeking posthumous notice, the latter directed that a collection of some two hundred woodcuts, which he entitled *Zwei Hundert berühmte Manner*, should be preserved in his skin, as well as three other favorites from his shelves. These are said to have belonged to Dr. Wood, but have long since disappeared.

A number of epidermic volumes were once owned by Dr. John Stockton-Hough of Trenton, who died in 1900, having been associated with the Philadelphia General Hospital where he did the tanning himself. Four of these volumes are on gynecology and are said to have been covered in the thigh skin of a woman who died of consumption in the hospital. His *Catalogue des Sciences Médicales* was half-bound in skin from a man's back, and a smaller volume was half-bound in the tattooed skin from a man's arm. All trace of these volumes has been lost, but the year after his death Dr. Stockton-Hough's library was sold in part to the College of Physicians in Philadelphia, which now has two of the other volumes from his collection. The College also owns Dr. Joseph Leidy's personal copy of his *Elementary Treatise on Anatomy*, published in 1861, with inscription stating it was bound in the skin of a Civil War soldier.

Dard Hunter, who at the turn of the century was designing books for Elbert Hubbard at East Aurora, tells of so clothing a volume, at the insistence of a young widow as a memorial of her late husband, for which she furnished a rolled parcel of skin from the back of the deceased. Obliged to comply, a hand-lettered memento was made of the testimonial letters and verses. Later, on learning of the lady's remarriage, Hunter ruminated whether the second husband, conning the tribute, pondered how he might look as Volume Two.

As an avocation, the late Maurice Hommoneau, who for years conducted a bookshop at the American Museum of Natural History in New York, tanned and bound animal skins for works of pertaining subjects, such as Mrs. Martin Johnson's narrative in the thinned elephant hide which she supplied. An early American treatise on cutaneous diseases is described by him as bound in "full morocco" in that the skin he used came from a Moroccan mulatto. America, it will be noted, has a varied assortment of these specimens of mortal membrane that enclose man's transient tenement.

In England, during the period when more than a hundred crimes met with capital punishment, the populace became conditioned to cruelty. In the hanging of criminals there was frequent provision for dissection, with occasional flaying on the part of the surgeon. Such corpses were legally consigned to hospitals for autopsy in the medical schools. Among such skins, tanned as leather but not used on books, are recorded those of Cadwallader about 1816, and of Thurtell, executed in 1823 for the murder of one Weare. That there were others is seen from entries such as the following in the sale catalogue of an Edinburgh collector: "Lot 10. . . . A most curious and unique book, being the particulars of the trial and execution of Charles Smith, who was hanged at Newcastle for murder, containing a piece of his skin tanned into leather for the purpose."

Issues of *Notes and Queries* from 1818 recite accounts of executions followed by dissection and skin tanning. It appears that volumes so bound found favor with early British physicians: from Dibdin we learn that Dr. Anthony Askew, bibliophile who died in 1773, had a cutis-bound *Traité d' Anatomie,* and Dr. John Hunter, who died in 1794, had an *Abhandlung über die Hautkrankheiten.* About 1870 the British Law Library is said to have had several such volumes, being tokens of trials and local executions, and the Bristol Infirmary one or more.

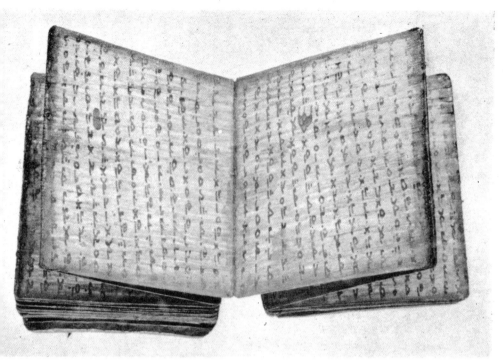

RK (OR BAMBOO) MANUSCRIPT

A queer eighteenth-century volume in the Toba dialect of the Batta language on favorable days and epochs; written on extended strip of bark (or bamboo) and folded in oriental manner between wooden boards; measures four inches square.

A "TRIPITAKA" OR PORTION OF THE KAMAVACA

Pali work in square Burmese characters on fifteen lacquered palm leaves (each 5" x 20") between richly gilded board covers with elaborate designs in red ink.

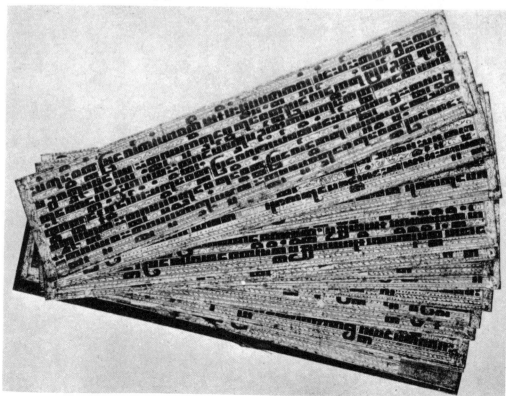

FACTS ABOUT GEORGIA

Made in the shape of the state, and published by the
Georgia Department of Commerce (Atlanta, 1916, 277 pp.)
with colored frontispiece of Georgia products.

NOT FOR THE THIN-SKINNED

In the Albert Memorial Library, Exeter, is a copy of Milton's *Poetical Works,* an inscription on the flyleaf stating the binding was part of the skin of George Cudmore, executed at Devon County Gaol in 1830 for the murder of his wife Grace. Sarah Dunn, his accessory, was acquitted but at the "especial prayer" of Cudmore she was brought to the prison yard with other female convicts to witness the hanging. Chronicle tells "she fell into hysterics and fainted when the drop fell." Cudmore's sentence included dissection, carried into effect by the Devon and Exeter Hospital. Subsequently the tanned skin came into the hands of W. Clifford, a bookdealer of Exeter, who used it to bind a copy of Tegg's 1852 edition of Milton. The skin is dressed white, resembling pigskin in grain and texture. It was acquired by the Albert Memorial Museum about 1885 from the library of Ralph Sanders of Exeter.

Formerly, and perhaps still, in the public library at Bury St. Edmunds is a record of the trial and execution of William Corder, aged 24, who in 1828 murdered a young woman named Maria Martin and disposed of her body under the Red Barn. The inner front cover bore a certification by Dr. George Creed, surgeon at the Suffolk Hospital (where Corder's skeleton was still preserved in 1949), that he had removed a large section of skin from the murderer's back, tanned it himself, and had it used to bind a history of the crime and trial by Curtis, published in 1834. The Red Barn murder excited great interest. When Maria Martin disappeared after answering Corder's matrimonial advertisement, her mother "had a dream on three successive nights" that her daughter had been buried under the Red Barn in a neighboring village. Persuading her husband to seek the body, he unearthed Maria's corpse. Corder was arrested while breakfasting with another bride.

Another instance concerns a youth of eighteen, John Horwood, hanged in 1821 at Bristol for the murder of Eliza Balsum. A volume in the Royal Infirmary there contains documents relating to the case. Dr. Richard Smith was authorized to use the body for dissection in lecturing to medical students. The skeleton was preserved in a cabinet of other relics of executed criminals, and a segment of skin was tanned by the surgeons. The binder charged £1 10s. for garbing the volume, including tooled borderlines in gold, with a skull and crossbones stamped in each corner, and a gilt inscription: "Cutis Vera Johannis Horwood."

In the library of Marlborough House, residence of Edward VII as Prince of Wales, were two volumes—possibly added as an eccentric gift during his time—supposedly encased in the skin of Mary Patman, so-called witch of Yorkshire, who was hanged for murder early in the nineteenth century.

In France as in England the bodies of executed murderers were long given over to medical schools for dissection, and occasionally, as in the case of Campi in the 1880's, the tanned skin under official instructions or sanction was used to bind documents, briefs, and clippings relating to the case.

Another telltale volume known only in that it was reported as having been seen by Henri de Halsalle in his *Romance of First Editions* is described as an almost black copy of the *Histoire Générale des Larrons*. It was said to be in the hide of a Negro sailor who "had run amok aboard ship and hacked to death with a cutlass half of the crew before the survivors could swing him aloft and riddle his carcass with shot—corroborative marks you may observe on the binding."

A French collector early in the century possessed a copy of Ernest Renan's *Life of Jesus*, bound at Nantes in human skin. Its present whereabouts are unknown. W. S. Brassington, nineteenth-century authority on bookbinding, mentions that in a bookseller's catalogue he saw listed at 200 francs a copy so bound of Suard's *Les Opuscules Philosophiques*. He also states that the poet De Musset prized such a book vesture bound by Derome in 1796. Hearsay has it that in an obscure antiquarian shop near St. Augustin's Church in Paris about 1900 an anonymous volume had a butterfly inlay of the author's own epidermis.

In the annals of book oddity one example leads to another, the second often excelling the first in peculiarity. So speaking of human skin bindings, we are reminded of the reputed action of a certain Russian poet who was severely injured in an equestrian accident. When he was about to lose a limb by amputation, he ordered the skin of the limb to be tanned and used as a binding for a collection of his sonnets to be presented to the Circe of his affections as a token of his devotion.

Following the death of the eighteenth-century poet Jacques Delille, it is reliably recorded that a young law student, André Leroy, having made his way into the mortuary where the embalmer was at work, contrived to cut two strips from his friend's remains, which he had tanned and inlaid on the covers of a sumptuous copy of the poet's rendition of Vergil's *Georgica.* Eighty years later the volume was in the possession of Edmund Leroy, attorney at Valenciennes.

Eugene Sue had the copy of the two-volume *Les Mysteres de Paris* garbed in the skin of a Parisian beauty who had loved him. Inside the cover an inscription in French reads in translation: "This binding is from the skin of a woman, and was made by M. Alberic Bautaille, 1874."

Notable among skin-garbed volumes is the famous "lady-bound book" which was owned by Camille Flammarion until, at his death, inherited by his widow. Although the identity of the donor who gave her skin remains uncertain, the circumstances, though grievously mauled by journalistic retelling and hedged with hearsay, are authentic. In 1882 a young French Countess, hopelessly afflicted with tuberculosis, on her deathbed is reputed to have made this strange request of her doctor:

> I have a confidential confession to make to you. I have loved Camille Flammarion with a flaming devotion, and now that I am dying I want him to have a souvenir from me. It will astonish you to know that I have never been presented to him, or talked to him, or even seen him, but I developed such an intense admiration for Monsieur Flammarion from reading his books and following his work that I secretly fell in love with him. I worshipped him day and night for five years. I want to remain with him, and so I beg you that as soon as I die, you cut a big piece of skin off my shoulders and send it to him as a binding for one of his books. I want my name

kept a secret, however, and you must promise that if he comes
and asks questions you will not reveal my identity.

However distorted or apocryphal the details of this deathbed
confidence, when the Countess passed away in the autumn, the doctor, a
noted practitioner named Ravaud, cut an ample oblong of tissue, twelve
by eighteen inches, from the torso, rolled it up in a packet, and
personally carried it to the astronomer's house, where he left it with an
explanatory note.

Flammarion, after the first shock of astonishment, did as the
anonymous lady wished; he had the skin tanned and used to bind a copy
of his *Terres du Ciel*, in the front cover of which he had lettered in gold
a transcription which when translated from the French, reads:

PIOUS FULFILLMENT OF AN ANONYMOUS WISH,
BINDING IN HUMAN SKIN (WOMAN) 1882.

The mystery which surrounds the book and the identity of the
charming Countess has never abated. According to another romantic
version when Flammarion, at a décolleté reception, admired the lady's
complexion she promised to leave it to him as a legacy.

In 1927 Mme Camille Flammarion, the astronomer's second wife,
gave this account of the affair:

> I often talked to my husband about this mystery before
> his death in 1925. He said that when he was living in the Rue
> Cassini, beside the Paris Observatory, in 1882 he returned
> home late one morning after a night spent in looking at the
> stars.
> As he passed the concierge's lodge she handed him a
> little packet, saying that a professional-looking man had
> come with it and left explicit instructions that it be given to
> him personally.
> My husband said that he smelled a curious odor and had
> a momentary shiver, as though he sensed something ghastly,

and when he reached his apartment he opened the package
with nervous fingers, wondering what he would find. As he
undid the wrappings of oiled paper and red ribbons he felt a
sickening sensation come over him. He was so excited, that
the package dropped to the floor and a big piece of soft
human skin unfolded before his eyes. He was amazed at first
and then concluded that some medical students had played a
trick on him; but as he looked through the wrappings, a note
dropped out. [Long in the possession of Mme Flammarion,
the note in translation reads:]

MONSIEUR:
True to my promise, I have carefully carried out the
request of the dead Countess who always loved you. She
begged me to send you, the day after her death, the skin of
her lovely shoulders. This is the skin, and you must promise
that you will use it to bind a copy of the first book you may
publish now, after her death. I have delivered this souvenir to
you, Monsieur, as I faithfully promised.

DR. RAVAUD

[Monsieur Flammarion immediately hurried to see Dr.
Ravaud, who was one of the fashionable practitioners of
Paris at the time.] "I gave her my word of honor while she
was dying that I would not reveal her name," [the physician
is alleged to have told the astronomer.] "All I can tell you is
that she was a marvelously attractive young woman, a
member of one of the first families of France, and that she
secretly adored you from the time she was a young girl. I had
a horror of mutilating such lovely shoulders, but I promised
the Countess to do it and I had to keep my promise. A few
minutes after she passed on, I took off the skin and
personally delivered it to your house to make sure you would
get it. I did not even tell her family about her strange
request, and I will carry the secret of her identity to the
grave with me."

From such evidence, the fact of the incident appears to be true, which makes it even more strange that the identity of the Countess continued to be a mystery. It would seem reasonable to expect that Flammarion, a social lion in Paris, would not find it difficult to discover what gentlewoman in the fashionable world of the city died at that time and to have put the facts together. Several years before Flammarion himself died, Dr. Cabanès, editor of a French medical journal, received this answer to the letter he wrote the astronomer asking the facts:

> MY DEAR DOCTOR:
>
> *The story has been somewhat elaborated. I don't know the name of the person whose dorsal skin was delivered to me by a physician to use for binding. It was a matter of carrying out a pious vow. Some newspapers, especially in America, published the portrait, the name, and even the photograph of the chateau where "the Countess" dwelt. All of that is pure invention.*
>
> *The binding was successfully executed by Engel, and from then on the skin was unchanging. I recollect I had to carry this relic to a tanner in the Rue de la Reine-Blanche, and three months were required for the job. Such an idea was assuredly bizarre. However, in point of fact, this vestige of a beautiful body is all that survives of it today, and it can endure lastingly in a perfect state of respectful preservation.*
>
> *The desire of the unknown woman was to have my last book published at the time of her death bound in this skin: the octavo edition of the* Terres du ciel, *published by Didier enjoys this honor.*
>
> *Your reader and admirer,*
>
> FLAMMARION.

Doubting the whole story, the present scribe wrote to Madame Flammarion many years ago and in due course received from her a photograph of the volume and a missive of authentication. Though she did not disclose the name of the donor, an article in the Boston *Transcript* (May 31, 1924) identified her as the Countess St. Agnes, while a contributor to *Notes and Queries* (1944, vol. 187), mentions the Countess de Saint-Auge.

The most frequent use of human skin was during the French Reign of Terror, if persistent tradition is to be believed. A report of September 20, 1794, concerns a tannery at Meudon which made into leather the skin of many of those guillotined, and the National Convention is said to have subsidized this industry with forty-five thousand francs. The historian De Cassagnac, who died in 1880, had a copy so bound of the *Constitution de la République Française de l'an I*. In the *Journal des Lois*, the editor, M. Galetti, inserted an announcement which read: "One of our subscribers has sent us, as a signal memorial of the tyranny of the Decemvirs, a copy of 'The Constitution of 1793,' printed by Causse at Dijon, and bound in human skin resembling tawny calf. We shall be pleased to show it to those who may be curious to see it."

The latter volume was acquired by the Carnavalet Museum in 1889 following its possession by several bookmen, including Targot and Villeneuve. Exhibited in the so-called Bastille Room of the Museum, the leather of this relic is polished and tooled with a lacelike pattern on the doublures. A note in Villeneuve's hand attests its nature. In 1872 at the Drouot auction rooms a *Constitution* of 1791, similarly bound, was sold. There is a strong presumption that there were other copies of the Revolutionary code clothed in cured gentility.

The Princess de Lamballe, intimate friend of Marie Antoinette, was a victim of the Revolution. Brutally murdered on September 3, 1792, her head was paraded on a pike before the prison window of the captive Queen, and her hacked and nude corpse dragged by the legs through the streets and subjected to obscene indignities, a volume being bound of her loins (*mons Veneris*) —according to tradition. Several bookmen who have alluded to the alleged flaying of guillotined aristocrats express doubt as to the truth of the legend, or, if true, as to the extent of truth. Richard Le Gallienne declares he saw one such volume of the period put up at the auction rooms of the Hotel Drouot, and recalls Carlyle's grim jest that the French nobles laughed at Rousseau's theories, but that their skins went to bind the second edition of his book.

That the tannery at Meudon made human leather is put down as Royalist propaganda by one recent spokesman who says the allegation was revived by Paul Lacroix (Bibliophile Jacob) and others. Yet in a preceding admission he conceded "the impetus to anthropodermic bibliopegy and related arts by the French Revolution." Summing up the meager evidence it seems not unlikely that some such volumes and other gruesome items came from the Terror tannery. Of the Meudon question, V. Valta Parma, former curator of the rare book collection in the Library of Congress, stated: "The bodies were taken direct from the guillotine to the tannery. It is said that a complete set of a famous author's work was bound in skin supplied by this tannery."

Iwan Bloch, former noted authority on sex life, declared the female breast has been employed for the binding of books. Bloch alleged that certain bibliomaniacs with an erotic bent had volumes bound with woman's skin taken from the region of the breast, "so that the nipple forms a characteristic swelling on the cover." An informant relates he saw a specimen in Paris many years ago at the Carnavalet.

Edmond and Jules de Goncourt in their *Mémoires* recall that in 1866 hospital internes at the Clamart were dismissed for selling skin of deceased females to a binder in the Faubourg Saint-Germain for fetishists. And we are told by Lawrence S. Thompson that: "The publisher of obscene books, Isidore Liseux, claimed to have seen the one-volume octavo edition of 1793 of *Justine et Juliette*, by the Marquis de Sade, bound in female breasts."

It is related that a former professor at Geneva, August Reverdin, was willed the skin of a friend, together with a small bequest. The legatee removed a segment of breast skin which was tanned by a leatherworker in Annecy. The professor, however, found the product lusterless, oily, and revolting, but when he begged a friend, Marcellin Pettet, to relieve him of it, Pettet used it to bind a copy of the *Almanac of the Prisoners Under Robespierre*.

The Germans led in erotomania of the library, even hinting at an appropriate binding for the medieval tractate *De serto virginum*. Robert Briffault, to indicate the decadence of one of the characters in his *Europa* assumes a number of volumes bound in human skin. One of the presumed collection was said to be so artfully bound in a nun's skin that a natural fold of the body served for the opening of the volume. Since this novelist was previously a bookseller, there is remote possibility that the depravity was not fabulous.

Pre-war Germany had its share of skin bindings, and among these the library at Göttingen had a rare copy of *Hippocrates* so bound. It is related by Lady Mary Wortley Montagu that in a visit to Prince Eugène de Ligne in 1717 she was shown several quartos on the art of warfare, bound with the skins of spahis and janissaries, in the Prince's booty library at Brussels.

Writing in 1804, Gabriel Peignot stated the Bibliothèque électorale at Dresden had a manuscript "*sur peau humaine*," consisting of a calendar and historical fragments about the Incas; also that the Imperial Library of Vienna had a Mexican manuscript in colors, similarly on human skin.

Much newspaper publicity attended the trial of Ilse Koch, widow of the Buchenwald camp commandant, on charges that she instigated the death of tattooed prisoners so that lampshades and book covers might be made at the pathological laboratory for her apartment. However, alleged lack of tangible evidence before the court of review led to commutation of the life sentence of Frau Koch.

That copies of *Mein Kampf* were bound at this notorious concentration camp in the skin of the slaughtered was reported by a correspondent of the London *Daily Mail* and recounted by the United Press under date of April 20, 1945. The correspondent added that the tattooed skin of butchered victims was tanned and used for lampshades for officers' wives. At the trial, a former inmate of Buchenwald, Herbert Froboess, having recognized a tattooed four-masted ship on the volume, testified that the Koch family album or journal had been bound in the

skin of a fellow-prisoner named Jean who disappeared. Sir Bernard
Spilsbury, pathologist, declared certain evidence bore out the charge of
the prosecution. But since the alleged products, done by a prisoner
named Wernerbach and confiscated by the occupation military authorities
in 1945, had vanished, they could not be presented as evidence.

Tanning increases the thickness of the skin and gives it a fine-
grained and soft texture. Holbrook Jackson saw a piece of human
leather from a hide tanned in London about thirty years before, which,
when seen by him, was in the possession of Zaehnsdorf. This specimen, he
says, resembled soft pigskin and was almost an eighth of an inch thick.
For those who are curious enough to desire the method of tanning, the
following may suffice: "The skin should be saturated for several days in
a strong solution of alum, Roman vitriol and common salt, dried in the
shade, and dressed in ordinary fashion."

Prior to World War II, in a German museum annexed to the
Zittauer Ratsbibliothek, was a tanned human skin flayed from an
executed highwayman. Of dull oyster-gray tone, it was pliable and felt
like sturdy glove leather. Similarly, a complete human skin dressed like
chamois was formerly in Hermann Boerhaave's surgical collection at his
Leyden museum. One also hears tell of a Graf von Erbach, in Hessen,
who stipulated that after his death a sportsman's breeches should be
made of his mortal coating. Earlier, in that region, belts, braces, and
hunting-knife sheaths—the booty of feuds—were sometimes made of
human leather and worn by foresters in princely retinues. In the
Bavarian Armèe-Museum is, or was, a janissary drum spanned with the
skin of a Hussite general named Ziska who ordered that after his death
a section of his own integument be stretched on a drum, so that its rat-a-
tat should goad on his troops.

But only scattered material has been encountered in the course of
twenty years' pursuit of data on this queasy subject. The printed
contributions of Lawrence S. Thompson on the topic are salient.
Scattered notations in *Notes and Queries*, both British and American,
and elusive articles in German and French periodicals for bookbinders

and booklovers virtually cover the field, with repetition in press and periodical. These rather meager allusions to a bizarre aspect of bibliomania are supplemented by the résumé in the late Holbrook Jackson's all-embracing exposition of the anatomy of collecting.

Concluding this somewhat repulsive theme and recalling the instance in which three volumes were bound from the exterior of one departed Negro, one might expect that some day a five-volume chef d'oeuvre, with each volume garbed in the skin of one of the supposed five primary races of mankind, will be someone's aspiration.

GOLIATHS OF BOOKDOM

THE MASSIVE BIBLE which an irate Samuel Johnson heaved at the head of the London bookseller Thomas Osborne settled that altercation, but in size it was pigmy compared with some colossal tomes. Gargantuan specimens that stand upright on castors, or open on an easel, or repose in flat ponderosity, are far removed from the dainty minims that can be ensconced in the hollow of a signet ring. Some there are with a taste whetted for broiled hummingbirds and "the delights that are bred in a lyttle booke." Others, like Heine, envy the titan of myth who would relish to partake of the elephant of Hindustani, correct his teeth with the spire of Strasbourg Cathedral, and thereupon toy with a Nuremburg Chronicle, or mull over an original Audubon, bound by Bedford, and nicely held 'twixt thumb and forefinger.

Up the River Nile at Thebes, on two massy walls of the second pylon of the main temple of Rameses III, is chiseled the largest "book" in all the world. Its "pages" are 138′ wide, and none among mortals may turn the outspread relic to discover if aught is glyphed beneath! Though victor and vanquished are as dust in the desert, this ancient chronicle of triumph has defied obliteration and oblivion for more than three thousand years.

Of all the products of the monastic houses during those centuries before printing when art and restricted learning centered in the omnipresent Church, the least lovely among the varieties of book painting were those cumbersome whales of volumes, known as Antiphonaries, that reposed on sturdy lecterns. Intended to be seen by each of the choristers as they sat in a group or stood clustered, the most expansive of these hefty tomes included musical notation which perched on the page like a row of blackbirds on a fence. The music recorded is that of the Gregorian chants, and the square- and diamond-shaped notes indicate pitch.

Occasional other medieval books for the holy offices were unseemly large, but the art of illumination was at its best·in less ponderous examples of the scribe's and colorer's craftsmanship. Ornamentation was lavished on these devotional manuscripts and their enclosures, which varied in size from exquisite and diminutive Books of Hours that could be laid in the palm of one's hand to devout, jewel-studded, bulky, bossed folios.

But there came a time when, to supplement religious literature, the surviving texts of the classics, rescued from long neglect and thwarted oblivion, were copied in massive volumes by scribes under regal patronage or with ecclesiastical sanction. Petrarch is said to have possessed a massive transcription of Cicero's *Letters*, made by himself, and other weighty volumes, which with much reading and his habit of propping them on his knees caused a trauma in one of the limbs.

In *The Art of Bookbinding*, Brassington tells us that most of the unwieldy works with musical settings, and similar monastic books of the period of the English Reformation, suffered a dire fate. Not only were the libraries sacked, but the huge volumes which contained the ancient services, and which abounded in most churches and monasteries, were destroyed without compunction and with fanatical zeal. Many of these books had been brought from Rome, where such works had been made continuously from the thirteenth century. When one of these immense volumes was laid upon the reading-desk (lutrin) in the middle of the choir, the letters and musical notes which accompanied the words were so huge and black they could easily be read by the canons as they sat in their stalls. Seldom removed from the desk, and then only to be borne to the nearby sacristy, they became fixtures of the churches sometimes for centuries (yet generally these Antiphonaries are not so ancient as at first sight might be surmised). They were protected with brass corners and studded with bosses and brass nails to preserve the heavy bindings from injury, and were further equipped with massive brazen clasps. A few of the largest reposed upon rollers. Subjected to daily use, sometimes for generations, utility rather than embellishment and artistry dominated their making. In some instances belted bands girded the backs and were fastened to either side to safeguard joints which might otherwise break under the strain and weight of the hefted sides. Yet none of these precautions against the ravages of time and use could save them from the holocausts and vandalism meted out to most of the repositories of the Church of Rome in the excesses of the Reformation.

The number of volumes of great bulk is rather small, but one of the largest of these certainly is the Grosse Kurfürst *Atlas* of the Great Elector of Brandenburg, a collection of enormous maps bound in boards. Until restored by the master bookbinding firm of Jacob Kohnert in Berlin, iron braces supported the boards as they began to fall apart. The restoration was finished in 1931, and in the beauty of its cartography and the artistry of its hide-covered and ornamented binding (on a par with the massiveness of its proportions), the work is impressive.

Taller than the average human, this volume is almost seventy inches high, forty-two inches wide, and weighs two hundred seventy-five pounds. It contains maps only, but these by reason of their origin and nature are precious. Made in the middle of the seventeenth century, the latest map bears the date 1661. Each map was proofed or printed by means of a number of sectional copperplates, and the individual prints were pasted together in perfect jointure. Names of places were written in by hand; armorial shields and quaint pictures were hand-painted. Various curious cartouches of the denizens of strange lands portray their raiment and customs, while vignettes of wild animals deck different regions. Thus the map of Brazil shows sugarcane being prepared and, nearby, man-eating headhunters.

This "German Prince Atlas" was exhibited at the Chicago World's Fair in 1893, but on its homeward trip suffered broken binding and water stains. After Jacob and Wilhelm Kohnert and their expert helpers had devoted seven months of intermittent work to its repair—as they later did to other book treasures that had been hidden by the Nazis in the salt mines—it remained in Berlin's Staatsbibliothek until the bombardment of that city. Perhaps it is still extant. The five-foot-ten old covers are virtual portals. They are made of wood cased with two enormous hides, and the reconstructed binding uses the fine metal embellishments of the original. The thirty-seven maps, made in Holland by such great mapmakers of the period as Blaeu, De Witt, Janssonius, and Allardt, are masterpieces of craftsmanship.

The esteemed Grosse Kurfürst of Brandenburg, Frederick Wilhelm, was almost as colorful as the great *Atlas* that was his stalwart possession. Though the territory he inherited from his father had been devastated by the Swedes in the Thirty Years' War, this prince nevertheless became a power through his military exploits and his lapses into *Kultur* between military campaigns. In 1666, Johann Moritz, a former governor of the Dutch West Indies Company, aware of Frederick's interest in all manner of maps, presented the *Atlas* to him.

Of similar size, and likewise of Dutch origin, is the *Atlas* of Charles II, the largest volume in the British Museum and, indeed, in the British Empire. Its maps are as fresh as on the day they issued forth. Measuring 5′ 9½″ by 3′ 2½″, and standing on castors so that it may be readily opened, this huge volume required eight large morocco skins for its binding. Each map is in twenty copperplate sections, almost invisibly joined, and the binding is well preserved. Under what circumstances it came to the English monarch is no longer certain; but it and the German *Atlas* vie in size and were possibly made from the same Dutch plates.

Our restriction here to a consideration of tangible big books excludes fabulous and celestial tomes such as, for example, the "huge pantoufled or thick covered breviary," weighing 1106 pounds, which Rabelais' Gargantua tells us they carried before him to church "in a great basket." Dean Swift in his "Battle of the Books" speculates as to the binding of the "Book of Fate" which Mercury lay before Jupiter.

From the lore of the Near East come tales of the Great Koran in Samarkand Palace courtyard, made about 1403 for Bibi-Khanum, the Empress of Tamerlane, which, according to unlikely legend, the Empress wanted large enough to enable her to read it from her upper window (another version declares it was made in her memory). After the earthquake of 1886, the stone lectern on which it is said to have rested was moved out of the mosque and into the open for safety. It still stands in the central court of the mosque measuring 7½′ by 6½′. The Koran which lay upon it is said to have been removed to the Eremitage (the National Museum) of St. Petersburg, now Leningrad, during the Russian conquest of Turkestan in 1868. But uncertainty hedges it about. Also in Samarkand, on the edge of the oasis, is the mosque of Shakh-Zinda, cousin of Mahomet, with its turquoise domes and mosaic façades. In a lofty vaulted chamber is the tomb of the revered Shakh-Zinda. Here to this day in a railed-off antechamber is an immense Koran, at least six feet wide, like that tome that once rested on a stone altar in the courtyard of Bibi-Khanum.

Of legendary proportions, too, is a gigantic copy of the Koran mentioned by D'Israeli. Transcribed by a certain Gholam Mohgoodeen, it is described as a foot thick, five feet high, and a yard wide, with individual characters three inches tall.

Among the real Goliaths of bookdom is a monumental collection of engravings on ancient and modern art published by Vivant-Denon, who accompanied Napoleon and advised the conqueror what art booty to appropriate from pillaged territory. The cumbrous bulk of this collection defies the loftiest library shelf and reposes instead in flat amplitude.

At an exhibition of Italian literature at the Casa Italiana, New York, in 1928, more than two hundred editions of Dante's *Divine Comedy*

Taller than the average human, the "German Prince Atlas" is almost seventy inches high, forty-two inches wide, and weighs 275 pounds. It contains maps only, with handpainted vignettes. This 1666 volume was restored in 1931 after seven months' work.

BROBDINGNAGIANS

The giant Atlas of Charles II, largest book in the British Museum, measures 5 feet, 9½ inches, by 3 feet, 2½ inches, and required eight morocco goatskins for its binding. Each map was engraved on twenty separate copperplates; the printed sections were then carefully joined and hand-colored.

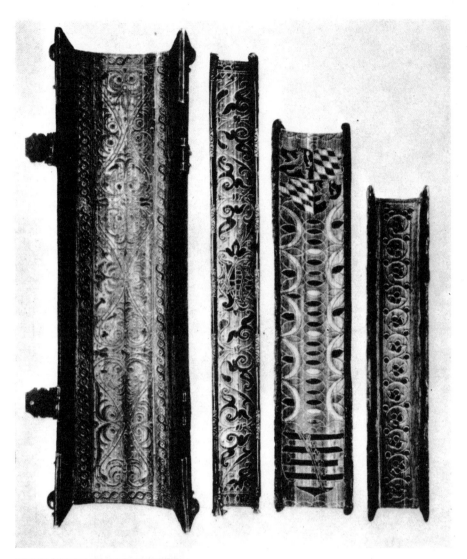

FORE-EDGE DECORATIONS

Rich and lasting colors over gold; executed in late sixteenth-century Saxony; largest specimen that of a Luther Bible 16⅝" tall. (Specimens from the Preussische Staatsbibliothek of Berlin.)

were displayed, ranging in time through six centuries and in size from a
vest pocket version to the superb volume illustrated in aquaforte by
Amos Mattini, with pages measuring twenty-four by thirty-six inches
and weighing forty-five pounds. Of course, neither size nor poundage are
earmarks of bookmaking excellence, but this handwrought edition,
dedicated to King Victor Emmanuel, was blessed by His Holiness who
declared: "It is a truly Michaelangelesque work, the honor and glory of
our century." Engraved on copperplates with the artwork gilded in gold,
it contained only the *Inferno* and *Purgatorio*, being half-bound in loose-
leaf fashion so that the *Paradiso* could be inserted when completed. An
edition of nine hundred copies was issued.

Among big books one must also mention John Boydell's collection of
Illustrations for the Dramatic Works of Shakespeare, a flawless, tall copy
of which measures not less than thirty by thirty-four inches, and sells for
about four hundred dollars. Boydell, an affluent Lord Mayor of London,
commissioned the leading artists of his day to illustrate Shakespeare.
Romney, Smirke, Peters, Zucchi, and Rigaud were among those who
painted the original oils. The engravers, too, were masters of their craft.
A huge engraving of George III, a bit bulgy about the midriff, adorns
the forefront of this work, into the making of which Boydell tossed his
fortune. When he could not meet his debts the sheriffs impounded his
last painting. The plates still have vigor and charm, the largest
measuring 25¼″ by 19½″. In some respects the American edition of
1852 excels the original 1803 edition. One wonders about the expression
on Will Shakespeare's face could he have pored over these delineations
of the characters and scenes he conjured from the bony vessel that held
his voyaging mind.

The original price of the Boydell work was £37 16s. He
commissioned thirty-three British painters to produce the gallery during
the years 1789–1802. These were then engraved and published with the
text of the plays in 22-point type. The volumes, on heavy rag paper
and extra heavy plate paper, are unwieldy in their solid leather covers.
The cost of the paintings and drawings was £42,266, of the Shakespeare

Gallery, £30,000, of the copperplates, a large sum. At eighty-five, to avoid bankruptcy, Boydell petitioned Parliament on February 4, 1804, for permission to clear himself from debt by lottery—thereby to dispose of the Shakespeare Gallery, the paintings therein, the copperplates, prints and drawings. Permission was accorded and twenty-two thousand tickets were sold. Boydell paid his debts pro rata, but died before the lottery was drawn. When the drawing took place on January 28, 1805, the chief prizewinner was a Mr. Tassie, who sold the Boydell property at Christie's famous London auction establishment.

By reason of their technique and size, the celebrated etchings and engravings of Piranesi have excited the admiration of artists and connoisseurs from their appearance during the latter half of the eighteenth century to the present day. The 137 plates of his *Vedute di Roma*, in imperial folio, are seldom found intact. Competent authorities have expressed amazement at their large dimensions and at the number of plates executed. Over a period of thirty-nine years they exceeded thirteen hundred in number, and during two-score years every fortnight or so he produced a matchless plate, noble in proportions and precise in details.

Another example of big books one must not fail to include is the nine-volume elephant folio *Mexican Antiquities* of Lord Kingsborough, who died in the debtors' gaol of Dublin through inability to pay for the costly paper and presswork which went into his portly thesis on the Aztecs, the set scaling almost two hundredweight. Seventeen years elapsed between the appearance of the first and last of the volumes (1831–1848), the text of which served his lordship's purpose to "prove" that the ancient Mexicans were derived from the "lost tribes of Israel."

In the Royal Library at Stockholm is a ponderous medieval volume, brought from Prague as the spoils of war, containing in twelfth-century illumination a Vulgate, commentary on Josephus, and other related matter. Strange because of its parchment of asses' skin, it is all the stranger because of the legend that, though the monk who worked on it was dying, through the aid of Beelzebub it was finished in a night. This

satanic copy of the Scriptures, forbidding to the fearful, is celebrated
as *The Devil's Bible*, and has an image of a squatting diabolic imp on
the last yard-high page.

A modern handwritten Bible was exhibited in 1921 in connection
with a religious crusade in England to win churchgoers. This behemoth,
5′ 2″ by 3′ 6″, consisted of the Scripture verses inscribed by twelve
thousand contributors, among whom were the King and Queen.

Another huge book, not intended for the library, was displayed in
1895 at the Cotton States and International Exposition by the Brown
Paper Company of Adams, Massachusetts. Made by William Mann of
Philadelphia, this exhibition piece, since lost to view, was a business
register weighing 360 pounds, and was made as a specimen of blankbook
manufacture. Each leaf handsomely bordered, the back and sides were
substantially bound in embossed Russian leather embellished with gold-
tooled rules. Such publicity display monsters are not uncommon, but when
they lack text, or are mere hollow shams of basswood or cardboard, aping
the appearance of a book, they do not come within the compass of
libraria.

It was the wild turkey cock (which Franklin desired to be the
national emblem rather than the bald eagle) that led to the huge size of
Audubon's *The Birds of America*, with its famous wild turkey cock
frontispiece. The double elephant folio amplitude of this work stems
undoubtedly from a prospectus drafted soon after the outset of the
undertaking which stipulated: "The Engravings in every instance to be
of the exact dimensions of the Drawings, which, without any
exception, represent the Birds of their natural size." It was planned to
issue five plates to a number and five numbers to a year until all the four
hundred drawings should be published; in actual accomplishment,
however, 435 plates were issued in twelve years from the appearance of
the first number in 1827.

Rebuffed in America, Audubon sailed in 1826 from New Orleans to
Liverpool, a trip of sixty-five days. Adventure and adversity had
attended him so long that his determined struggles to bring this

sumptuous work to completion refused to yield to the threats of failure. After William Lizars of Edinburgh made the first ten plates, he stopped, dissuaded by the difficulties. In the end it was the talent and enthusiasm of Robert Havell, the young London engraver, in fortunate alliance with this natural son of a French sea captain and a creole woman of Santo Domingo, where Audubon was born in 1785, that brought the remarkable enterprise to culmination. The friendship of these two decided Havell to come to America with his wife, and here for ten years the tedious work was pursued.

The cost to British subscribers was £182 14s, to Americans one thousand dollars. Fewer than two hundred sets were issued, and in course of time many of these were broken up for the individual plates; with others overtrimmed in binding, there are perhaps but one hundred sound sets left. The untrimmed plates, measuring $39\frac{1}{2}''$ by $29\frac{1}{2}''$, have an expanse of almost eight square feet. The famous wild turkey cock as plate number one and frontispiece is indispensable to a sound copy of this amazing achievement which, with the five smaller volumes of text, brings upwards of seven thousand dollars at book sales (even when the margins of the plates have been somewhat trimmed in binding), if the first ten plates by Lizars are in their earliest state. Unmarred sets have brought thousands more—£9,200 ($25,760) at London in 1955.

One must be a very Briareus to handle these huge volumes, and merely turning the leaves of the 435 plates requires unusual care. The subsequently published three folio volumes of the *Quadrupeds*, massive in their own right, seem diminished alongside the larger work. And these two productions with their meticulous coloring somewhat eclipsed in popular esteem the five volumes of text in the Audubon *Ornithological Biography* with its close to a million words, in which "an account of the habits of the birds of the United States" is interspersed with essays and adventures full of the tang of backwoods America.

The vicissitudes of Audubon's career made all the more romantic his granite determination with respect to completion of the prodigious *Birds of America*, in which the artist-naturalist accomplished the flawless drawing, engraving, coloring, and presswork that depicted more than one thousand feathered specimens. Like Catlin, whose Indian drawings also suffered long neglect, and like Rafinesque, the versatile but erratic American scientist, Audubon wandered hither and yon through the pioneer wilderness of the American frontiers, most of the time with meager resources. From Florida to the Canadian outposts, from the Atlantic seaboard to the Mississippi, he traversed the sparsely settled regions of the time as perhaps no other man of his generation did. Meantime in the stripling cities or straggling towns he eked out a pittance in a dozen ways. As his biographer tells us in *Audacious Audubon* he "worked as a clerk, merchant, miller and taxidermist; earned money painting portraits, landscapes, street signs, birds, plants, flowers, and the interior of an Ohio River steamboat; gave lessons in French, fencing, drawing, dancing, and music . . . and was the author, illustrator, publisher and chief salesman of a number of books."

As with Catlin and Rafinesque, he was insatiable in the pursuit of his quest, not as a dry-as-dust type of academic scientist but as a picturesque and passionate seeker, inured to the ups and downs of fortune. His capable wife advanced his vexed career to its crest by her faith and devotion. The intense love of nature that inspired him overshadowed his rare lapses of observation, as in his challenged portrayal of a rattlesnake attacking a mocking-bird nest, or his famous description of a rattlesnake pursuing a squirrel into a treetop.

The century that has passed since the final plates of *The Birds of America* were distributed to subscribers has witnessed a steadily increasing esteem for the figure of Audubon and the growing monetary value of the four gigantic volumes (there were four title pages) that are his crowning work. Their size—scaling up to 3' 3" high—made most people deem them the largest books in the world, and Gladstone so designated them. Incidentally, some of the subscribers, including the King of England, the Marquis of Londonderry, and the Duchess of Clarence, it has been reported, neglected to pay.

But the bigger big books are eclipsed by what is undoubtedly the

biggest book in the world, entitled *The Story of the South* and made for
the exposition of Southern industries held at the Grand Central Palace,
New York, in 1925. At last report it was on display at the City Hall of
Baltimore. Bulking 6′ 10″ in height, 12″ in thickness, 4′ 7″ in width,
this Brobdingnagian tome measures 9′ 2″ outspread. It weighs
approximately five hundred pounds and stands on an easel which,
together with the mechanism that turns the leaves, brings the weight to
considerably in excess of half a ton. The vertical easel upon which the
upright book rests is 12′ 2″ high and is equipped with two motors
developing twelve horsepower to turn the book and the consecutive leaves.
The bookbinders were faced with the problem of finding a hide for the
"backbone" of this work, but Texas afforded a way out by furnishing an
oxhide twelve feet long and of sufficient acreage for the purpose. This
mighty curiosity consists of nineteen pages, each featuring some phase of
the South's contribution to the building of the Republic. These are
photographic enlargements, mounted on the thickest cardboard. An
octavo reproduction was issued in 1925 by the Baltimore publishers,
Norman, Remington Company, with a foreword telling of the difficulties
overcome in making the biggest of all books.

For those to whom comparisons are not odious, it may be pointed
out that the disparity of size in the world of books is at its greatest
extreme between *The Story of the South* and the smallest printed book
in the cosmos—the Omar Khayyám quatrains brought out at Worcester
in 1933, of which perhaps fifteen bound copies could be laid side by side
in three rows of five on a postage stamp. Or, to vary the figure, some
five million of the Omars would just about bulk to the immensity of the
mastodon of the South!

Singular indeed is the titanic Bible that was fashioned by a devout
gentleman of Los Angeles. Louis Waynai made the work so that by this
application he might the better absorb the contents of the Scriptures.
With an outspread stretch of 8′ 2″, this Cyclops had a thickness of 34″,
and a weight with stand of 1,094 pounds. Each page was 43½″ high.
Begun in 1928 and completed in 1930, it contained 8,084 pages. What

made it unique apart from its size is the fact that it was imprinted throughout with rubber type, hand-stamped letter by huge letter, in laborious zeal. The rubber alphabet was fixed on the rim of a wheel having a fourteen-inch diameter. Rotated by hand, a threaded shaft of this wheel permitted movement from left to right, and each letter was stamped separately by lowering the wheel into contact with the open page beneath.

Somewhere in Hollywood is a six-hundred-pound volume originated by the motion picture industry in 1944 to present a review of the accomplishments of moviedom in selling bonds in the fourth War Loan drive. It is 5′ 2″ tall, 10″ thick, and has fifty leaves of compressed fibre board for pages. The cover is all leather, sixty square feet of it, and the rounded spine was equipped with six brass piano hinges.

But giants such as these are not legitimate literary or art works and must be distinguished from those authentic massive products of the printing art that are monuments of the craft and are published in editions. Several of the latter merit mention. There is the *Pinakothek zu München*, usually called "The Munich Gallery," which appeared a century ago in three volumes thirty-six inches in height. Even taller by an inch or two are the *Pyramids of Gizeh*, and Fénelon's views of the ancient tabernacle and temple of Jerusalem. Visitors to the Vatican Library see displayed under glass an elaborately bound folio Vulgate Bible bulking fourteen inches thick. Perched upon its center by way of contrast is a tiny tome: a St. Francis mass, 1½″ by 1¼″, ensconced on a diminutive pedestal.

Though size alone has little to commend it, those who revel in *Gulliver's Travels* will recall with relish those Brobdingnagian books that were read in Jonathan Swift's conjured kingdom.

LILLIPUTS OR MIDGET BOOKS

IN THE SIDESHOWS of bookdom huge elephantine folios—in which a city couple might wellnigh set up light housekeeping—vie, with wee midgets—volumes as tiny as a hummingbird's egg. Since the cradle days of printing, small books have come from the presses of the masters, but these little Elzevirs and other tiny masterpieces take on almost an aspect of ponderosity beside those delectable miniature books on which from time to time renowned printers and binders have spent their ingenuity. Books *in petto* from the 1627 *Horace* to the Pickering *Diamond Classics*, are classic treasures of intrinsic charm in type and format, but the truly miniature volumes are really articles of *virtu*, book bibelots that may be classed as *curiosa*, at least in respect to the tininess of their proportions. Here, our concern will be with these superlatively small literary chits, those which range downward from a not too rigid maximum of three inches tall, of which there have been, all in all, several hundred published or privately printed, to the ultra half-dozen bantams, the supreme Tom Thumbs, which even a postage stamp dwarfs. These are the books that never grew up, especially attractive, perhaps, to those who never outgrow a childhood affection for tiny things.

Many a wee volume must have lain lost and undisturbed in a neglected chest through a procession of years, but many a precious literary Lilliput, hidden in secret secretaires and handed down from parent to child with the family laces and jewels, finally finds its way to alien but appreciative hands.

A winning little book written by an unknown "Microphilus" and printed in London by "N. & J. Okes, dwelling in Little St. Bartholmewes, 1636," bears the quaint title: *The New Yeres Gift presented at Court from the Lady Parvula to the Lord Minimus commonly called Little Jefferie, Her Majesty's Servant, with a letter as it was penned in shorthand, wherein is proved Little Things are better than Great.* The little gem of a portrait of that famous midget, the Court favorite of Charles I, which adorns this rare minim was engraved by John Droeshout, brother of Martin, famous as the engraver of the portrait of Shakespeare which appears in the first folio of the bard's works. Lines under the frontispiece instruct us to "Gaze on with wonder, and discern in *me*, The abstract of the world's Epitome." "Little Jefferie" [Jeffrey Hudson] be it remembered, was once served up to royalty in a make-believe plum pudding; he fought a duel with a spurred turkey cock and, when the ladies-in-waiting desired to chastise him for boudoir eavesdropping in a bandbox, spared himself the riding whip by the quip: "Let her who was my last mistress strike the first blow!"

Tortoise-shell, enamelled, mother-of-pearl, silver, and embroidered book covers are charming and cherishable variations and departures from conventional bindings; and when such embellishment or protection is found adorning miniature books, the heartstrings and pursestrings of collectors of the exquisitely minute are subjected to a particularly strong tug. Tortoise-shell bindings edged and clasped with silver were characteristic in the late seventeenth century and were mostly of Dutch workmanship; German workmen used *repoussé* and engraved silver bindings under such titles as "Rosengartlein." A *petit bijou* with delicate chiseling was a desirable metal-craft *reliure* of the silversmith's art. One book shepherd of tortoise-shell bindings informs us that "This testudinatious material makes a neat, light and durable book-cover,

108

BOOKMEN'S BEDLAM

pleasant to the touch, but it is brittle as glass, and must be handled as gingerly." These tortoise-shell and silver-bound books are all of a devotional character, usually missals.

It is recorded of Mevrouw Philipse, widow of one of New York's merchant princes in the good old Dutch days of cocked hats and eelskin queues, that she possessed one of these tiny cherished psalm-books, clasped with gold, which hung by a golden chain from her presumably plump arm, or ample girdle, and swayed to and fro in rhythmic measure with her stately (or mincing) step, as she wended her way on the Sabbath to the newly erected Middle Dutch Church in Nassau Street.

Embroidered small books of the seventeenth century are highly prized and their needlework is usually ascribed to one of the fair inmates of the Protestant Nunnery of Little Gidding in Huntingdonshire, England. Several are preserved in the British Museum, though the colors of their silken threads are fast fading. We even hear of little books in crimson velvet, embroidered with silver thread, and other marvels of the deft bodkin.

Earliest in point of age among tiny books is the *Officium Beatae Mariae Virginis* (Venice, Nicholas Jenson, 1475), a black-letter little volume, 2¼″ tall, a choice copy of which sold for £42 a generation ago. Ornamented with three borders and many richly illuminated initial letters, it is printed on vellum in red and black, with twelve lines to the page, the morocco sides richly tooled and painted. Jenson's first book is supposed to have been printed at Venice in 1470, five years earlier. Although this great Venetian typographer produced many a larger volume, none was more lovely than the *Offices of the Blessed Virgin*, which Andrews calls a "miniature epitome of the whole art of book-making."

The Morgan Library has among its treasures an undated fifteenth-century Latin exemplar of these devotional miniatures, which is one of the smallest complete illuminated manuscripts known, the text measuring 1⅛″ by ¾″. The miniatures are in grisaille, heightened with gold.

Orlando Furioso (Venice, 1570) is the smallest edition of Ariosto ever printed. About two inches tall, it contains 1151 pages, and is half an inch thicker than it is wide! Still it is a comely book and quite legible. Substantially bound in brown calf with goffered edges, the leather is rich in tone and so lustrous with age that it invites the caress of eye and touch.

The *Psalmorum Liber* of Christopher Plantin (Antwerp, 1584), another miniature volume, is also a superb classic specimen of typography. The copy formerly possessed by William Loring Andrews came from a famous library and is bound in crimson morocco covered with a network of gold tooling, with delicately modeled silver clasps in the form of mussel shells.

Next in point of antiquity is Bishop Andrewes' *Manual of Directions for the Visitation of the Sicke, with sweete Meditations and Prayers* (London, 1642), a thumb-wide pocket edition of a religious compendium prepared by this prelate for the use of his clergy in their ministrations. Of Bishop Lancelot Andrewes, says an old chronicle, "God translated him to heaven, not, however, before he had narrowly escaped another translation on earth to the primacy of all England."

And now a word of the Book of Books in miniature, the extraordinary Bible excerpts printed in shorthand by Jeremiah Rich in London about 1660. It is about 1¾″ wide, 2¼″ tall, and an inch thick. The New York Public Library treasures one of these little curiosities. Among other petite Bible rarities is a beautiful *Newe Testament* printed in London by Christopher Barker in 1593. It is about three inches tall and quite bulky, being over an inch and one-half thick. Another is the Newberry *Bible in Miniature* (London, 1780) which is 1⅝″ tall.

The earliest tiny books known to be printed in America were histories of the New Testament, as they were called, in fact abridged selections paraphrased for children. Perhaps the first with date was that published in Boston in 1765 by the firm of Mein and Fleming, which measures 1⅜″ by 2″.

David Bryce and Son of Glasgow, who perfected the process of making India paper (prized for its opaque thinness), in 1896 published a little Bible not over 1¾″ tall and 1¼″ wide, which was accompanied by a small reading glass. It has 936 pages and 28 illustrations delightfully executed. The same firm in 1895 issued a New Testament which when opened flat is no larger than a postage stamp. The specimen of this diminutive oddity is kept in a protective locket but may be read under the tripod enlarging glass which belongs with it.

Wilbur Macey Stone in 1926 issued through the Carteret Book Club a delightful little treatise, limited to two hundred copies, entitled *A Snuff-Boxful of Bibles*, which recounts the salient facts about miniature Bibles, including the history of John Taylor's "Tom Thumb Bible," as it was called. John Taylor was a Thames waterman with literary addictions.

Various editions of these Biblical minims appear; the first edition, in 1614, measured 1¼″ by 1⅛″ and bore the formidable title *Verbum Sempiternum* for the Old Testament, and *Salvator Mundi* for the New Testament. Stone recalled: "The only copy of this first edition which has survived the weight of years is a ragged little volume lacking two leaves, but having both title-pages intact. This book was at one time owned by Colonel James Allardyce of Scotland in whose family it was an heirloom. It now rests in the Aberdeen University Library, to which institution it was bequeathed by Colonel Allardyce, who died in 1910." Between 1614 and 1720 several later editions of this wee Bible appeared. Thumb Bibles in early editions, whether of British or American imprint, are highly prized and costly. Most copies are defective from hard handling.

A still earlier miniature book was John Weever's life of Jesus which appeared in 1601 under the title *Agnus Dei*. Only one or two copies of this have survived, as is true of a similar 1610 edition. In rhyme and of the same diminutive size as the later *Verbum* of Taylor, it is perhaps the most valuable of miniature books.

Apart from tiny format Testaments and Scriptural excerpts, one finds a range of literary Lilliputiana. A Koran in Arabic, measuring 1″ by ¾″ and printed on India paper, was issued by Bryce and Son in 1896

and was worn as a charm by Mohammedan officers during World War I.
But more unusual and precious is the manuscript Koran written in
Persian about 1800 in characters of almost microscopic fineness, with
each of its pages edged with a narrow gold border. What makes it the
showpiece of a collection is that this tiny manuscript is in the shape of
an octagon, and there are probably fewer octagonal books extant than
Gutenberg Bibles. It measures 1½″ across and is bound in lacquered
covers on which rose designs have been painted. Though one bookseller
did part with this rarity for $25, it would be difficult to find one for
$250.

Miniatures that are made small by photo-reduction are less esteemed
than those set in movable type, and minims in manuscript are usually
unattainable. The Bibliothéque Nationale has an Ethiopian prayerbook
in manuscript within wooden covers 1″ by 1¾″. A Bablylonian clay
tablet of 2000 B.C., which measures 1″ by 1½″ and about a half inch
thick, is listed in one bookseller's catalogue at twenty dollars. Or one may
prefer the smallest set of Shakespeare, the Ellen Terry Miniature
Edition in twenty volumes on India paper, which though easily legible
can be shelved in an oaken stand no larger than a one-pound candy box.
It must be confessed that it is rarity rather than readability of content
which is sought by the several score Americans who garner little books,
or books about little books like *The Queen's Dolls' House Library*
(1924).

A bibliopegic freak is the bizarre production of a modern bookbinder
—a twin book—like a three-panelled screen folded. Even larger twin books
are a rarity, so that a specimen of Siamese Lilliputs may be accounted
doubly delectable and an epitome *in parvo* of the art of bookmaking.
This oddity contains *Walton's Lives* and *The Compleat Angler*, bound
in dark green morocco with only three covers—a tête-à-tête style of
binding exhibiting neat and dexterous handicraft on the part of the
French bookbinder Marius Michel.

In the first half of the nineteenth century not a few small almanacs
vied in popularity with such tiny song books as *The Little Warbler* and

The Caledonian Siren. Most of the latter were published in Edinburgh in 1803–1805. The little-known *Alarm Almanac* appeared in Paris in 1781; it was engraved and measured ¾″ by ⁹⁄₁₆″.

A noted English series is Schloss's English *Bijou Almanacs*, several of which measure less than an inch tall and contain plates of much beauty. The first one appeared in 1837 as a souvenir of Queen Victoria's accession to the throne. Its thirty-seven pages contain, in addition to the almanac proper, several leaves of music, a list of theatres and museums in London, verse by a now forgotten poetess, and several portraits, including one of James Fenimore Cooper. It is bound in gold-tooled morocco with gilt edges.

These *Bijou Almanacs* were engraved, however, not printed from type, and vary in the extent of their littleness. The 1837, smallest of them all, is therefore eclipsed by the type-printed *The Mite;* although an eighth of an inch wider than the Queen's almanac, *The Mite* until the Padua Galileo was the world's smallest book printed from movable type. It consists of twenty-eight pages and was published at Grimsby, England, in 1891. The text measures ⁹⁄₁₆″ by ⁷⁄₁₆″ and there are several illustrations and a tinted title page. Artisanship as well as small size gives these gems appeal.

In 1894 Georges Salomon of Paris dispersed a collection of seven hundred miniature books, a library which could be carried in a moderate-sized portmanteau. The largest book in the Salomon collection, about 3¹⁄₁₆″ by 2¼″, was a work of Lafontaine. M. Salomon thought he possessed the acme of tiny books, a Dutch work printed at Amsterdam in 1674, entitled *Bloem Hof je Door* (The Court of Flowers). With a text height of ⁹⁄₁₆″ and width of ⁷⁄₁₆″ its forty-nine pages were contained in an exquisite binding of silver filigree, with clasp. It was preserved in a little morocco cabinet, lettered with the title. About 1915 it reappeared in a famous London bookseller's catalogue at £35.

But in 1896 was published a tome of 208 pages about half the size of a postage stamp—⅝″ by ⁷⁄₁₆″; each page had nine lines of about a hundred letters. Printed by the Salmin Brothers of Padua from "fly's eye" (*occhio di mosca*) type it contains in Italian a hitherto unpublished letter written by Galileo in 1615 to Madame Christine of Lorraine, to wed whom a cardinal relinquished his red hat. In this smallest known font of type, four thousand *i*'s weigh only a pound.

The same firm of Padua printers in 1878 printed a famous diminutive edition of Dante's *La Divina Commedia*. Although the edition consisted of one thousand copies, specimens are now seldom encountered and are worth approximately fifty dollars if morocco-bound. It is 2½" tall and 1½" wide, with thirty-one lines to the text page. Two folded sheets of paper sufficed to contain all the 14,323 verses of the poem, thirty-one verses occupying a space something less than 3¼ square inches. The type from which this curiosity was printed was cut as long ago as 1834, but no complete book had hitherto been turned out in it, the difficulties for compositor and proofreader being so enormous that attempts were abandoned time after time. The setting of the *Commedia* was started in 1873 and some notion of the difficulties experienced may be gathered from the fact that the work occupied the spare hours of five years for completion.

The text is that of Fracatelli; the proofreader was a certain Signor Luigi Busato, and the compositor Giuseppe Geche, whose eyesight was seriously impaired by the task. One is unable to form a judgment as to how corrections were handled, for even with the best magnifying glass it is difficult to follow the text continuously. It took one month to print thirty-two pages, and new types were necessary for every new form of the 499 pages. This is the smallest substantial and impressive work ever printed from type, having no semblance to the toy book.

Several decades ago, at a book auction dispersal, the Sir Julius Caesar Traveling Library—presented by Sir Julius Caesar to John Madden, Esq., attorney to King James I—comprising forty-three little volumes was sold for $3,500. Sir Julius Caesar, Master of the Rolls, invented this postchaise library which fitted into a case, made to resemble a folio, bound in olive-green leather with an Italian design; it is 16" high, 11" wide and 3" deep. The little books are packed in three compartments; they are all bound alike in vellum stamped with gold, but subjects are distinguished by colored silk ribbons in red, blue, and green. Blue indicates theology and philosophy, and includes the *Imitation*, the *Meditations of St. Augustine*, the moralities of Epictetus, the philosophical books of Cicero, and others—sixteen in all. Red indicates the fourteen ancient historians, including Caesar's *Commentaries*, Sallust, and Tacitus. The green of the third shelf in the box is devoted to sixteen poets, among whom are Catullus and Ovid, and the historical Lucan. Inside the bottom division of the case the date January 1617 and a coat-of-arms may be faintly discerned in letters of gold.

One sought-after little book is an edition of *Omar Khayyám* with an introduction by Nathan Haskell Dole, which was privately issued by Charles H. Meigs of Cleveland in 1900 and dedicated to John Hay. The bound volume measures $1\frac{3}{32}''$ high and $\frac{5}{16}''$ broad, approximately one-fourth the size of a postage stamp. There were only fifty-seven copies published, and these on Japan paper. For a time this was the smallest book in existence, but since it is a facsimile reduced through the medium of photography it cannot be accounted a tour de force such as the precious Lilliputs set from type. Set in a boldface type larger than ordinary book size, it was then reduced by photography and reproduced by photogravure on copperplates. It is, of course, only readable with a magnifying glass, the individual letters being illegible to the naked eye. The whole edition of fifty-seven copies weighed slightly over three ounces avoirdupois, or about twenty-five grains Troy per copy! The volume was printed from the plates only after many difficulties had been surmounted; some copies are bound in cloth. One was sold at auction for $225; another, a perfect copy set in the bezel of a signet ring, was purchased for $420 at an auction sale of miniature books.

America has had other triumphs in little books, for example, *Brilliants*, a setting of humorous poetry in so-called brilliant (3-point) types, with a most interesting preface by De Vinne, onetime dean of American printers. Printed at the De Vinne Press in New York in 1895, there are about twelve hundred distinct pieces of metal in a square inch of this type. Copies are of considerable rarity.

Another fragile American Lilliput, copies of which occasionally pass to new possessors, is called the *Life and Services of General Pierce* and was printed by the Gazette Press of Concord in 1852. It has fourteen pages, is unbound, and measures 1⅝″ by 1″.

A facetious volume entitled *Quads*, printed on English banknote paper in pearl type, is not over 1½″ square. It is a miniature replica of a volume of conventional size containing printers' jokes, and the small book reposes in a receptacle hollowed out in the major volume.

It may or may not be true, as stated in the Harleian manuscripts in the British Museum, that Peter Bales, a sixteenth-century Englishman, made a handwritten copy of the Bible so small it was kept in a walnut shell. But an American craftsman, Burt Randle, made handwritten books bound in leather with a wire clasp, containing the Gettysburg Address and bulking less than ⅛″ square.

The Grolier Club possesses one of the finest American showings of these masterpieces in miniature, including 176 examples presented by the noted nineteenth-century bibliophile Samuel P. Avery. A catalogue of these was issued soon after their acquisition, and the collection was augmented to some three hundred and fifty specimens. James D. Henderson of Boston and Wilbur Macey Stone also had notable collections.

The ultimate in littleness was achieved in 1933 by the Commonwealth Press of Worcester, Massachusetts, in their photo-reduced edition of Omar's quatrains, each copy weighing a third of a carat and bound in full crimson morocco. The whole edition of 150 would go into an old-fashioned watchcase, and twenty-four are a heaping thimbleful.

There is a growing fondness for these literary morsels; the relish for tiny tomes, once acquired, is like the legendary taste for peacocks' tongues! As one collector of another day said condescendingly of Samuel Johnson's penchant for folios: "Sir, he hath never fed of the dainties that are bred in a lyttle booke."

OLIO OF ODDITIES

VETERAN BOOK COLLECTORS, devoted with exclusive ardor to their own specialties, are often amazingly uninformed on fields of bibliophily other than their own. This is natural enough by reason of the range and variety of collecting penchants. There are men who boast a hundred editions of *The Compleat Angler*, yet would balk when asked the century in which Audubon wrought his work on birds. There are bibliognostes who covet every vestige of Aldines, almanacs, or Algers, yet would scratch perplexed heads if asked to say concerning Roger Payne, Tom Paine, John Howard Payne, and John Payne, which was binder, which disbeliever, which playwright, and which translator of the *Rubáiyát*. There are those who garner Lincolniana, but would hesitate to distinguish Montaigne from Montesquieu. Small wonder, then, that many who are expert in one or another phase of booklovers' arcana should raise an inquiring eyebrow at the mention of so little known a topic as cut (bisected)-hymnbooks, or at citations of those queer revolving discs known as volvelles. Even bibliographica has neglected these latter curious and intriguing byways, for, so far as could be ascertained, each variety has but a solitary article devoted to its charm and oddity.

No phase of the expansive subject of book oddities is more neglected than that pertaining to unusual formats and to those singular trimmings

that occasionally are found as embellishments of the text. In outward
form these unconventional items range from the volume on Georgia that
has the outlines of that state to books having object or animal shapes.
Among varieties of curious inner forms there are those early tomes with
movable discs, bisected hymnbooks, and, latterly, juvenile "pop-ups"
from which colored cardboard figures and folded scenes spring as the
book is opened. The collection varies in artistry as it does in form; some
are mere trifles for children or booklets of commercial inspiration,
others have genuine merit as eccentric but artistic craft estrays of the
bookbinder.

To the last group belong those superfine specimens bound by
Caspar Meuser, a court binder for Kurfürst August of Saxony, princely
patron of the arts. A superb and unique heart-shaped binding by this old
craftsman (who died in 1593) is or was preserved in the Landesbibliothek
of Dresden, having been executed about 1590 for the Kurfürstin Anna
von Sachsen. It is a "Betbüchlein" or small prayerbook, and contains also
domestic household rules entitled *Oeconomia oder Bericht vom
Christlichen Hausswesen.* A singular circular book is another of the
extant Meuser creations. We are told that such unusual forms were
sometimes indulged in during the French Renaissance before they
became favorites in sixteenth-century Germany. One lovely illuminated
manuscript Book of Hours, which was bound in 1555 for Diana of
Poitiers, opens in the shape of a lily. To call these "Spielereien" (playful
trifles), as does a contributor to the Loubier volume on bookbinding, is
belittling a delightful and too seldom ventured *jeu d'esprit* of inspired
binders whose work achieves the reaches of a fine art. Such truly artistic
specimens of the past must be distinguished, however, from those
extravagant or grotesque examples that occasionally crop up as the
product of commercial binderies or are intended as playful curios for
youngsters.

No one has hitherto deigned to give consideration, in a surveying
article, to books of bizarre shape. Meuser's unique circular binding
elicited a brief description by Christel Schmidt in the *Festschrift*

Loubier, from which we learn that this volume so oddly fashioned more than three centuries ago was last known to be in the collection of Olga Hirsch of Frankfurt, who exhibited it with other specimens of bookbinding in 1920. Like the lily-shaped book this circular binding is bisected, the contents (containing five religious tractates of the period) being bound back to back. The covers, hinged at the middle radius, are of dark brown calf, richly gilded. The diameter of this strange volume is 10⅖", and the rounded fore-edges are elaborately decorated. The original semicircular leaves were brought to the present form by neatly added arcs of paper and the hinges and outer rim of the binding were restored at a later date. No other artistic binding in this round format is known to this writer.

Such of the early craft specimens of unusual shape that have survived may be counted on the fingers of one hand. The lily-shaped Book of Hours of Henry II was, and is, a thing of beauty, and though one may regard as extravagant the heart-shaped, lozenge-shaped, triangular and octagonal bindings of sixteenth-century craftsmanship, they have a curious appeal all their own. Even if modern bookbinding should seek to imitate these unconventional forms, the early specimens would still retain their allure and their rarity.

Discussion of this matter of odd shapes is difficult, in that the subject is too enticing to be dismissed cursorily, and necessarily too heavy with bibliographical detail if encompassed adequately. In compromise, distinction of binding, period of issue, as well as association will operate in choices made. An exquisite hand-tooled book that is rare in shape may be all the more a charming *trouvaille* when it hails from the long ago; whereas a book of similar contour in die-cut format of recent guise may be no more than an example of "literary didoes" or advertising doodling.

Precious both in point of age and in small proportions are four octagonal books. One of these, bound in gold-yellow silk, with gilt edges, is the *Christliches Kleinot vñ Geschmeid zur Andacht und Gebett,* which on its engraved title pages gives the compiler as Johann Haberman, the printer as Johann Carolo, and the provenance as Strassburg, 1613. Its eighty-odd leaves have the type set to conform with the cross-cut corners of the format which measures about 3½″ tall by 2½″ wide. Surrounding the black letterpress, each page has an ochre-red frame in octagonal ornamental design.

The second is a *Gita-Govinda*, being a 2½-inch manuscript written in Sanskrit on Indian paper, with sixteen full-page miniatures, in an octagonal red velvet binding embroidered in silver. The third is in the miniature collection of the Library of Congress, an undated Mohammedan manuscript Koran, octagonal in shape, bound in golden-brown tooled leather, and measuring less than two inches square. The fourth, a seventeenth-century Koran, engrossed by Bel El Kadi Abogeid of Fez, similarly shaped and about four inches square, is in England.

An unusual item having the heraldic form of a cross patté has been reported; and there is record of a royal bibelot in cruciform shape. The latter is said to be a miniature album containing pictures of the Nativity and the Holy Eucharist, painted by Princess Sophia, daughter of George III. It is bound in gold-tooled green morocco, with white silk end-leaves, the thirty-four leaves held by three silver clasps of which the uppermost has a small ring so that it could be worn suspended from a chain attached to the girdle. Such devotional girdle-books were once common to noble waistbands, and if this cross-shaped specimen is not alone of its kind, one may be a lifelong bibliophile without encountering another such binding.

In the Morgan Library the collection of illuminated manuscripts includes a lectionary in Greek which was lettered and illuminated at Constantinople about 1160, and in which the text on each leaf is disposed in the shape of a cross. Such cruciform texts in devotional manuscripts are few.

At least one modern item having the outline of a six-pointed star may be noted, although it is a mere twelve-page sheaf of minor verse in illustrated paper covers, bound with a thong. Scarcely meriting inclusion as a book, this oddity, entitled *The Christmas Star*, appeared in New York in 1882 with Annie H. Mercur as author.

Far more valid is the genuine *Facts About Georgia*, mentioned earlier in this chapter; edited by Louis D. Geldert and published in Atlanta in 1916, it has in text and binding the shape of that state. Its colored frontispiece pictures all the products of Georgia, including fair women, and the 277 pages extol the resources and opportunities of that Commonwealth as set forth by the Georgia Chamber of Commerce under the auspices of which the book was issued. Somewhat less pretentious is *The State of Maine* issued at Bangor in 1894 by the Bangor and Aroostook Railroad. This is an eighty-page guidebook having the outlines of the Pine Tree State, with type set to follow the contours.

Among the commercial curiosities is a booklet shaped like an automobile, and the *Football Souvenir of the 1911 Yale-Harvard Game*, a forty-eight page oval piece, the size of a football, bound in tan cloth with a thong through punched holes. Undoubtedly there are other examples of odd items published for similar purposes.

Then there are occasional trifles with leaves folded in expansible accordion-pleat after the Oriental manner. Odd, too, is the Italian *Decameron*, 13½" tall and only 3" wide; only a hundred copies of this extraordinary volume were printed and tastefully bound at Florence in 1820. Some elongated books are printed lengthwise (parallel to the backbone), instead of across the page in the conventional way. And a novel of 1899, *A Hero of Manila*, was printed in Detroit and bound with three edges serrated.

Queer, indeed, are the few animal profiles that have come to notice. There is a slim book by Thomas Wallace Jones, published in Cincinnati in 1904 and entitled *Bull Fighting*, which was made in the outline of a bull's head with paper covers bearing an appropriate likeness. Another such has the shape of a buffalo; still another, of a bird (aviform, as the learned cataloguer of the Library of Congress cards it). Such items are doubtless die-cut, like a bell-shaped history of the Liberty Bell.

Among fetching oddities for children was Peter Newell's *Topsys and Turvys* (1893), with two columns to the page, one upside down, and with color illustrations of twofold aspect: each picture, when inverted, reveals another semblance. On the last page the caption reads:

AND NOW APPEARS A MYSTIC WORD, BUT IF IT BE INVERTED

WE FIND THE ENDING OF THIS BOOK IN PLAINEST TEXT ASSERTED.

Juvenilia has produced not a few oddities of form and fandango. There is the volume in which the perforated circle, which constitutes a part of the cover illustration, on one page makes a huge open mouth in the picture, on the next a hoop, on another a cave, and so on. In Peter Newell's *Hole Book* of 1908, according to the story, a bullet is fired through the volume when a gun goes off in the hands of the boy, Tom Potts, and the small hole appears with different effect on each page. Newell's *Slant Book* of 1910 was a quaint conceit, cut on the bias. It is difficult to find copies of these and his *Rocket Book* (1912) in good condition.

Though of few leaves and in paper covers, R. A. Garman's *Moving Picture Circus* (Chicago, 1909) is included here because it has the outlines of an elephant, with the pages cut in many pieces from the fore-edge to the spine, in order for the pieces to be turned back and forth independently of each other to show, the title legend discloses, "120 wonderful animals performing."

Cyril Davenport in his *Byways Among English Books* (London, 1927), states: "A few years ago a considerable number of small children's books were made in the shapes of animals, birds, and other objects. I think this output was not a success as it does not appear to have been continued. In that case good and clean specimens will become rare and one or two examples might well be procured and kept as curiosities."

Singular features in the make-up of books are sometimes encountered. Thus a tiny French Almanac of 1745, formerly in the collection of the late Wilbur Macey Stone, measuring only $5/16''$ by $1\frac{1}{2}''$, has its folded leaves opening out into fours. This diminutive curiosity is engraved throughout and morocco-bound. And at the Caxton Celebration in 1877 were exhibited two small eighteenth-century English Bibles with folded-in notes at the bottom to be retained or perforated off.

Other oddities, not elsewhere mentioned, come to mind. An extremely scarce *Kipling Handbook* was published in 1899 by the San Francisco *Examiner*, to be folded, stitched, and cut by the subscriber. An unusual —indeed unique—item is the thin sheaf of poems issued about 1925 by Phillips Russell, in which the inner margin of each leaf is perforated, while a prefatory note invites the reader to discard any of the poems that do not please and to pass on to friends such pages as may invite further reading. A little Italian catechism on vellum, dated 1659 and printed on one side only, has the separate questions so cut that they are attached by the inner margins only. This *Industria Spirituale*, prepared by Serafino Giorgi at Bologna, is the only one of its kind this writer has seen.

Of a different nature is John Eliot Hodgkin's *Monograms, Ancient and Modern* (London, 1866) ; though bound in usual fashion, the text is printed in the form of a shield on each page, thus giving it membership in the group of books having effigy verse or prose in odd type forms. Odd shapes of text, both in manuscripts and printed works, is a subject meriting separate consideration ; they range from love lyrics having the typographical appearance of a heart, to a portrait made of type ornaments. Such effigy printing was once quite the vogue.

In a collection of occult books belonging to M. Lionel Hauser of Paris was a vellum manuscript written and cut in triangular shape. This French treatise of ceremonial magic and alchemy was executed in cipher and cabalistic symbols about 1750 by the Comte de St. Germain (Marquis de Betmar), and is known as a *grimoire*, or book of magic spells and ritual of the black art. This curious work gives instructions for prolonging life, for the discovery of treasure lost at sea, and for locating diamond, gold, and silver mines. A key to the cipher had been worked out by previous owners. The manuscript is ten inches square and was sold at Southeby's in 1934, when the Parisian collector's library was dispersed. Triangular formats like this are exceedingly rare.

With respect to oddity of format it would be impossible to surpass an Oriental palm-leaf specimen once in the British Museum but now reported disintegrated. It was a Tamil manuscript of rounded form—a veritable book-ball. The layers of leaves at the center were longest; those above and below gradually tapering in length. Around the circumference was a metal band secured by a hook having small projecting handles. A strange denizen of the library, this fragile item was suspended like a cocoanut hanging from a nail.

Another freak form is found in the Library of Aberdeen University —an Indian Makassar manuscript, written on palm leaves cut to the shape of a ribbon about one inch wide and rolled up and fastened in a bamboo fork.

Occidental panoramas are outdone by those of the East. A hand-painted Japanese panorama depicts scenes of a military and naval campaign in vivid colors; when extended it measures sixty-two feet, but folds to a compact square between silk covers.

The variety of these unusual formats is as great as their acquisition is difficult; most are beyond the reach of the average private collector. The Jewish Seminary of America has an elongated oblong Hebrew prayerbook, printed in Spain about 1490, which was used by the Marranos or secret Jews, who underwent enforced conversion but clung to their ancient faith and devised this form in order to slip the book easily up a sleeve should a stranger come in while the devout were at prayer.

There is a booklet by the owner of an ostrich farm which is shaped like an ostrich egg; one on the Siwash Indians is in the form of a tepee; and *Love's Garland,* a ninety-six-page volume of poetic inscriptions copied from rings and bracelets, is bound in the outline of a garland of roses, a facsimile of which is embossed in colors on the cover. The *Gems of American Scenery—White Mountains* (New York, 1878) has two small lenses fixed in a flap of the front cover which may be held at right angles to see the stereoscopic views interspersed in the text.

One of famous binder Berthelet's bills for binding a New Testament and a Psalter for Henry VIII describes the dual volumes as "bounde backe to backe"; one middle cover is common to both books which in being read are reversed, so that the fore-edge of one is next to the spine of the other.

These curious twin bindings when stood on end remind one somewhat of a Z-shaped tête-à-tête settee or a three-panelled screen folded. Known also as dos-à-dos bindings, they open on opposite sides and inverted. Such Siamese-twin specimens of the book world are infrequently encountered. In their choicest examples they comprise a New Testament and Book of Common Prayer (perhaps the Psalms) in an eighteenth-century or earlier English binding of embroidered satin, or with covers adorned in seed pearls or sequins, or delighting the eyes in velvet. Occasionally two other closely related works are twin-bound, for example, *Walton's Lives* and *The Compleat Angler*, delightful in the little Pickering edition of 1825. A diminutive dual specimen, so small that a postage stamp will cover the letterpress of a page, is the early, and often reprinted, Thumb Bible, containing Scriptural couplets by John Taylor, the Water Poet who hawked his works in the byways of London in Shakespeare's day. The only known copy of the 1616 original is in the British Museum. Among the curiosities in the famous but long since dispersed Salomon collection of tiny books was another such twin work, entitled respectively *Catechismus Handlung* and *Vom Christlichen Hausstand*, printed in 1666 at Nuremberg; 1¼″ tall and richly bound, it is, indeed, a prize.

Unlike the above in rarity or binding artistry are those quite common volumes which contain contrary lucubrations printed in a single inexpensive book in reverse directions. Two modern American examples are both facetious. In one, dated 1920, Irvin S. Cobb was allotted one side of the leaves to discourse on *Oh, well, you know how women are!* while Mary Roberts Rinehart inverts the volume to reply, from Cobb's last word forward, on *Isn't that just like a man!* The other, in imitation, is entitled *Men I'm Not Married To*, by Dorothy Parker, and, in reverse, *Women I'm Not Married To*, by Franklin P. Adams. Either end is right side up, according to one's attitude!

A correspondent in *Notes and Queries,* referring to these dual books, ventures with mock gravity to term them "amphisbænic volumes." Other examples include: Hereward Carrington's *Spiritualism a Fact* which, when turned upside down becomes James J. Walsh's *Spiritualism a Fake,* with the stunt extended to the spine and pagination. The London bookseller Frank Hollings in 1932 issued a catalogue, the one part *Books of Recent Vintage,* the reverse, *Books of Mature Vintage.* A devotional textbook with London imprint, entitled *The Anchor: The Haven,* contains Scriptural selections interspersed with verse for each morning of a month, and, inverted, for each evening. And finally, a book appearing at London in 1909 bears the title *The Great Question: Tariff Reform or Free Trade?* by L. Amery, and in reverse *The Great Question: Free Trade or Tariff Reform?* by J. M. Robertson, M.P.

These topsy-turvy printings are of small consequence, although it is surprising that they have not been more often resorted to for controversial matters, for when the contending themes approximate one another in length, it is an admirable method of presentation. The authentic twin binding, however, is in a different category, cherishable for beauty of needlework embroidery or dainty bullion ornamentation together with age and sometimes midget size. The twin binding concerns two separate books, perhaps printed years apart but bound with the inner cover common to both. This is quite different, of course, from those single volumes in which the text by opposing authors—whether grave or gay—runs in reverse direction between ordinary covers. Moreover, the true twin book blends in mutual contents within its three covers, whereas the other type contends between its two covers.

As items for the collector, the tête-à-tête binding is one of those oddities of bookdom that inveigle the susceptible. One must be, indeed, cold to the lure and pursuit who would not yearn to possess an example of this curious craftsmanship, for instance, such a one as Thomas Berthelet's already alluded to. Quaintly designated in the bill for binding submitted by that master of the craft to his sovereign Henry VIII, dated January 15th, 1542, he charged, among other items, six shillings for "a

New Testament in latyne, and a Psalter englisshe and latyne, bounde backe to backe, in white leather, gorgiously gilted on the leather."

After all, matters of forward and backward can be made most confusing by the metaphysician. All Hebrew works begin at what is termed the back of a book and are read forward to what is called the front. What is the end and what the beginning in anything that lingers in time and space? And perhaps it were better if many a book had never been begun, much less ended! Not without warrant was it that beneath the word Finis, at the end of a stupid book, a wit added the following barbed couplet:

> *Finis! An error, or a lie, my friend!*
> *In writing foolish books there is no end.*

Of all eccentric formats, what may be deemed the most extraordinary group of kindred specimens known has seldom been chronicled. Each of these specimens consists of six volumes in one sextuple binding, opening six ways. One specimen contains six religious works in German, with imprints between 1570 and 1579. This *Vexierband* (surprise or tease binding) is believed to have been made in Breslau, and its seventeenth-century Saxon cover is adorned with colored ornamental enamel plaques, even the gilt edges of the rarity being goffered. Of octavo page size, it contains three prayerbooks, the fifty-first Psalm of David, and two tracts of Martin Luther, one a Passio, the other *Der Kleine Catechismus.* Together, the six bear either Breslau, Frankford, or Leipsig imprints. The very queerness of this aggregate binding defeats description; only an illustration can do it justice. Imagine two small volumes at top and two small ones at bottom side by side, with two large center books dos-à-dos. In other words, the upper pair and the lower pair are attached to the outside covers of the inner twin binding. Thus from six sides this sextet of devotional books may be perused by anyone who has the inclination, the mastery of crabbed old German, and possession of the strange multiple volume that contains them. Some seven such agglomerated bindings are known, most of the sextuples being in libraries of Sweden and Denmark.

What for want of a better term have been called cut-hymnbooks, were a product of Yankee ingenuity for which there is only one known old-world counterpart. The pages of this variety of book curiosities were split to the spine of the binding, about midway across the book or two-thirds down. On the upper leaves were printed the stanzas of various hymns, while the lower part bore the musical notation. This permitted various hymns to be sung to the same tune and vice versa, with the announced two juxtaposed in the hand of the devout worshipper. There seem to have been four such bisected works published.

Most of the early hymnbooks contained only the words to be sung, the tunes being learned by ear. Though not devised to supplant the conventional hymnbook, prior to 1800 several books of tunes having a single verse of each hymn were printed with the musical notation. *The Essex Harmony*, printed in 1770 by Daniel Bayley, was one such. This made two books necessary for the singer, one for the words, another for the tunes. Still earlier there were also numerous songbooks, not always liturgical, in which the printed page was so disposed as to show respective parts to musicians standing on all sides of the opened book. Of this variety a typical example, sometimes giving five or six parts for a song, was Thomas Morley's *A plaine and easie introdvction to practicall musicke, set down in forme of a dialogue* (London, 1597). The huge antiphonaries of monastic origin often were in musical parts also.

First honors for the innovation of the cut-hymnbook go to John J. Williams, printer at Exeter, New Hampshire, who in 1818 put out a bisected edition of Isaac Watts' *Hymns and Spiritual Songs*, of which there is a copy in the Clements Library of Americana at the University of Michigan. Midway in the volume another title reads: *The Psalms of David, Imitated in the Language of the New Testament, and Applied to the Christian State and Worship, by Isaac Watts*. Throughout both portions the upper part contains the text, the lower the musical arrangement. The lower half of the split title page reads: "A Valuable Collection of Sacred Musick, adapted to the Various Metres in Watts." The "Advertisement" is signed in October, 1818, by the inventor of this "construction," Moses Elliott, who wrote that he had secured a patent on the basis that the leaves could be turned "in such a manner that any tune may be presented to the eye with any psalm or hymn." Each musical score is marked "L.M." (long meter) or "S.M." (short meter).

But the split books do not seem to have been popular, for the next one published was not until 1880 when *Unity Hymns and Chorals* appeared at Chicago, jointly compiled by William C. Gannett, James V. Blake, and Frederick L. Hosmer, all Unitarian clergymen. The tunes are above, the words below, and the preface states: "The cut page enables a few noble tunes to serve conveniently many hymns and secures to every hymn the range of all the music in the book to find its best adaptations." The editors do not mention the earlier Watts item, though it does not seem likely that they were unaware of it.

A *Hymn Book, for Jewish Worship* (Rochester, 1909) contains three hundred songs, of which about one third are in German. Many are designated for special holy days. The upper halves of the pages set forth ninety-six airs. This scarce work was a new edition, for the preface is dated "Rochester, 1880," and the compilers, "Dr. M. Landsberg and Sol. Wile," state that the early copies were all burned in "the destruction of the Temple Berith Kodesh by fire, April 13, 1909." No mention is made of the cut-hymnbook published also in 1880 at Chicago. The compilers express the hope that "the arrangement of the hymns and tunes on different sets of leaves will be found a great convenience, as it allows a choice of tunes for any hymn."

Abroad the only uncovered instance of the use of the cut page was in *The Psalter, being the Authorized Version of the Psalms*, which was issued at London in 1888 by Thomas Nelson and Sons. This was published "by authority of the General Assembly of the Church of Scotland." It seems strange that the device should not have been more freely adopted, both here and overseas.

Movable discs, forming part of the illustrations or embellishments of a volume, are a curious feature of certain early works. In a sixteenth-century astronomical treatise by Peter Apian are various diagrams and plaquettes with applied revolving plates of the constellations, the zodiac, and the like, in some copies colored by hand. This *Astronomicum Caesareum*, summarizing current knowledge of astronomy, was published at Ingolstadt in 1540 and is a masterpiece of typography. The John Carter Brown Library has a perfect copy of the first edition with thirty-seven full-page diagrams having complicated movable pieces richly colored by hand.

Such volvelles, as they are called, are found in sixteenth-century works on astrology, in which they served the purpose of casting nativities and the like. In an article on these curious literary accessories in the *Booklover's Magazine* (London, 1905), Gilbert R. Redgrave states: "Many of the diagrams are well worn and have evidently been frequently consulted. It is interesting to reflect upon the anxious fingers which have turned these fateful little wheels in the far distant past. . . ."

According to this authority, "perhaps the earliest known example" of the printer's use of a volvelle diagram is in the *Kalendarium* of Johannes Monteregio, printed by Ratdolt at Venice in 1476. The edition of 1482 has a double disc to indicate the moon's motions and, much more unusual, a small movable two-jointed brass arm securely fastened to another diagram. But their use antedates this, if we are to believe a writer in *Notes and Queries* who states: "Several astrological manuscripts and almanacs in the British Museum show early use of movable figures, often crude. The earliest, a manuscript copy of Raymund Lullii, *Ars Generalis*, dated 1306, has four astrological figures or tables, one of which has two round movable figures of parchment, attached through the center by a thread."

Volvelles with shifting concentric discs or other movable parts were used for Copernican astronomical charts showing movements of heavenly bodies and also for mathematical demonstrations, but more frequently for astrological hocus pocus. Often elaborately printed, with ornamental spandrels, they were usually in folios, though Johannes de Sacrobusto's *Libellus de Sphæra* (Wittenberg, 1543), printed by Petrus Seitz, is a duodecimo containing two. Zodiacal specimens are found also in the small work of M. Sebastiano Theodorico on the same general subject, dated Vitebergæ, 1564.

The ingenuity of the printer in the construction and use of these devices is seen in the *Organum Uranicum* of Sebastian Münster, printed at Basle by Henricus Petrus in 1536 and containing fourteen volvelles, besides various *instrumenta* in the form of superimposed concentric discs or semicircles, with threads deftly attached for manipulation. The silk guiding threads usually were secured by parchment wafers.

There are three movable attachments in *Mr. Blundevil, His Exercises* (1636). In *Renatus des Cartes de Homine* (Leyden, 1664), there is a heart with two flaps which lift to show the inner structure. Still earlier, in Bartisch's *Das ist Augendienst* (Dresden, 1583), the anatomy of the eye is illustrated by a series of woodcuts, imposed one over the over.

The most remarkable of these volumes is a folio by Johannes Paulus Gallucius entitled *Speculum Uranicum,* from the press of Damianus Zenarius and dated Venice, 1593. This work has seventeen of the contraptions, of which the first comprises no less than seven shifting circles.

With the decline of the vogue of the astrologer the device became more or less obsolete, being seldom encountered in eighteenth-century books. But it persisted in a few instances. Cowley's *Perspective* in 1766, and Harrington's *Science Improved* in 1774, were two such English works having applied movable figures to illustrate scientific subjects.

In 1932 an American travel bureau issued a colored booklet on the cover of which was a revolving cardboard wheel having apertures through which rates, duration of cruises, and itineraries were shown for various vessels according to the dates of sailings indicated by an arrow at the circumference. Occasional juvenile books have employed the disc device for one purpose or another, but its possibilities for graphic instruction

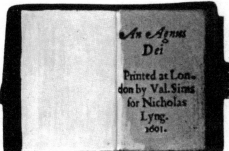

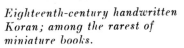

Rarest tiny book of the world; printed in 1601, only two copies are known to exist, one in the British Museum, the other in Philadelphia.

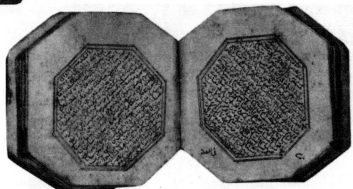

Eighteenth-century handwritten Koran; among the rarest of miniature books.

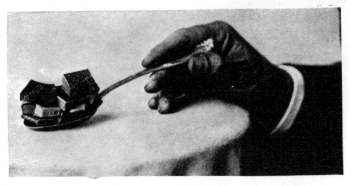

A spoonful of books. These dozen books hold world's record as smallest. They are the tiniest in the world in their respective fields, including: a Koran; English dictionary of 12,000 words; a Galileo (the smallest volume ever printed from actual type); a Testament; the Mite (up to 1896 the world's most diminutive book); Robert Burns (vellum); Petit Poucet; French Constitution (gold-stamped leather binding); Gita (Sanskrit); Tasche Kalender (1839); Toras Mosche or Laws of Moses (world's smallest Hebrew book); and Scotch-Irish Songs (with music).

Thimbleful of books. Quatrains of Omar Khayyam in leather covers (3/16" x 5/16"); printed from photo-engraved copper plates; the whole book weighs a third of a carat; an edition of about one hundred fifty copies executed by the Common-wealth Press at Worcester, Massachusetts, at $75 each.

Lincoln's Gettysburg address originally executed by Kingsport Press, Kingsport, Tennessee; this copy was printed on parchment and bound in red morocco with silk headband by Sangorski—a choice minim. Eight pages of text from the Kingsport Lincoln.

Shorthand Bible. Entire text in shorthand.

Early (1701) Dutch Bible.

Two early tiny tomes printed in England

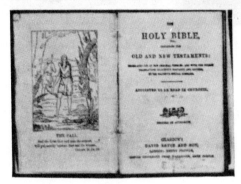

Published at Glasgow (1901) with twenty-seven plates and including full text.

Locket New Testament. Printed at Glasgow (1895) on a single sheet (24" x 38") of thinnest India paper ever made; an enlarging glass is set in the locket.

would seem to have been neglected by present-day textbook makers. Much ingenuity has been employed in the production of unusual books for children; but it is adult eccentrica that is most enticing.

The olio of oddities is of wide range. We have noted in this chapter but a trio among many—odd formats, cut-hymnbooks, volvelles. An assortment on the shelves—from a Hamlet in Hebrew to a medical treatise bound in human skin, from a volume printed at sea to a Bible in shorthand—constitute a veritable book circus.

CURIOUSER AND CURIOUSER

THOUGH WE KNOW of none, it would be possible to have books printed without actually using a type font made up of letters of the alphabet; they could be set either in Semaphore type or in Morse code. The first is an alphabet based on the accepted arms-signalling practice, in which the font of type embraces all units by showing a tiny human figure with arms positioned for each letter. Arranged in sequence, they carry a message as a series of animate-arms signals would do; in a similar fashion the Morse code of dots and dashes is a typographical medium. Moreover, the American Indians had a gesture medium of communication or sign language between tribes having wholly different vernaculars, and this gesticulation has been reduced to printed form by showing in outline the various positions of the hands and, by means of dotted lines, the movements. The deaf mute code is another instance.

Books printed in phonetic spelling are few in number, but the earliest go back three centuries in English and almost four in French. The first in England was a small quarto by Charles Butler concerning bees, printed at Oxford in 1634, entitled *The Feminin Monarchi, or the Histori of Bees: Shewing their admirable Nature and Propertis; Their Generation and Colonis; Their Government, Loyalti, Art, Industri, Enimies, Wars, Magnanimiti, &c.* The admirable nature of the bees seems not to pertain to the erratic phonetic system in which they are extolled.

Included in this curious work is the bees' threnody, a stave of musical
notes being arranged in triple time and alleged to represent the humming
of a swarming hive. In addition, the volume is prefixed with
commendatory verses by George Wither. Two years later Charles Butler
published a little treatise on music, printed in phonetics, with apologies
for its "od" appearance.

In this country shortly before the Civil War someone in Cincinnati
seceded from orthodox orthography and gave us *Ferst Lesonz in
Jeometri, bi Tomas Hil, Fakts befor Reznin, Sinsinati, 1858.* Evidently
emboldened, the Cincinnati simplifier in 1861 published a New Testament
in 343 pages of righteous phonetics. A similar Scriptural contortion had
appeared at Philadelphia in 1848.

But in France the idea of writing according to pronunciation goes
back to 1542, when Louis Meigret wrote a tractate suggesting it. His
suggestion, however, was in traditional spelling, and it was not until 1550
that he adopted his system in a phonetic effort entitled *Le Tretté de la
Grammere Francoeze.* This proposed reform started a controversy
between Meigret and Jacques Peletier, the latter writing a phonetic
opuscule that same year in a system of his own, printed in a special type.
Both were keen for phonetic transcription, but wrangled as to the
method, Peletier clinging to his Lyons accent, Meigret holding forth for
the pronunciation of Le Mans. In 1555 Peletier sought to further his
eccentric orthography by publishing at Lyons his *L'Art Poëtique,*
printed in a special italic font of phonetic type.

But the early movement for simplified spelling languished, despite
other disciples. One of these, J. P. de Ria, a Swiss, published a curious
book on the subject at St. Petersburg in 1788, with parallel columns of
ordinary French and a phonetic version thereof.

Allusion has been made to the manual communication of certain
advanced stocks of the American Indians, on which their pictography was
based, as exemplified in Brinton's notable study and transliteration of the
Walam Olum, the inscribed traditions of the Lenâpé. There have been
several volumes devoted to the elucidation of the American Indian gesture

speech and sign signals. Ernest Thompson Seton's *Sign Talk* conveys some 1,725 signs, based on their use by the Cheyenne Indians; and General Hugh L. Scott, who writes the Introduction, states: "The American Indian sign language is the best extant. It is theoretically perfect and practically complete. It is established over the whole area of the Great Plains, and, though varied locally, is essentially the same from Saskatchewan to the Rio Grande."

A curiosity pertinent to this theme is *The Sermon on the Mount in the Indian Sign-Talk,* published at Fort Smith, Arkansas, in 1890 in a four-page folio leaflet. It consists of a series of hand-signs in white outline on a background of small black blocks, interlined with explanatory text. The locutions may be judged from the sign-rendering that promises a blessed Hereafter, which in the English subscription reads: ". . . because you good: for the same you catch it kingdom of heaven." The twenty-third Psalm has been similarly done in sign-talk symbols.

Allied is the sign language of the deaf. About fifteen hundred signs used by the deaf are contained in J. Schuyler Long's manual on the subject. And this, too, comes within the purview of strange books.

The zigzag jamboree of a booklover extends to Esperanto and those other universal language systems into which books esteemed by all the world have been rendered; estimates vary as to the extent of this literature. Although a complete bibliography of Esperanto would embrace seventy-five hundred books and booklets, noteworthy titles are probably fewer than one hundred; of them, our consideration here, limited to books, excludes excerpts and fragments.

Surprising as it may seem, there have been some two hundred such schemes, the majority of which were merely projects. Esperanto and its offspring, Ido, have been "reformed" by a number of other modified versions. Though such artificial languages as Volapük (1880), Orba (1893), Veltparl (1896), Europal (1911), Novial (1928), and many another have been suggested, few have had standard works of literature printed in their idioms. *Paul and Virginia* was rendered into Dilpok (1898), but this is a curiosity and nothing more. Of them all, only

Esperanto appears to have a growing literature of rendered and original works.

Hamlet (Hamleto) was put into Esperanto by Zamenhof himself, and there exists a number of other Shakespearean plays in this "language" including *King Lear* (La Reĝo Lear), *Midsummer Night's Dream* (Sonĝo de Someromeza Nokto), and *The Merchant of Venice* (La Venecia Komercisto). Not only the Bible, but the Psalms separately are published in Esperanto, as are also six books of the *Æneid*, in metrical version, which are said to be both faithful and sonorous. Goethe's *Iphigeneia* (Ifiĝenio en Taurido) and Lessing's *Nathan the Wise* (Natan la Saĝulo) are to be had, the former having been translated by Zamenhof and actually once given in a performance at Dresden by a professional company of actors.

Similarly from French literature, works have been rendered into Esperanto, from the *Song of Roland* to Renan's *Life of Christ*. And from Polish literature, closed to most of the cultured world by reason of the difficulties of language, several outstanding works have been published. Strangely enough, several original romances of the thriller variety, written by Dr. Vallienne, have been published in Esperanto and in no other language.

Shorthand is a form of cipher, as Pepys' *Diary* made evident by concealing the disclosures of its strokes and curlecues for a century and a half; but secrecy is not the object of these systems of abbreviated writing so much as speed. It is an amazing fact that sets of symbols have been devised for innumerable systems in various languages, and there have been renditions of literary works in more than fifty recognized shorthand systems the world over. Naturally, among notable works published in one or another of these mediums, the Bible takes leading place, a number of versions having been published of the Scriptures, some of the New Testament alone. Of these, several in tiny format are doubly odd. Some of these shorthand Bibles are in phonetic symbols of languages other than English.

Scores of renowned literary works have appeared in shorthand versions, perhaps the major number of those based on English being in the Benn Pitman or Isaac Pitman systems. But one of the earliest was in Bertin's French system, a rendition of La Fontaine's *Fables*, published at Paris in 1796. Among well-known writings published in English shorthand may be mentioned Moore's *Lalla Rookh* (London, 1846), More's *Utopia* (London, 1857), Bunyan's *Pilgrim's Progress* (London, 1866), Richard Locke's *The Great Moon Hoax* (Rochester, 1886), Defoe's *Robinson Crusoe* (London, 1900), Franklin's *Autobiography* (Cincinnati, 1916), Conan Doyle's *The Sign of the Four* (New York, 1916), and Dickens' *Christmas Carol* (New York, 1918).

Abbreviated writing harks back to the earliest efforts at recording. Archeologists in 1903 unearthed a number of papyri at a site south of Cairo, and among these was a contract, with a date equivalent in our chronology to 137 c.e., arranging with a teacher of shorthand to instruct a boy for the sum of 120 drachmae (about $25). One third of this was stipulated to be paid in advance, another third when the boy showed evidence of progress, and the final third when he had achieved proficiency.

Naturally, the nations of classical antiquity resorted to abbreviated writing. Tiro, an educated slave of Cicero, devised a system of signs for contracted writing and, according to Plutarch, took down the Ciceronian orations by means of a stylus on tablets covered with a layer of wax. These tablets had wooden edges somewhat resembling the school slate of a later day, and two or more were frequently fastened together by means of rings. As many as twenty tablets were sometimes so joined, but usually they were fewer. Two tablets so fastened were called a *diploma*, and were commonly used to confer appointments or honors. The Roman poet Quintus Ennius, more than a century before Cicero lived, devised a scheme of eleven hundred signs for his own use.

Among the early Christians, St. Augustine and St. Jerome employed a corps of stenographers. The former records the fact that the stenographers of Rome went on strike on one occasion and secured the concessions they demanded.

In what is termed modern times, the earliest system of shorthand was that of Dr. Timothy Bright entitled *Characterie: An Arte of Shorte, Swifte and Secrete Writing by Character* (London, 1588), dedicated to Queen Elizabeth. It was made up of arbitrary symbols having no phonetic relation to the alphabet. In a similar fashion he wrote *A Treatise on Melancholy* published in 1586, one with which Shakespeare was doubtless familiar, for the word "characterie" occurs in two of the plays, as well as phrases common to both, such as "discourse of reason."

J. R. Gregg reports in a masterly article, "Julius Caesar's Stenographer" (*Century Magazine*, May, 1921), that the earliest mention of the term shorthand occurs in a Westminster Abbey epitaph to William Lawrence, who died in 1661. It reads:

> *Shorthand he wrot, his flowre in prime did fade,*
> *And hasty death shorthand of him hath made.*

If immortality was his reward, he doubtless found no need for the art with all of eternity at his disposal.

Between 1600 and 1750 more than two hundred systems were published. Pepys' *Diary* was in the Shelton system and included accounts of the Great Plague and the Great Fire of London. Naturally, with shorthand systems so popular in England of that period, the settlers of Colonial America brought with them knowledge and practise of the art. Gregg states: "There is evidence that the art of shorthand was in use in this country within half a dozen years of the landing of the Pilgrims. Roger Williams was an accomplished shorthand writer." The Brown University Library has in its collections a copy of the Eliot Indian Bible of 1663 which belonged to Roger Williams and in which he made annotations in shorthand. These notes, which have never been deciphered, are in narrow columns on the back flyleaves.

Gregg relates further: "John Winthrop, Jr., son of the first Governor of Massachusetts, and who was himself afterward Governor of Connecticut, was an accomplished shorthand writer. When he arrived in Boston in 1631 he proceeded to superintend the settlement of the town of Ipswich, Massachusetts, while his wife, Martha, remained in Boston. They corresponded in shorthand, and many of these shorthand letters, written in 1633, are preserved by the Winthrop families. I mention this particularly because Martha Winthrop is the first American shorthand writer of the gentler sex of whom we have record." It seems that it became quite a common practice for young women to take shorthand notations of sermons when they attended church.

Benjamin Franklin was another early American worthy of mention in this connection. In his *Autobiography* he says: "My uncle Benjamin had formed a shorthand of his own, which he taught me. He was very pious and a very great attender of the best preachers which he took down in shorthand, and he had many volumes of them. My father intended to devote me to the service of the Church. My uncle offered to give me his collection of sermons as a sort of stock-in-trade with which to start."

Jefferson, like many of his contemporaries, occasionally resorted to cipher in his correspondence and he, also, seems to have been accomplished in shorthand. In a letter to his friend Page, dated January 23, 1764, he proposed that they should study Shelton's system and use it in mutual correspondence. Jefferson wrote: "I will send you some of these days *Shelton's Tachygraphical Alphabet and directions.*"

No one not conversant with shorthand literature can conceive how voluminous it is. Thirty-six Bibles and New Testaments printed in shorthand are listed in the card catalogue of the New York Public Library, and about twenty-five versions of the Psalms.

There are oddities in this field, too, such as a number of shorthand tracts, catechisms, and prayerbooks done by a missionary in Chinook and other dialects of the British Columbia Indians. Under the title *The Oddities of Shorthand* (New York, 1891), John B. Carey wrote fictional sketches based on the manipulation of shorthand in plots as an aid in crime or its detection. It is a little-known and ingenious volume, with stenographic illustrations intrinsic to the narrative.

There is even shorthand poetry of a sort. *Pitman's Shorthand Rhymes* (London, 1922), by E. Tracey Archer, is a quaint sextodecimo of forty-eight pages published as "a valuable aid in memorizing the principles of the system."

Perhaps one can in no way better indicate the diversity of technical shorthand textbooks than to say that, in the respective languages, expositions pertaining to indigenous systems have been printed in Japanese and in Gaelic, in Bengalese and Bohemian, in Chinese, Hebrew, Scottish, Siamese, Latin, Maori, Slavonic and Welsh!

And finally, one of the rarest English books on the subject, in which instead of being printed the shorthand characters have been filled in with the pen. The title reads: *A Pen Pluck'd from an Eagles Wing; or, The most Swift, Compendious, and Speedy Method of Short-Writing that ever was yet Composed by any in this Kingdom; is at length (through the blessing of God) brought to Perfection, by the Indefatigable Industry of William Mason, Authour and Teacher of the said Art* (London, 1672). Good William Mason is now doubtless busy with his crabbed shorthand assisting the Recording Angel!

Inkless printing by electrical contact is a development that has now gone beyond the experimental stage. Such an electrical inkless process was patented in 1899 by W. Friese-Greene, the method consisting in the impregnation of paper with certain chemicals and the application of current at the moment of impression. Demonstrations of the process evoked much interest, especially among inkmakers, who foresaw the possible doom of their business. But they seem to have survived, and the inkless menace is now almost forgotten. Still, in 1932 a German electrical firm patented a method of making impressions by a metal (silver or an alloy) which will leave a mark. Though intended only for printing the recording bands of electric meters, the process might be extended to a wider range of printing. There is one oddity in this field of typographical technique, a little-known specimen of only twelve pages dated 1900, entitled *Interesting Dovercourt, Essex, with a description of the Miraculous Rood of Dovercourt.* Written by Friese-Greene, this curious production bears the legend: "This entire pamphlet is printed by electricity without ink," and has as imprint: "The Electrical Inkless Printing Syndicate, Ltd., Clifton Mansions, Brixton, S.W." In at least one copy of this rarity the lettering had an unpleasant lead-colored or faded impression, and the paper was brittle. Apparently, nothing more ever came of his invention.

The first book stereotyped in America was *The Larger Catechism, received by the Presbyterian Churches in America. Revised by Rev. Alex. McLeod.* This was stereotyped and printed by J. Watts & Co. of New York in June, 1813, and a copy is occasionally noted in booksellers' catalogues. But Britain used this process much earlier; according to the records, a Latin version of Sallust was produced in 1739 by William Ged, a goldsmith of Edinburgh, regarded in England as the inventor of stereotype printing which he first employed for a book in that year.

The Anatomy of Sleep, or the Art of Procuring Sound and Refreshing Slumber at Will by Edward Binns, M.D. and published in 1842 by John Churchill, was "Printed by J. H. Young by a Patent Composing Machine, 110 Chancery Lane." There were five hundred copies of this four-hundred-page book; though the exact process is uncertain, a prefatory note states:

> It would be unjust to the ingenious inventors of the
> Machine by which this work has been composed, not to say,
> that we believe it must and will, at no very distant period,
> supersede in many departments of typography composition
> in the usual mode. But the use of compositors can never be
> entirely dispensed with, even supposing the machine to be ten
> times more perfect than it is. The opposition with which its
> inventors have had to contend, is what might have been
> anticipated, but was certainly unexpected by the author. But
> that in time it will come generally into use, he thinks there
> cannot be a shadow of doubt. He consequently looks upon the
> publication of the 'Anatomy of Sleep' as an epoch in the
> history of typography, from which it is possible to conceive
> a new era in the history of literature may be dated.

The first book composed on the linotype was *The Tribune Book of Open-Air Sports*, edited by Henry Hall and published by the New York Tribune Association in 1887. That five-hundred-page volume has on the verso of the title page, under the copyright notice, the following: "This book is printed without type, being the first product in book form of the Mergenthaler Machine which wholly supersedes the use of movable type."

The monotype was first used for book publication by Morrison & Gibb of Edinburgh in July, 1889 and then by Butler & Tanner in August, 1901. Stanley Morrison states: "These are the earliest dates of the use of the machine by printers specializing in books. Messrs. Wyman used the Monotype in 1897, and claimed to have composed 'two volumes of high-class book work for London publishers' between June and November of that year."

The first book printed on a cylinder press was Dr. John Elliotson's translation from the Latin of Blumenbach's *The Institutions of Physiology* (second edition, London, 1817). The end of the translator's preface informs us that "The volume may be considered a typographical curiosity, being the first book ever printed by machinery. It is executed by Messrs. Bensley and Son's patent machine, which prints both sides of the sheet by one operation, at the rate of 900 an hour, and is the only one of the kind ever constructed." Author J. F. Blumenbach was professor of medicine at the University of Goettingen. In the preface of a 1828 edition of Elliotson's rendition, reference is made to the 1817 version as "the first book printed by steam."

Experiments in typeless printing have proceeded at a good rate since 1925, including the employment of a photographic film base and an operator's keyboard that projects letters and symbols in rapid sequence. In 1933 the first complete book to have all its type matter set up by means of the Teletypesetter was Max Brand's *Slow Joe*, which was issued by Dodd, Mead, and Co. and produced at the Burr Printing House, New York. This device automatically operates slug-line casting machines by means of code-perforated tape, the perforator having a keyboard resembling a typewriter.

The first book printed in this country from rubber plates was published in 1934 at the plant of Charles Scribner's Sons, New York, after two years of experiment; the process is said to afford economies in initial cost, in make-ready, and in ink consumption. The book was Jackson Gregory's *The Emerald Murder Trap*. Rubber-coated paper, too, has been developed, the use of latex or raw rubber in the preparation of the stock preventing curling and shrinking, and the nonabsorbent coating requiring less ink.

This serves to recall the rubber-covered books used by Gabriel D'Annunzio, poet, soldier, and aviator (and a bit of a poseur), as he read while bathing with goldfish in his huge sunken tiled bath. If John Wesley read on horseback, Leigh Hunt prone, and Lincoln at closet, why not a tale in a tub? and why not one protected by rubber from inspired splashing? Malcolm Macmillan, in his *Letters* relates that when he was in Athens he met a German pundit who was reputed to have a Homer printed on India rubber, to read during his bath; though there's reason to suspect the report, a patent for rubber bindings *was* granted to a Paris inventor in 1935.

The first volume composed with the revolutionary Higgonet-Moyroud, photo-electric type-composing machine was issued in 1953. It is entitled *The Wonder World of Insects*, by Albro Gaul. The mechanism, commonly called Photon, was a project of the Graphic Arts Research Foundation; it is an electronic device that delivers film negatives instead of metal type and at high speed.

The virtues of brevity have been often lauded, and instances abound. Balfour epitomizes the history of the human race as "a brief and discreditable episode in the life of one of the meaner planets." Madame de Staël wrote to a friend: "Pardon this long letter. I had no time to write a short one." Hugo engaged in a duel of brevity with his publisher. Absent from Paris and anxious to know how his new novel, *Les Miserables*, was selling, he wrote "?" and received in reply an expressive and triumphant "!." This reminds us that the note of interrogation is said to have been formed from the first and last letters of the Latin word *Quaestio* (question) placed one over the other thus: $\frac{Q}{o}$; and that the exclamation was derived from *Io* (joy) written vertically thus: $\frac{I}{o}$.

Which leads us on our laggard way to the long and short of it in literature. In fiction the palm might be awarded Marcel Proust, who wrote an eleven-volume novel in bed. The nine hundred pages of Thomas Wolfe's *Of Time and the River* (curtailed in manuscript) is outdone by the twelve hundred pages of Hervey Allen's *Anthony Adverse* and the 1514 pages of *House Divided* by Ben Ames Williams. The original edition of Eugene Sue's *The Wandering Jew* is of appalling length, while Hugo's tale of Jean Valjean is no trifle.

The legend over which Sue waxed so prolix appears to have been a fancy first expressed in a mere leaflet of four leaves printed at Leyden in 1602, and inspired by a tradition that when Jesus, bearing the cross, passed a spectator who taunted him "Go on quicker," he replied, "I go, but thou shalt wait till I return."

The Hugo masterpiece remains a contender against all comers. As James Bennett says in *Much Loved Books*, this colossal novel "in easily readable type runs to five pages less than two thousand." Moreover, we are told, "On April 3, 1862, 'Les Miserables' was published in whole or in part in Paris, Brussels, London, Madrid, Rotterdam, Leipsic, Budapest, Warsaw, and Rio de Janeiro." A year before its publication the author himself wrote that "The entire work revolves around one central character. It is a kind of planetary system moving around a giant soul, which is an incarnation of all the social misery of the time." "A book may be as great a thing as a battle," Disraeli remarked, and verily the Hugo opus was one such, as was also *Don Quixote,* which in its entirety is of redoubtable length.

Waiving quality, fiction on the quantitative side has no parallel, in so far as a single work is concerned, with the more than three million words devoted to the novel, *Free Lances in Diplomacy,* by Clarence Herbert New. Adventures recounted under this title ran serially in *Blue Book Magazine* from 1909 until the death of the narrator in 1933, skipping an issue only twice in over twenty-three years, and being by all odds the longest story ever written with the same set of characters. After the author's death at seventy, installments continued to appear for several months, for he had written ahead of schedule. A world traveler and engineer, as well as onetime editor and newspaper correspondent, this writer's novels and short stories were noted for accuracy in the geography, navigation, and engineering which entered into the plots of many of them. The shelfful of adventures he crowded into this unprecedented serial were in part at least the chronicle of his own life.

When it comes to serious works, no literary production is half so voluminous as the original edition of the Chinese Encyclopedia or *Yung-Lo-Ta-Tien;* unfortunately, in 1900, during the Boxer outbreak, the original 11,100 tall slender volumes were reduced to about one hundred volumes by wanton incendiarism at Peking. The British Museum now has five volumes of this colossal compendium, the Bodleian Library six, and about sixty remain in Peking.

The manuscript of the Persian poem *Shahnamah* by Firdausi, longest in all literature, consisting of one hundred twenty thousand lines, was sold in London in 1949 for £1,040.

The Bodleian possesses what is doubtless the longest occidental poem in the world. The more than sixty-eight thousand lines were written by Robert Barret; the work, dated 1610, is entitled: *The Sacred War, an History conteyning the Christian Conquest of the Holy Land from 568 till 1588: Reduced into a Poem Epike.* It treated the Crusades in rhymed quatrains, and such readers as this volume may have had must have been grateful that it was reduced to a mere thirty-two "bookes." Other bards pale beside such sustained poetic flight: Homer wrote only 27,881 lines, 15,774 in the *Iliad* and 12,107 in the *Odyssey;* the *Divine Comedy* achieves 14,533 (*Inferno*, 4,992; *Purgatorio*, 4,740; *Paradiso*, 4,801); Spenser's *The Faerie Queene* about 32,390; Milton's *Paradise Lost* a mere 10,565.

Continuing the statistics, the *Ring and the Book* provoked 21,000 lines from Browning. A further tabulation shows Shakespeare's total, taking twenty-nine plays as authentic, and neglecting the Sonnets and other miscellany, is 83,643 lines, of which 26,067 are prose. The shortest play is *The Comedy of Errors,* with 1,770 lines, and the longest *Hamlet,* with 3,924. Finally, the tally of words is about 670,000, as compared with the 724,000 of the Bible. For those who have an appetite for this kind of fodder, *Gone With the Wind* has about 500,000 words, *War and Peace* about 670,000. But *Sironia, Texas* (1952), by Madison Cooper, has about 840,000 words, more than the Old and New Testaments combined.

And so to the longest play ever published. This twenty-one-act drama of the year 1499 was a forerunner of *Romeo and Juliet* and, indeed, of the modern realistic novel. The Spanish text of El Bachiller Fernanda de Roxas, whose name is revealed in a prefatory acrostic, was "Englished" in 1631 by James Mabbe, who tricks himself out as a Spaniard by assuming the name of Don Diego Pued-ser (James May-be). The translation is reputed to be superb, though few among the living have read *The Spanish Bawd represented in Celestina, or, the Tragicke-Comedy of Calisto and Melibea; Wherein is contained, besides the pleasantnesse and sweetenesse of the stile, many Philosophicall Sentences and profitable Instructions necessary for the younger sort.* Appearing originally in the Mabbe rendition as a folio, this extraordinary drama was reprinted in 1894 in the Tudor Translations, with an Introduction by James Fitzmaurice-Kelly, translator of *Don Quixote.*

By way of contrast, a word about the shortest of all plays, *The Exile* by Tristan Bernard, which concerns a mountaineer and an exile. When the curtain rises, the mountaineer is shown sitting before the fire in his mountain cabin near the frontier. There is a knock on the door, and when he opens it the exile enters. This is the entire dialogue of the play:

EXILE: "Whoever you are, have pity on a hunted man.
There is a price on my head."
MOUNTAINEER: "How much?"

As for the longest sentence in the English language, the palm in the field of reputable letters may well be awarded the first sentence in Edward Phillips's *Preface to Theatrum Poetarum*, written in 1675. This elaborate weave of clauses runs to a total of 1,012 words, quite exceeding the 842 in Hazlitt's climactic sentence on Coleridge in *The Spirit of the Age*.

The words "engraved throughout" have a cabalistic appeal for certain haunters of book auctions and conners of dealers' catalogues. The reaction against inferior printing in eighteenth-century France and England, as well as the decline in the woodcut, led to a vogue of text and and illustration engraved on copperplate. In the production of such works, from the seventeenth century on, there were several score having genuine artistry and pleasant appeal. From Moreau's *Dévotes prières* of 1640 to the three-volume *Chants et Chansons Populaires de la France* of 1843, the range is inviting. Who would not cherish the complete engraved work of Piranesi? John Pine's two-volume *Horace* (1733–1737) is perhaps the most attractive edition of that work and the most beautiful of the "engraved throughout" books. In like manner, Pine engraved text and illustrations of a volume describing *Tapestry Hangings of the House of Lords*.

A shelf of these typeless volumes might include Fénelon's *Les Aventures de Télémaque* (1781), and Rousseau's operatic effort, *Pygmalion* (1775), with its series of exquisite copperplate illustrations by Moreau and text engraved by Drouet. The fastidious collector might acquire Justice's version of the works of Virgil (1757), *Calliope, or English Harmony* (2 vols., 1739), and the early folio of *Historischer Bilder Bibel*, with its delicate pictorial interludes, which was issued at Augsburg in 1705. One might be regaled by Burns' *Cotter's Saturday Night*, put out by the Bibliophile Society; another might find delight in the unpretentious but precious Billings' *New England Psalm Singer*, engraved in 1770 by Paul Revere—in, let us hope, its original binding; or in Montesquieu's *Le Temple de Gnide* (1772), with designs by Eisen.

A number of tiny books were so produced and are esteemed by

GLORY or GRAVITY,

The Second or

MECHANICAL PART:

WHEREIN

The Operations and Power of LIGHT in GRAVITY, SEEING and COLOURS, with some OBSERVATIONS on its joint Operators, FIRE and SPIRIT,

Are Explained and Demonſtrated.

SO

Vulgar Errors about the Title of the SECOND PERSON, and the Actions performed by his Emblem in the Rule and Motion of Matter, Detected and Corrected.

Taken from the Original MSS. of

JOHN HUTCHINSON, Eſq;

Late of the Meuſe, Charing-Croſs.

LONDON:

Printed by J. BETTENHAM, And Sold by GEORGE STRAHAN, at the Golden Ball in Cornhill. MDCCXXXVIII. Where the reſt of Mr. Hutchinſon's Works may be had.

In all the one hundred fifty-four pages of this volume, there is none more lucid than this title page.

The mystic number 666 gave rise to other such lucubrations from the sixteenth century onward.

AN EXPOSITION OF THE

Fisheries Commission Frauds;

SHOWING HOW THE FRAUDS WERE CONCEALED BY THE USE OF THE NUMBER

666,

AND THE MASKING NUMBERS

42, 10, 7, 2,

TAKEN FROM THE 13TH CHAPTER OF REVELATION.

EMBODIED IN LETTERS ADDRESSED TO

THE PRESIDENT OF THE UNITED STATES

——AND——

THE RIGHT HON. W. E. GLADSTONE, M. P.,

PREMIER OF HER MAJESTY'S GOVERNMENT,

With an appeal for Official Publication in the interests of RELIGION and GOOD-NEIGHBORHOOD.

——BY——

HENRY YOULE HIND, M. A.,

(FORMERLY PROFESSOR OF CHEMISTRY AND GEOLOGY IN THE UNIVERSITY OF TRINITY COLLEGE, TORONTO.)

British Scientific Witness at the Halifax Fisheries Commission ; and Official Compiler of the Analytical Index to the Documents of the

HALIFAX FISHERIES COMMISSION.

Geologist to the RED RIVER EXPEDITION of 1857.—In charge of the ASSINIBOINE and SASKATCHE-WAN EXPEDITION of 1858.—Author of the Narrative of the Canadian Expeditions in the North West, 1860.—Explorations in the Interior of the LABRADOR PENINSULAR, 1861.—Official Report on the Geology of New Brunswick, 1865.—Official Reports on Waverley, 1869.—Sherbrook, 1870.—Mount Uniacke, Oldham and Renfrew Gold Districts of Nova Scotia, 1872. &c., &c., &c. On the Fishing Grounds of the Northern Labrador, 1876.—Official Papers on—The Effect of the Fishery Clauses of the Treaty of Washington, on the Fisheries and Fishermen of British North America; Parts I and II, 1877.—Recipient of Gold Medal and Diploma, Paris Exhibition, 1878, for Maps and Charts illustrating the Fisheries of British North America, and the movements of Fish in the Sea, 1878.

WINDSOR, NOVA SCOTIA, 1883

Not so much a strange type face, as a strange idea: A poem on baldness with each line starting with c.

ORATIO DOMINICA

PHOENICIE,

SAMARITANA DIALECTO.

A sample page from Didot's Type Specimen Book in Phoenician (Samaritan dialect).

A Torah scroll, of course in Hebrew and handwritten, as tradition demands.

Extract from SACRED EDICT *in Chinese Braille with Chinese ideographic equivalents.*

collecters of lilliputiana. Early in the nineteenth century an engraved *Mignon Almanach* appeared at Vienna, with text page half the size of a postage stamp. In England the series of Schloss's *Bijou Almanacs* were similar gems, appearing annually from 1836 to 1854, and including engraved frontispieces, with the text also engraved in minute but legible characters.

Notable in the province of completely engraved books is the name of John Sturt, who in 1717 executed a *Book of Common Prayer and Psalms* on 188 silver plates, each page having a vignette and emblematic border. Moreover, the frontispiece, an engraved portrait of George I, is unusual in that within the lineaments and bust is inscribed in minute lettering the Lord's Prayer, the Creed, the Commandments, prayers for the King and the Royal family, and the Twenty-first Psalm. Four years later he engraved on copperplates *The Orthodox Communicant*, each of the eighty-six pages illustrated with a vignette view of the Biblical subject and adorned with a border. Sturt had come by his skill through his earlier work in engraving for John Ayres several of that once famous writing master's manuals on calligraphy.

The nineteenth century produced few of these engraved books. However, as recently as 1934 a collection of poems by Siegfried Sassoon, entitled *Vigils*, appeared in England with the complete text engraved on copper by Charles Sigrist, the script meant to simulate the author's own handwriting. Similar, though not engraved, was a German volume of Rainer Maria Rilke's poems in facsimile of the author's own handwriting.

The craftsmanship of the early printers is a matter for endless marvel. A seeming full-sprung technical efficiency overleaped at a bound the usual trial-and-error period of a new art. The impeccable pages of a Gutenberg were so sure a semblance of the toilsome lettering of monkish scriptoria that diabolical assistance was suspected by benighted scholasticism.

Erhard Ratdolt and Aldus Manutius, both of Venice, were the Columbus and Magellan of typography; the enduring artistry of their work is monument perpetual of their mastery. In 1495 Aldus began printing the first of nineteen classics that bear the familiar emblem of the Aldine Press—the anchor with a dolphin entwined on its shaft, the anchor being a symbol of firmness and stability, and the dolphin, the swiftness and activity of the new craft. This first of the famous series was the *Aristotle* of 1495–1498, in five folio volumes. The type was cut to Aldus' design, Greek penmanship serving as a model, for his proficiency in Greek was the incentive of his desire to transmit the masterpieces of that literature in flawless form. The ink for this most notable of the Aldines was made on the premises, and the handmade paper, durable as ever after more than four centuries, was, as he tells us, "of pure linen and hempen rags beaten in pieces by dint of wood and made stiff with glue gotten from boiled hides."

A scholar himself, scholars frequented his place and scholars manned his shop; instructions to compositors, pressmen, and binders were given in Greek. Not profit but perfection motivated him, and he died in 1515 an immortal but poor man. Well might he have had as motto: *Trifles make perfection, but perfection is no trifle.*

Not only did Aldus print the *editiones principes* of Demosthenes, Aristophanes, Euripides, Herodotus, Pindar, and Sophocles, but his successors, son and grandson, gave us the Latins and Renaissance Italians. Though he also made adept advances in binding, it was the exemplary letterpress that was his first and last love. He made first use of the semicolon as an expedient to refine the punctuation hitherto restricted to colon and period.

But above all, it was Aldus who first employed italic, which it is thought was suggested to him by the handwriting of Petrarch. This character of type was called Aldino by the Italians and italic by those who later appropriated it. The first book printed in italic type has been assumed to be the rare Aldine *Virgil* of 1501, although an earlier broadside in Aldus italic is said to have been discovered, probably from the year 1499. Various of the Aldine classics were subsequently printed in italic, with roman capitals, chapter headings, and running heads, notably the Juvenal and the Tacitus. Copies of the precious *Virgil* are in the New

York Public Library and in Princeton University Library, and there was
a counterfeit imitation of it. Printing books in small format was also an
innovation of Aldine, possibly more important than his employment of
italic.

The *civilité* introduced by the Lyons printer Robert Granjon in
1557 was another departure based on cursive handwriting; it was first
used in books for children. Though a French invention, this script was
known in France as *Anglaise,* and in form was a close imitation of the
handwriting used in a class of documents by early scribes. It was a face
that came to be known as copperplate; modeled on penmanship, the
characters were so designed as to join, giving the effect of continuous
writing.

Sixteenth-century books in script type were fewer than those in
italic, and specimens of either style are rare. The earliest American book
in italic seems to have been *The History of Ink* (New York, 1860),
devoted to specimens of writing from ancient times onward. Never widely
employed, even in modern times, script has now become virtually obsolete,
and italic almost completely restricted to special phrases and words in
ordinary book text. Bruce Rogers, however, did use italics in *Theocritus*
and in *The Night Before Christmas;* and the delicacy of cursive pen work
is achieved in the completely italic face known as Arrighi. Also in 1928
the American Society of Calligraphers published *Paraphs* printed
entirely in italic.

The range of collectibles is virtually endless; human nature is such
that the devotee who confines his chase to twentieth-century firsts, or to
association copies, or to any other of the score of conventional diversions
of the quest will be inclined to indifference or a disdainful eyebrow at the
foibles of his fellows in other alcoves of bibliobsession. He who plucks out
his purse to possess an incunable of the cradle days of printing may
refuse a tithe of its worth for an inscribed first of Joyce's *Ulysses,* and
vice versa. This could not be otherwise.

Eccentric Timothy Dexter's *Pickle for the Knowing Ones* had the
last pages of the editions of 1838 and 1858 devoted to rows of

punctuation marks. By contrast, meticulous departures from the norm have sought to quicken typography with new ventures. Back in 1792 one of the most superb publications of Bodoni was printed entirely in capitals. In 1895 those distinctive publishers, Copeland and Day, issued a small edition of Stephen Crane's *Night Riders* in green ink and set throughout in caps. To the other extreme Elias Molee produced *Molee's Wandering* (Tacoma, 1919) wholly dispensing with capital letters. And a more recent volume of verse entitled *Soul,* by June Jamison King, is not only devoid of punctuation, but the initial letter of every word is capitalized. Finally, in José Garcia Villa's new collection of poems, *Volume Two* (1949), commas are used to separate each word from the next; Villa explains this affectation as the literary counterpart of Seurat's pointilism in painting. E. E. Cummings published one novel lacking a title, another called *.&.* (1925), and his *Eimi* (1933) and $\frac{1}{20}$ *Poems* (1936) indulge idiosyncracies of an experimental nature.

Good form in typography requires that as few words as possible break at the end of lines to reduce hyphenation that would mar the harmony of the page. Perfection cannot be obtained, but there are at least close approximations. In 1826 the famous Didot press at Brussels published and printed a practical typographical manual, treating of every branch of composition and presswork. Written by Marcelin Brun and produced under the supervision of Firmin Didot, this gem possesses the singular feature of not having one divided word in the whole text. That precedent is followed in these pages.

Evincing the richness of the Spanish language, as Brunet points out, a number of stories were gathered by Isidro de Robles and published at Madrid in 1709. The first five of these, attributed to Lope de Vega, are each written without the use of one of the vowels. A century earlier the *Proverbios Morales* of Barros appeared, with all but six of its 1,062 proverbs beginning with the word "*ni.*" Insomnia is the only answer as to why he included the six and missed a perfect score!

The church Latinists also indulged in these tours de force. Peter de Riga, a canon of Rheims, summarized the Scriptures in twenty-three chapters, each consecutively omitting a letter of the alphabet. And he had imitators. A quaint life of Jesus, *Christus Crucifixus* by Christian Pierius, appeared at Frankfort in 1576 with charming woodcuts; each word of the long title and every word of the Latin text commenced with the letter "C." Thirty years earlier at Basle was first printed that curious ninth-century poem *Ecloga de calvis* of Hugbaldus, a Benedictine monk, whose hexameters on bald-headed men, dedicated to Charles the Bald, also begin every word with a "C." From Germany in 1690 came a volume of four satires on the Pope, of which the first, *Papa Pariens!* in prose, and the second, *Porcus Pugnans!* in verse, begin every word with "P." Also, a half century before, there was the *Pugna Porcorum Poetica* in a volume of student facetiae. Of other varieties of literary contortion, effigy verse, such as song to wine in flagon shape, was a favorite.

Less common were the centos (or centons) and their makers, in which a hundred scattered lines from Virgil or Horace were chosen to form the continuity of a new poem on another theme. Thus Petrus Spera in his *De Passione D. Nostri Iesu Christi* (Naples, 1647) uses for his poems only lines selected from various works of Virgil.

Of these devices, anagrams and acrostics were done to death. In 1906 a collection was made and published by Walter Begley which included Latin hymns of the early church turned into metrical anagrams.

To round out this little excursus concerning books that toy with the alphabet, or with letters thereof, it may be pointed out that Jacques Arago dowered Paris in the year 1853 with his *Voyage autour du monde sans la lettre A*, which but for one slip came up to promise. A reprint of this little *jeu d'esprit* in 1883 confessed in the errata that the author had overlooked one word, "ser*a*it." And so we say "Selah" to this crooked alley of inquiry among the bypaths of bookish queerness.

HOT STAKE OR COLD CHOP

THROUGH THE CENTURIES, authorship has been beset with risks. There are the sometimes flaming works that had their origin behind prison bars, and the resented tracts and treatises that were consumed by ecclesiastical fires or on parliamentary pyres. And there were those hapless ones, the authors who were consigned to the flames along with their books. The pillory, the gibbet, the faggot, the dungeon have ever been among the bays of authorship. A volume written with all the tenderness these remembered wounds inspire could not tell the tithe of it. Of man's vindictive nature none can bear surer testament than those literary offenders who affronted the authorities of their day. Of the many, only a few can be cited here.

What an array of anguish is rehearsed in Ditchfield's *Books Fatal to Their Authors*. Not only has the progress of learning been achieved in the ivory towers of the mind, but in spite of stake and stock, prison cell and suppression. Penury was the constant guerdon of most of the too rabid exponents of opinion or unwary searchers after knowledge, and posthumous recognition was the belated meed of many.

Fortunately, the atrocities to which books and bookmen have been subjected are not wholly devoid of the saving grace of humor. But there is all too little food for laughter in the sorry tale. Dibdin tells us about bibliophagia, the vice of book-hunger, to satisfy which many a booklover will suffer an empty stomach. But he overlooks one aspect of devoured reading, one little calculated to nourish either soul or body, that is, the enforced eating of books. Many an author has been compelled actually to eat his words—perhaps many another should be!

First in this category was the Scandinavian writer, Theodore Reinking, who, in a Latin political tract dated 1644 concerning the shorn power of Denmark, aroused the ire of the Swedes, whom he maligned as responsible for the Danish débâcle. He was imprisoned and after a time subjected to the ignoble choice of either losing his head or eating his provoking work. To have wilfully suffered the first would have shown a flash of the heroic, but he chose instead to devour the corpus of his own volume after it had been rendered somewhat less unpalatable by a sauce—or, as another account has it, "he ate his manuscript boiled in broth." Unfortunately, there is no evidence as to whether this literary entrée was a bulky tome or just a delicate morsel of a brochure.

From more remote times the relics of anecdotage relate that in 1370 Barnabo Visconti forced two Papal delegates to eat the Bull of excommunication they had brought him, together with its silken cord and leaden seal. As it was presumably on parchment, only a saintly stomach could have failed to rebel.

Not unlike this story is the one told by Oelrich, in his *Dissertatio de Bibliothecarum et Librorum Fatis* (1756) concerning an Austrian general who having signed a note for two thousand florins was compelled by his unpaid creditor to eat it when it fell due.

Add to these Frederic R. Marvin's account in *The Excursions of a Book-lover* (Boston, 1910) to the effect that Isaac Volmar, who wrote some satirical pieces against Bernard, Duke of Saxony, "was not allowed the courtesy of the kitchen, but was forced to swallow his literary productions uncooked." And Philip Oldenburger, a once renowned jurist, suffered an even worse fate. He was condemned not only to eat a pamphlet of his composition, "but also to be flogged during his repast, with orders that the flogging should not cease until he had swallowed the last crumb."

Does all this seem like an echo out of dark bygone days? In the year of grace 1934 gruesome details of how he was tortured in a Hitler concentration camp were given by Ernst Toller, German playwright and one of the most distinguished younger writers in that country until the Nazis came into power. His political beliefs brought him afoul of the swastika henchmen. "It was terrible and inhuman," Toller said. "The guards forced me to swallow almost a complete volume of one of my latest novels. In addition, several irresponsible Nazi sadists, all of whom were youths, poured castor oil down my throat."

To round out this gustatory theme, it is worth mentioning that not all eaters of books have been reluctant to partake of their fare. Primitive tribes regard the book as a fetish, and Livingstone relates that he so excited the awe of African natives by his perusal of a volume he had taken along into the heart of the dark continent, that they, seeking to share the white man's satisfaction, stole and ate it.

Before taking leave of this theme, we must recall the gift of prophecy acquired by Ezekiel through the eating of a heavenly book. In this curious act of commensality he is told by the spirit to fill his bowels with the "roll of a book" given him, and in his mouth it was "as honey for sweetness." In Revelations there is a similar instance in which the book comes from the hand of an angel with the words: "Take it, and eat it up; and it shall make thy belly bitter, but it shall be in thy mouth sweet as honey."

Antiquity yields many instances of the fatalities and suppressions of authorship, but first among the vanguard of the long ago was the incomparable Roger Bacon. This philosopher and physicist in benighted 1267 sent his *Opus Magnus* to Pope Clement IV. Following the death cf that pontiff, Bacon was summoned by the headship of the Franciscan order to be judged in Paris for his heresies. The penalty for his scientific gropings was imprisonment, exacted for fourteen years; and thus he languished, dying at Oxford the year of his release. His soaring spirit had been pinioned by those unable to realize his genius. Posterity acclaimed his work the *Novum Organum* of the thirteenth century.

Three hundred years later there emerged into the intellectual firmament Galileo, peerless pioneer in experimental philosophy. Made professor of mathematics at the University of Pisa when he was twenty-four, his first work set forth astronomical speculations which provoked the disfavor of the Inquisition; and a subsequent writing, published in 1632, confirming the Copernican theory, was the cause of his undoing. Refusing to renounce his findings, he suffered incarceration for five years before recanting. To him are ascribed the principle of the telescope, the first thermometer, the hydrostatic balance, and the pendulum. But it would seem that he was fettered less than many another by the shackles of men who gave their lives to religion but feared to search for God.

So, too, does posterity devote a willing paragraph to Giordano Bruno. A contemporary of Galileo, he also rebelled against the monastic affiliations of his earlier years and, infused with the groping spirit of the new learning, sought knowledge apart from theology. Casting off the shackles of scholasticism, this courageous figure of scientific bent travelled through the Europe of his day, searching for those keys to the Unknown that were the grail of many an unfettered seeker.

Bruno sought kindred souls in France, thence found himself in London as the intimate of Sir Philip Sidney. Here, at the time the stripling Shakespeare was poaching deer, this strange ecclesiastic, urgent with the doubts that devoured him, wrote a work entitled *Spaccio della Bestia Triomphante* (Expulsion of the Triumphant Beast). A title and an attack typical of those times, this onslaught launched allegorical arrows at Catholicism, scoffed at tenets of theology, and, indeed, blasphemed quite beyond redemption. Soon Germany heard him lecture, but on his venturing back to Italy to teach at Padua, the Inquisition took its score. Imprisoned in 1595, he languished for two years and then was consigned to the stake. With detached fortitude he told his tonsured accusers: "You pronounce sentence upon me with greater fear than I receive it."

One extraordinary martyrdom in the annals of books fatal to their authors is that of Kazimir Liszinski, a cultured Pole, who in 1689 was burnt for his heresies, his ashes being then placed in a cannon and shot into the air. His doctrines were unbalanced rather than unorthodox; but the iniquitous and atheistic ideas he expressed in manuscripts found in his possession sufficed to bring him to the stake at the instigation of the Bishop of Potsdam. One reflects with satisfaction that no hapless author has been compelled to eat his own ashes.

Queen Elizabeth issued numerous proclamations against seditious writings. An instance of the temper of her disapproval occurred in the case of the hot-headed Puritan John Stubbes and William Page his bookseller, the first for having written and the other for having published a tract aimed at the incognito visit of the Duke of Anjou to England, after the favorable reception of his proxy by the Queen. Printed in 1579 and entitled *The Discoverie of the Gaping Gulph, whereinto England Is like to Be Swallowed by a French Marriage, if the Lorde Forbid not the Bands by Letting Her Majestie See the Sin and Punishment Thereof*, the diatribe protested against this "Imp of the crown of France" venturing to pay Elizabeth a courtly visit with the object of what is stoutly denounced as "an unman-like, unprince-like, French kind of wooing."

Elizabeth's wrath was so great that author, publisher, and printer were tried and condemned to suffer the loss of their right hands. The printer secured a remittance of his sentence, but the right hands of Stubbes and of Page were chopped off with a butcher's knife and mallet in the marketplace at Westminster. Stubbes displayed remarkable fortitude and loyalty, for as soon as his one hand was off, he doffed his hat with the other, and cried, "God save the Queen!" and thereupon fainted. But this display of courage and devotion did not save him from further misery, for the bleeding stump was then seared with a red-hot iron. Taken to the Tower insensible, he was confined there for eighteen months, during which he learned to write with his left hand.

It comes as something of a surprise to learn that in the flourishing Elizabethan era, cruel punishment was meted out to writers who infringed upon political topics. Marlow barely missed a dire fate at the hands of the Privy Council by his sudden death; fleeing from the warrant issued by the Privy Council summoning him for utterance of heretical opinions, he died by the dagger-thrust of the servingman, Francis Archer. From one who has studied censorship under Elizabeth and James I we learn that "A paper of information from one of the 'State decipherers' lay before the Council, accusing him of heresy and blasphemy, and of receiving seditious and libelous books." Four years earlier, for opinions similar to those imputed to Marlow, a fellow-undergraduate of his had been burnt to death at Norwich.

Extreme severity was meted out to those accused writers who were unable to prove their innocence. Any utterance construed as political heresy was liable to be regarded as seditious and treasonable, and to be so accused was to be liable, before conviction, to imprisonment and torture. These implacable severities of censorship brought many to punishment. Thus, on May 11, 1593, an order was issued by the Privy Council to search for the author and publisher of certain supposed seditious placards. If the suspected persons refused to confess the truth, the order ran, "you shall by authority hereof put them to torture in Bridewell, and by the extremity thereof . . . draw them to discover their knowledge."

Alexander Briant, in efforts to extort his confession concerning a suspected secret press, was subjected to the agonies of the rack and "the scavenger's daughter."

Those were gory days—though now and then they were also glorious days. To be drawn and quartered was rather a crude procedure; yet offenders had short shrift, for constituted authority did "draw them" to elicit confession. And this in a generation graced by Shakespeare and Cervantes! Relic of this mad world, "the scavenger's daughter" is now an exhibit in the Tower of London. One is reminded of the facetious quip concerning the erring scrivener of harsher days who, when asked whether he preferred death on the block or by faggot, is presumed to have replied: "Fire, since a hot stake is preferable to a cold chop!"

England, indeed, had its share of literary punishment; Gillett required two volumes merely to narrate the book burnings. Justice was not always equitable; the most flagrant offenders did not always meet with the most drastic reckoning. Thus a rabid but obscure clergyman named Leighton, in an unreadable diatribe entitled *Zion's Plea Against Prelacy* (1630), saw fit to denounce the hallowed Bishops of Britain as satanical, and the Queen herself as "a daughter of Heth." It was an outspoken era and one of condign answer. By way of rebuttal to his printed opinion, the Rev. Leighton was fined ten thousand pounds sterling, unfrocked, pilloried, branded, whipped; after an ear was cropped off and his nostrils slit, he was sent to Fleet Prison for life— surely acute literary criticism! But, as in other instances of those politically violent days, the House of Commons after eleven years reversed the sentence that had been pronounced on the manhandled cleric, released him, and informed him that his mutilation and confinement had been illegal.

Any consideration, however casual, of the calamities that have befallen authors calls for inclusion of splenetic William Prynne, who was a victim of the Star Chamber. His celebrated *Histrio-mastix, or, the Player's Scourge* in 1633, a blast of more than a thousand closely printed quarto pages against the wickedness of play-acting, masques, and revels, aroused the ire of the Court by its indiscretions. Pilloried at Westminster and at Cheapside, Prynne had an ear lopped off at each place, was fined five thousand pounds and condemned to life imprisonment. The deft executioner who sliced off his ears did, however, spare the stumps; when a few years later, because of his *News from Ipswich*, the undissuadable scribe was again fined five thousand pounds, he was shorn of the rest of his ears and branded *S.L.* (Schismatical Libeller) on both cheeks. Although once again sentenced to duress for life, a change of political affairs brought about his release and he became a member of Commons! This prolific pamphleteer launched some forty volumes of miscellaneous controversy on the disturbed Britain of his day.

But the infliction of penalties was by no means limited to the field of polemics. The estimable De Lisle de Sales in 1769 had published his *De la Philosophie de la Nature, ou Traité de morale pour l'espèce humaine,* seemingly an inoffensive title. Yet, not only was the philosopher punished for his concern for the human species, but the bookseller, two of the printers, and the censors who had sanctioned the disquisition were jailed. Sympathetic savants of Paris were indignant and visited the imprisoned philosopher. Eight years later, the sentences of all the parties principal and accessory to the treatise on morals were revoked by the Parliament of Paris. Meantime, as was to be expected, the extenuated essay had been translated into several languages. During the reign of terror in later France, De Lisle de Sales suffered a second term of imprisonment for another book entitled *Eponine.*

Perusal of the chronicles concerning the pangs and penalties of authorship does not show that men were deterred from an expression of their opinions by fear of shackles or bars, and gradually the punishment of offending authors grew less harsh, or at least the torture of their flesh more uncommon. Musty passages that seem harmless enough today once brought their sponsors to the pyre. Henri Estienne suffered a typical fate. A century after François Villon, Estienne was condemned to be burnt to death for his *Traité de la Conformité,* which in 1566 tilted at the monks and the Church and hinted at the pleasures of ecclesiastical concubinage. The latter observations, so says an annotator, occur in the twenty-first chapter, "which is castrated in all other editions, even in the counterfeits of this edition, of which there were three."

Ancient and terrible was the fiery displeasure. Caligula, deeming himself Jupiter's very own brother, resented a satirical allusion in one of the Atellane farces which he construed as a reflection on his purple, and had the author burned alive in the arena. The soldiers of the Roman Caesars, annoyed by the teachings of the revered Jewish mentor, Rabbi Akiba, sentenced him to death; though eighty years of wisdom was his, he was burned at the stake with the Holy Scroll wrapped around his body.

Smoke ascended from many a pyre. Still preserved with its leaves charred is the Bible which the Rev. John Rogers had with him when in 1555 he was burned at the stake at Smithfield, London, as the first Protestant martyr in the reign of Bloody Mary.

At least one instance may be noted here of fatalities not to authors but to readers! It is said that the dubiously devoted mother of Charles IX of France, noticing that her royal son had a habit of wetting his thumb before turning the leaves of occasional volumes he conned, had the lower corners of a favorite book nicely poisoned and then presented it to him. When he scanned the pages and lingered over the curious pictures of this particular book, we are told, he suffered a mysterious colic to which he finally succumbed. "But not," says the frank commentator, "until after celebrating the Eve of St. Bartholomew." The story is told by Dumas in his *Marguerite de Valois*.

The fatal habit of Charles recalls an illuminated vellum psalter once fondled by this writer, in which the lower corner of each recto had become polished like yellow horn from its many encounters with one or more reverent thumbs.

Bibliophiles, too, have suffered hardships, sometimes yielding their lives and falling from high estate for love of books. Witness the testimony of Fertiault who, in *Les Amoureux du Livre* (1877), mentioned the mortal injury of several booklovers who toppled from their lofty library ladders. Curiously, the list of those who fell from perilous perches is singularly lacking in Anglo-Saxon names. Is it possible that the British worthies of an older day, given no less to great private libraries and inaccessible reaches of literature to the ceilings, were steadier in their ladder researches? Or should one conclude that British bookmen have been less keen to scale the heights, or that the English boot has a firmer grip on the teetering treads?

Like a counterpoint to the tempestuous times that have swept men since the annals of history began, the vicissitudes of authorship attend the strife and the strivings of the generations. Take no more volumes than the fingers of one hand; obliterate all others and intimations of the past could readily be gleaned sufficient to form a mental mosaic:

HOT STAKE OR COLD CHOP

D'Israeli on calamities of writers; Ditchfield on books fatal to their authors; Farrer and Gillett on the burning of condemned works; Vickers in his moving chronicle of the martyrdoms of literature. From their pages might be filled in much of the political and religious rancors of the past, merely through their record of literary devastation.

SIGHTLESS AUTHORS
OF INNER VISION

FROM HENRY THE MINSTREL to Booth Tarkington, temporary
and partial blindness have hampered many in the ranks of authorship.
Pepys, the incomparable diarist, was tormented by two plagues, his
termagant wife and his desperate fear of blindness. Oliver Wendell
Holmes curtailed his extensive correspondence because of impaired
eyesight, but for many years afterward was still able to use his pen.
Jules Janin was virtually blind; John Addington Symonds scarcely less
so. James Joyce and Aldous Huxley would not let defective vision stand
in the way of their work. Lafcadio Hearn, blind in one eye and
grievously myopic in the other, was almost sightless during the last
decade of his life, spending a month at a time in a darkened room.

As Dr. Axel Munthe wrote *The Story of San Michele* he was
growing blind. Though entirely sightless for a time, an operation
restored his sight, and when he died in 1949 he was acting as the palace
physician of Swedish royalty. As the apostle of pity he was by devoted
followers termed "the modern St. Francis of Assisi." While awaiting the
return of light after the operation, Munthe related how the Umbrian
saint, faced with blindness, had submitted with mystic calm when the
fiery brand was brought to cauterize his eyes.

Only those conversant with books of merit written by the sightless

can realize how heroic have been the careers of many of those so
handicapped. Not only among the illustrious have there been such, but
in the common byways of life many a notable figure, though deprived of
sight, has a well-earned place in the world of letters. The human epic
has no more spirited chapter than the untold tale of those who with
inner vision have prevailed over the enclosing veil of outer darkness.
There are many who have eyes and see not, but their are others who,
deprived of their eyesight, can yet behold the wondrous and o'erleap the
chasms of despair, and these are not blind.

Over a century ago Louis Braille, humble blind Frenchman, opened
a new vista for the sightless. After patient effort he perfected the 6-point
tangible system since adapted and in common use. Born near Paris, the
son of a saddler, he lost his sight through an accident in his father's
workshop. He became a teacher and organist and wrote several treatises,
including an esteemed one on arithmetic. In 1840, at the age of thirty-
one, Braille made public his system of sixty-three combinations of six
raised dots, but it was not until 1852, the year of his death, that his
method was widely adopted, though later modified. The influence of his
spirit survives in the hearts of countless blind readers; in America alone
they have at their disposal Braille editions which total several thousand
English-language titles. Braille was perhaps indebted to the much
cruder point system of Charles Barbier, an officer of artillery who in
1829 devised a rough phonetic series of thirty-six pricked-paper dot
clusters for the use of the military intelligence service in sending
messages that could be read in the dark (*écriture nocturne*).

A notable forerunner, too, was Valentin Hauy, not himself sightless,
who first raised characters, although he used ordinary roman lettering in
the form familiar to the sighted. It was "high printing," but not a code
system. It was this pioneer teacher of the blind in France who first
thought of making tangible letters in embossed relief large enough to be
recognized by touch. In 1785 Hauy founded the French institute for
blind youth and began the first printing for the blind in raised
characters. In 1786 he was able to make a good exhibition of the

progress of his pupils before Louis XVI and his Court, and in the same year published his *Essai sur l'Éducation des Aveugles*, with exposition and 111 pages in raised lettering, the first book printed for and by the blind.

The career of François Huber, the Swiss savant who though he lost his sight at fifteen became an authority on the life and habits of bees, exemplifies how a man of courage can triumph over blindness. Born in Geneva in 1750, his scientific bent led him to train his manservant, François Burnens, as his research assistant. The story of Huber's work is remarkable. The success of his faithful servitor in becoming his eyes elicited a tribute from Maurice Maeterlinck in his *Life of the Bee*. Huber's contribution to the apiarian science of his day began with the publication of a volume of his letters to his friend Charles Bonnet, in which he gave an account of his labors and discoveries in this field. Four years later, in 1796, his *Nouvelles Observations sur les Abeilles* appeared; in 1808 it was printed in English at Edinburgh. First to discover and explain the mystery of the making of wax by bees, he embodied his findings in a second volume in 1810. He also collaborated with a fellow scientist of his day, Senebier, and their joint researches were published. The curious interest of their mutual research consisted in the fact that it was his confrère, with good eyesight, who suggested the experiments, but it was Huber the sightless one who carried them out. The mettle of the man is shown by the fact that at this early date he contrived a primitive sort of typewriter for his private correspondence. He died in 1831, his work being republished in a London edition of 1841 with a memoir of the author.

The mathematician Nicholas Saunderson, who at thirty became a professor at Cambridge, was blind from infancy. This early scientist's *Elements of Algebra* was published posthumously in 1740; it consisted of two volumes with an introductory memoir. His lectures in illustration of the Newtonian theories were highly esteemed, and from his manuscripts there was printed, in 1751, "an explanation of the principal propositions of Sir Isaac Newton's philosophy."

John Stanley, blind organist and composer, held by some to have been compère and successor of Handel, in 1742 published a collection of cantatas, and subsequently composed three oratorios, "Jephthah," "Zimri" (which was produced at Covent Garden), and "The Fall of Egypt." The original scores of the latter two are preserved in the Royal College of Music.

Another figure in this category was that of Thomas Blacklock, who became a personage in Edinburgh society and in 1767 was granted the degree of Doctor of Divinity by the University of Aberdeen. Although his poetry was mediocre, Robert Burns owed much to him, for it was Blacklock's appreciation of him that deterred Burns when early in his career he was on the point of emigrating to the West Indies. Blacklock wrote the article "Blind" in the first edition of the *Encyclopædia Britannica*.

In this cursory chronicle of authorship by the sightless it must be left to the reader to infer the fortitude of those men and women who sought a way out of their darkness through the medium of writing. No less than heroic, for instance, is the life story of James Wilson, whose humble triumph over odds that would have conquered most men gives the pulse an extra beat. Wilson was born in Richmond, Virginia, in 1779. His father, a Scotsman, enlisted under Cornwallis as one of the loyalists. After the War of the Revolution, the family were returning to Liverpool aboard a sailing vessel when the father died of injuries resulting from his military service, and his wife followed him in death a day or two later. James, suddenly an orphan, contracted smallpox either during the voyage or soon thereafter and, as was so frequently then a result of this disease, lost his vision. He was taken by kindly hands to Belfast, and later, in a blind asylum, was taught the trade of upholsterer. In early manhood he married a good helpmate. He comes within the purview of this sketch because in 1820 he published a *Biography of the Blind: Including the Lives of All Who Have Distinguished Themselves as Poets, Philosophers, Artists, etc.* This volume was sold only by the author, as was the second and third edition (Birmingham, 1833 and 1835). The latter editions, much improved and enlarged, are prefaced by an autobiography in which Wilson tells in simple language the story of his handicapped life. In America, writing on the same subject, William Artman gave us in 1854 *Beauties and Achievements of the Blind,* which also had several revised editions.

Other names come to mind in these brief annals of achievement among those so smitten. Dr. William Moon, afflicted in early manhood, evolved the Moon type of embossed printing. Sir John Fielding, brother of the novelist, was a pioneer in penology.

Henry Fawcett lost his sight by accident when he was twenty-five. Five years later in 1863 he became a professor at Cambridge, and at thirty-five a member of Parliament. A devoted angler before his affliction, he continued to pursue the sport with unabated zest after the loss of his eyesight. More remarkable still, his love of ice-skating led him to runs of many miles when occasion permitted. He skimmed fearlessly along, guided only by the voice of his wife or daughter. Made postmaster-general of England in 1880, he was a factor in establishing the system of parcel post in England. His able administration of this office added to his reputation. In 1883 he was elected Lord Rector of Glasgow University, but died the following year before he could deliver his Rectorial Address. A tablet in Westminster Abbey commemorates his life. Fawcett wrote books and articles on such economic topics as free trade, pauperism, and Indian finance. Sir Leslie Stephen wrote a biography of him, and another was written by Winifred Holt in 1914 with a foreword by Viscount Bryce who says: "There has been no more striking example in our time of how self-reliance can triumph over adverse fortune than that presented by the career of Henry Fawcett."

It is impossible to do justice to a career in the short paragraph that must be allotted here to some men. For example, the scientist Edward Livingston Youmans who refused to yield to misfortune. Using a writing machine of his own devising, he popularized scientific discoveries by his lucid interpretations. Losing his sight in early manhood, "he was not made of the stuff that acquiesces in defeat," wrote John Fiske in his *Century of Science.*

An American by birth, Sir Francis Joseph Campbell, himself blind from youth, devoted his life as an educator among those who too had lost their sight. His confidence that the sightless could pursue the profession of music led him to plan a conservatory for the blind which should be connected with one of the American universities. With this in mind he went to Leipsic in 1869 and also visited London, where he came in touch with Dr. Thomas Armitage, a social seer through whose efforts the system of educating the sightless in England was reformed. The result of their association was the foundation of a pioneer school in England, the Royal Normal College.

An outdoor devotee, Francis Campbell, incredible though it seem, ascended Mont Blanc in 1880. Narrating the adventure in the London *Times* he said: "With the exception of cutting very extraordinary steps for me, the guides during the ascent did not assist me in any way." His purpose was to build faith in himself and to convince his friends that the handicaps usually ascribed to the blind are exaggerated. Afterwards he scaled the Wetterhorn, Eiger, Jungfrau, and made an attempt at the Matterhorn that was frustrated when the party became weatherbound for forty-two hours in the uppermost hut on the mountain. Fragments of the autobiography of Sir Francis are incorporated by Mrs. Craik in her *Light and Darkness.* In 1909 Edward VII conferred the rank of knighthood upon him. His many addresses and papers before the international congresses of the blind and elsewhere evinced a gifted style.

William Hickling Prescott, revered American historian, wrote all his books with the aid of an ivory stylus used over carbon paper in a "noctograph," a framework of brass wires for guiding writing along straight lines. Because of an injury to his eyes while a student at Harvard, Prescott was rarely able to tax his failing eyesight for more than an hour a day, and he was often for protracted periods totally prevented from reading. He spent much of his life in a darkened room, and the mechanical appliance he devised permitted him to write his copy without seeing it. He probably was never surpassed in the ability to compose at great length before putting his words on paper. The choice of a literary career, despite his severe handicap, revealed a strength of mind superior to circumstances. His correspondence, much of it written with the same device, was posthumously published in later years.

The ten volumes of the historical works of Francis Parkman, who died in 1893, were written in much the same manner as those of Prescott. He constructed what he called a "gridiron," which was indispensable to all his labor until the completion of *La Salle,* when his sight improved slightly. Similarly handicapped was the French historian Augustin Thierry before the publication of his *History of England,* which William Hazlitt rendered into English in 1847.

The revivalist Ira David Sankey, who became blind in 1903, spent the subsequent two years in preparing the story of his evangelical life. Fanny (Frances) Crosby, who wrote hundreds of hymns, was sightless from infancy. Her *Bells at Evening and Other Verses* appeared in 1902, and her *Memories of Eighty Years* was widely read.

Joseph Pulitzer, founder of the New York *World,* began to lose his eyesight in his fortieth year, and thereafter, until his death a quarter century later, he was unable to read. His masterful journalism continued unabated and with dramatic intensity, a corps of secretaries aiding him.

Harper Scott was an American artist whose right hand was mangled and who executed admirable paintings with his remaining hand. Losing his sight at thirty, he took to dictating novels that were popular toward the close of the century, and "the word despair was not in his vocabulary."

Similarly, William Benjamin King, known to the reading public as Basil King, was a clergyman who on losing his sight resigned from the ministry and became a distinguished novelist. His *The Inner Shrine* was published anonymously, leading to much speculation as to the authorship. Among his other works were *The Wild Olive, The Street Called Straight, Earthbound,* and *Let Not Man Put Asunder.*

Numerous juvenile books as well as a history of Vermont, all
bearing Boston imprints, were written by the blind naturalist Rowland
Evans Robinson, who died in 1900; and Nina Rhoades of the same city,
in spite of her affliction, wrote appealing volumes for the young during
the early years of this century. In 1883, Dr. Clarence Hawkes, then only
twelve years old was blinded by a gunshot wound, but he grew up to
write a score or more of unpretentious books on wild life and the
outdoors, mostly for younger readers. His autobiography, *Hitting the
Dark Trail*, appeared in 1915. His *Dr. Thinkright* (1934) was as
likeable as Mr. Chips, and sensitive feeling imbued *The Light That Did
Not Fail*, which was published in 1935.

Laura Bridgman was another of those imprisoned souls who
acquired a measure of the fullness of life. Born in 1829 in New
Hampshire, it is said that she not only lacked sight, hearing, and normal
speech, but that her senses of smell and taste were also impaired. The
sense of touch alone remained in added delicacy. She met the celebrities
of her time, including Dickens, Kossuth, and Longfellow, and her letters
and *Journal*, groping in their efforts at expression and understanding of
the world, reveal her continual struggle with darkness until her death in
1889. Two biographies of her have appeared; one by Laura E. Richards
in 1928 was aptly subtitled *The Story of an Opened Door*. Mrs.
Richards was the daughter of Julia Ward Howe, who wrote the "Battle
Hymn of the Republic," and of Samuel Gridley Howe, and in her
biography she gives a graphic account of what Dr. Howe did for Laura
Bridgman, who had gradually become pietistic.

In 1868, Dr. Howe wrote to Charles Dickens asking him to pay for
the cost of embossing one of his novels. Dickens selected *The Old
Curiosity Shop* and donated $1,700 for 250 copies to be printed in
Boston Line Type, a reading system for the blind at that time. In three-
volume format, copies were popular for years.

A notable figure of the Old South was Judge François Xavier
Martin, who died in 1846 after serving thirty-one years as Justice of the
Supreme Court of Louisiana. Known as the father of Louisiana

jurisprudence, he was a brilliant eccentric who wrote legal compendiums, histories of Louisiana and of North Carolina, and translated lawbooks and novels from the French. His dim eyesight failed completely by 1836, so that he was compelled to dictate his opinions and employ help for his literary work. Virtually blind in the flush of his career, he pursued authorship in a gamut that ranged from statutes and almanacs to newspaper feuds and fiction.

Known the world over, Helen Keller, born in 1880, is, of course, the unique and heroic example. Her own writings, such as *Story of My Life, The World I Live In, The Song of the Stone Wall, Out of the Dark,* and *Midstream,* as well as those volumes by others concerning her extraordinary training and culture, form quite a bookshelf. Her book *My Religion* shows Miss Keller to be an inclined if not an avowed Swedenborgian. The versatile volumes that bear her name as author are an amazing revelation of her personality and the boundless possibilities for a human being to emerge from afflictions that might well seem to be insuperable. It was Mark Twain who said that the two most interesting characters of the nineteenth century were Napoleon and Helen Keller. Various of her books have been rendered into Braille as an inspiration to those others even less circumscribed than she. In her poem, "A Chant of Darkness," written at twenty-eight, we get a glimpse of the vision that has sustained her:

> *All sight is of the soul,*
> *Behold it in the upward flight*
> *Of the unfettered spirit.*

The morocco-bound personal copy of her book *Midstream,* which Helen Keller received from her publishers as a Christmas gift, had its title in Braille dots made with tiny brass airplane tacks. It is safe to say that this brave woman has been more extensively written about than any blind person in history, unless it be Homer.

Marie Huertin, born in 1885 and known as "Helen Keller's French sister," seems not to have published any writings. Arturo Giovannitti, also deaf and blind, wrote *Arrows in the Gale,* published in 1914 with an introduction by Helen Keller. One feels exalted by the groping for mental light of these imprisoned yet pinioned souls. Miss Keller speaks of "the bread of books for those who hunger in spirit."

Notable was *A Challenge to Darkness* in 1929 by J. Georges Scapini, the story of a French soldier who lost his sight in World War I, overcame his handicap, and was elected a member of the Chamber of Deputies. The volume in its English translation has an introduction by Helen Keller and a foreword by General Henri Gouraud. A work of fine balance that should be mentioned here is the *Memories of Sixty Years* of 1931 by Henry Sanderson Furniss, blind economist and educator.

Merely to cite titles of other volumes written by the sightless may admittedly be tedious, yet mention must be made of *Pour Wine for Us* (1932) by Dean Van Clute; Edwin Brant Frost's *An Astronomer's Life* (1933); and Thomas D. Cutsforth's *The Blind in School and Society* (1933) which urged a fresh approach in education for the sightless. The verse of Alice Adkins Johnson, *Fog Phantoms* (1934), was published by the Columbia University Press. Hector Chevigny who narrates his experiences in *My Eyes Have a Cold Nose* (1946), was also the author of *Lord of Alaska, Lost Empire,* and other volumes. Baynard Kendrick wrote *Lights Out* (1945) and *Blind Man's Bluff* (1946). Hans Habe's *Walk in Darkness* (1948) and several other titles were translated into English. Henry M. Barry recorded his war experiences in *I'll Be Seeing You* (1952), and Jacob Twersky wrote *The Face of the Deep* (1953).

From the dim vista of antiquity the figure of Homer, with all the legends that cluster about the composition of his *Iliad* and *Odyssey,* stands forth like an eternal Pharos. Dauntless, he said: "Let us follow whithersoever the Fates lead us. Whatever shall befall us, every kind of fortune is to be surmounted by patiently enduring it." Part of the *Iliad* may have been composed before his loss of sight, but he certainly was bereft of vision when he wrote the *Odyssey.*

Sightless Ossian was another legendary bard, whose ballads were transmitted by tradition. Son of the Caledonian hero-king Fingal, he lived in the remote past. And names of others have come down to us, for example, Blind Didymus of Alexandria, a learned figure in the fourth century who was celebrated as an expositor of the ancient world's wisdom.

The centuries that followed contain in their annals various sightless authors, now no longer esteemed. But John Gower, friend of Chaucer, must not be forgotten. The first edition of his *Confessio Amantis* was printed by Caxton at Westminster in 1493. Nor should William Jaggard be overlooked. Printer of Shakespeare's nine quartos and the folio, Jaggard in his later years became sightless, but kept at his business.

At the pinnacle of inspiration was Milton, who became blind in 1652 after years of waning vision. In total darkness from forty-three until his death at sixty-six, his ailment was described, in the peculiar terminology of the time, as the "gout struck in"; doubtless today it would be termed glaucoma. *Paradise Lost, Paradise Regained,* as well as *Samson Agonistes* and prose works were written after the loss of his sight. It is vain to conjecture if the greatest of epics in the English tongue would have been written had Milton, blind for twenty-two years, retained his vision of the objective world. He met Galileo at the latter's villa near Florence in 1638 when the aged astronomer, now sightless, was a forlorn figure.

His sonnet on blindness is eloquent. In *Milton's Blindness,* published in 1934, Eleanor Gertrude Brown, herself sightless, discussed the influence of blindness upon Milton's poetry. The fiery imagery, the massive design, the visionary proportions, she attributes to his handicap.

Contemporary with Milton but across the Channel was the Count of Pagan, who wrote several astronomical and military works. An army engineer, Blaise Francis de Pagan lost an eye in a siege and as Field Marshal became blind. Written in French after his retirement, his *Description of the Amazones in America* was translated and published at London in 1661.

Nothing is stranger, perhaps, in the annals pertaining to literate makeshifts than the facts concerning Blind Jacob, who lived about the middle of the eighteenth century and who hailed from Netra, a German village in Hesse. As a schoolboy he devised a curious system of notching small sticks, using these for his own peculiar *memoria technica*. With the passing of years his system grew to be more elaborate, until gradually, as an adult, he accumulated a small collection, whittled records of his lowly literacy, his repository of books being bundles or fascines of intricately notched sticks. Esteemed in his neighborhood as a man of parts, he made his living as an herb doctor. Even his curative preparations were distinguished by notched wooden labels. Though a man of little schooling, Blind Jacob by reason of his queer homemade library, using a personal system of symbols in relief, deserves recognition as a quaint character in booklore. He probably never knew that staves and tally sticks were used for recording from immemorial times. We hear of it in Ezekiel and among the American Indians. A Chinese record on wooden wands, undoubtedly ancient, was discovered in Mongolia in 1930 by Sven Hedin.

Among curious works shelved in the British Museum's manuscript division is a single set of fifteen large volumes in which the Psalms and New Testament are written in bold longhand characters an inch tall with white ink on specially made black paper. This Scriptural transcript was engrossed in 1745 at the expense of a prosperous London merchant named Harries, whose failing sight had precluded his reading the family Bible.

One of the curious earlier volumes meriting mention is *The Life of John Metcalf, Commonly Called Blind Jack of Knaresborough, with many entertaining anecdotes of his exploits in Hunting, Card-Playing, etc., and an account of his various contracts of making Roads, erecting Bridges, etc.* Born of Yorkshire stock in 1717, this sturdy individual, who was at home in the saddle, in 1753 inaugurated a stagecoach business between York and his home town, regularly driving the coach himself. Through this he became interested in new turnpike projects, and he contracted for and completed more than 180 miles of new roads, including viaducts and small bridges, being one of the first to use crushed stone for roadbeds. A detailed account of this remarkable man, who was also a skillful musician, is given by Bramah in *The Eyes of Max Carrados* wherein he says: "For energy, resource and sheer bravado under blindness, no age or country can shew anything to excel the record of John Metcalf." A chapter is devoted to him in *Heroes of the Darkness* by John B. Mannix. Though not himself an author, he was much written about.

In Ireland, lowly Blind Raftery was a celebrated itinerant Gaelic poet, whose poems and songs were translated and edited by Douglas Hyde, while Donn Byrne wrote a novel concerning him. Indeed, the annals of the sightless include many who wooed the muse, not forgetting Father John Bannister Tabb, the beloved poet-priest of Maryland, who became completely blind two years before his death in 1907 and after most of his cameo lyrics had been given to mankind.

Three types of books for the blind are in use: Braille, consisting of embossed dots; Moon, in raised lines forming angles and curves; and Talking Books or phonographic records. An adaptation of Braille, known as New York Point, came into use in the 1860's, but the system now used and known as Standard English Braille was adopted in 1932.

The first disc sound recordings of entire books was an innovation of 1934 under Congressional grant. It marked a new era for the sightless. Think of hearing a whole novel in a few hours instead of taking days to read it by touch in Braille. The Talking Books released the handicapped from the drudgery of pawing dull dots at snail's pace through volume after volume.

Some fifteen hundred titles are sound-recorded by selected professional voices. A book of average length may be heard in nine hours of aggregate playing time. Recordings of the Old and New Testaments, from Genesis to Revelation, were completed in 1944 on 169 double-sided phonographic discs, each of which plays for a half hour, making the total reading time of the Bible as a Talking Book 84½ hours. The Old Testament runs to 129 records and the New Testament to forty. The longest novel, Tolstoy's *War and Peace*, needs 119 records, each side playing fifteen minutes. A disc book on music will have the musical phrases and notations played out, and a book on birds will include their calls. A new sound recording of the complete King James version was finished early in 1951 by the American Foundation for the Blind. It is superior in tone and accuracy to the older venture. The prophet Isaiah himself testified to the efficacy of the Bible that talks when he said: "I will bring the blind by a way they know not; I will make darkness light before them." Many persons who become blind as adults are unable to master touch reading, and for them the Talking Book spells new life.

Bulk has been the great drawback of point printing, so that sound discs have the advantage not only of much speedier communication than finger reading, but of compactness. It was indeed an eventful date for the sightless when in 1923 the King James version of the revised Braille Bible was completed in twenty-one volumes. This achievement of international significance was the work of J. Robert Atkinson, embosser, called the "Blind Benjamin Franklin," and was accomplished against great odds. In 1925 the newer American Standard revised version of the scriptures was completed in twenty Braille volumes, each about the conventional size of the old family Bible, and taking up two yards of shelf space.

The American Bible Society Library has specimens of embossed Bibles or parts in more than forty languages and systems for the blind. The Braille Bible in Arabic, completed in England in 1931 by the National Institute for the Blind, required five years to complete and fills thirty-two volumes. The Koran has been embossed in Egypt. A Scottish missionary, Dr. Murray, adapted Braille for Chinese printing. The first Hebrew text in embossed type was *Hebrew Daily Prayers* in a code developed by H. Frees and published in 1889. The first Hebrew Braille book, containing selections from the Old Testament and Talmud and excerpts from later sources, was sponsored in 1936 by the Library of Congress. Among curious experiments in the past was Dr. Foulis's tangible ink, which produced raised characters on paper; it was devised in 1851 by the Edinburgh School for the Blind. The earliest writing machine was that of Pierre Foucald, himself blind, who received a gold medal in 1850. A Braille typewriter was perfected in 1934 by the American Foundation for the Blind of New York.

The Perkins Institution for the Blind has issued bibliographies (3rd Supplement, 1944) comprising a title array of books by English and American blind authors, as well as by the deaf-blind and the blind deaf-mute. All volumes cited are in the Library of the Institution at Watertown, Massachusetts. The "several thousand items in nineteen different languages," make the collection on this library's shelves the world's greatest source of material about the blind.

These annotated listings also include a tabulation of blind characters in books of fiction. There is Hugh Walpole's *The Blind Man's House* with its consummate character study, and Ernest Bramah's *The Specimen Case,* concerning the imagined Max Carrados, blind detective. Old Irons in Barrie's *Sentimental Tommy,* sightless figures in De Morgan's *It Never Can Happen Again,* Kipling's *They* and *The Light That Failed* are among characters and titles in the long tally. In the portrayal of these fictional folk many authors have captured and conveyed something of the inner light that makes the lives of the blind so often an inspiration of courage and cheer. Truly, they let not the vision perish.

ASTRAL AUTHORSHIP
AND AUTOMATIC WRITING

COMMUNION WITH THE DEAD is a touchy topic; spiritualism, a subject on which to avoid dogmatism. But there have been demised authors, so it is alleged, who, not content with the life of the Hereafter, pine for a celestial catharsis. These employ human mediums to convey their afterthoughts to mortal readers in a sort of discarnate dictation. While succinct messages from the lesser literary dead usually reach the receptive by way of the ouija board or planchette, some seem to find the inspirational slate inadequate and, accustomed in the flesh to reams of paper, require that their mundane amanuenses dispense with this "prop."

The shelf of such books is not large. Although several eminent writers now deceased are said to have grown restive in their Elysian retreats—Mark Twain, Oscar Wilde, William James, and Woodrow Wilson among others—the posthumous output of these notables is not distinguished. Strange perversions of style occur and lapses into the commonplace, even the maudlin, give rise to the suspicion that the afterlife is not especially stimulating to the literary spirit. Perhaps the distinct let-down may be accounted for either on the grounds that authors, inured to tribulation and contention during their lives, find immortality debilitating; or that the mediums who in automatic writing transmit the ghostly works are too frail instruments. The clairvoyance of the latter is too often misty; mystification in fact, plagues the entire field of deceased literature.

Eastern mysticism is more receptive to the esoteric than the practical Occident. The wisdom of the East accepts the incomprehensible; that of the West prefers to doubt it. The Omaresque concept of mortal man as earthen vessel, molded on the mystic wheel of the ineffable Potter, readily conceives outpouring of the spirit in supernatural guise.

Lore concerning the life of Mahomet narrates that the Koran was orally delivered under conditions of trance. Inert contemplation, visions, and a state verging on self-hypnosis, induced by prolonged fasting or otherwise, have long been a commonplace among various tribal cultural stocks and castes. Mahomet, prone, exclaimed, "I see a light and I hear a voice, beholding no man!" and in the exaltation of trance he dictated the Koran word by word to his scribe who wrote down the emanations. Mahomet is conceived as the medium of divine communication. Curiously, tradition records that his entranced utterances were preceded by copious perspiration, induced by blankets.

Spiritism in our own literature may be said to begin its critical approach with the ponderous but naïve *A True Account of Actions with Spirits* by Dr. John Dee, which, appearing in 1583, told (in twelve hundred quarto pages) of the clairvoyance, termed Spirits, of a certain "Childe Arthur," gifted with inner sight. Whether "revelation" or "communication," a human being is agent in the transmission. Hence, in a sense, messages from the dead impinge on mandates from the gods. But a sharp distinction must be drawn between such alleged contact with the Beyond and the faculties of psychic intercourse in a mundane sphere called clairvoyance and telepathy. As here referred to, automatic writing may derive from either source. The present theme eschews those supreme books that are said to have come from spiritual founts deemed divine; it is restricted to volumes claiming contact with post-mortem personality.

Strange, indeed, is the narrative of psychic experience and self-discipline expounded by May Wright Sewall in *Neither Dead nor Sleeping*, perhaps the most remarkable document on communion with the

A sixteenth-century specimen of Vexierband
*(tease binding) from Saxony, containing a sextet
of tractates and opening variously to each;
a singular example of perhaps misguided ingenuity.*

*Infrequently encountered in the book world,
such curious twin or dos-à-dos bindings open
on opposite sides and inverted.*

An extraordinary example of a book bound in human skin. The silver plaque inserted in the binding bears the name of the artist, Ladmiral; the name of the owner, Hans Friedenthal; and a Negro profile and skull. Three volumes were bound from the skin of this Negro which was removed at the post-mortem.

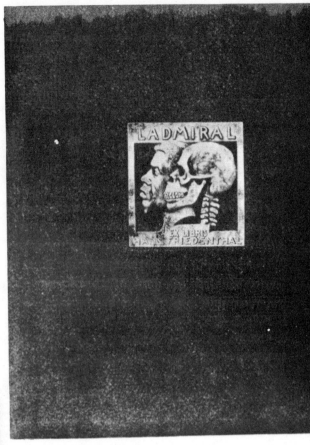

Terres Du Ciel (Lands in the Sky) was bound in the skin of a young Countess, who on her deathbed (1882) stipulated that a book by Camille Flammarion, an astronomer, should be so bound and presented to him. The volume was later in the possession of Flammarion's widow.

departed that America has produced. It appeared in 1920 at which time
the transmitter was honorary president of the International Council of
Women, and of the National Council of Women of the United States,
with numerous other affiliations. In his Introduction to this extraordinary
work, Booth Tarkington espoused the belief in "personal survival of
death," and opines: "We are dwelling in the night. To the man of ten
thousand years hence, who will not be able to distinguish through his
archæologic researches which of the forgotten tribes fought the Great
War that left the long line of bones in the subsoil from the Channel to
the Alps—to that enlightened modern we shall seem to have been formless
gropers in the dusk of ignorance."

Mrs. Sewall, who with her husband founded the Classical School for
Girls at Indianapolis in 1882, was for twenty-five years its principal.
Her receptive state seems to have followed the demise of her husband, for
the volume of self-revelation stems from ouija contact with his spirit.
The contents of the work tend to defy cursory abstract. Interwoven is
the disclosure of how through advice from the other world she overcame a
malady that had been pronounced fatal. She records having fasted for
eighty-five hours, during which she slept for only seven hours yet worked
"unabatedly every waking minute." She developed the faculty for
"magnetized sleep," which we are given to understand was a sort of
concentrated rest.

Mrs. Sewall is introduced by the wraith of her husband to the ghost
of the Greek demi-god Hermes. She meets the spiritualist William T.
Stead in the flesh in London, and other corporeal mediums abroad. But
her life is influenced by the disembodied control of Père Conde and
Rubinstein. The latter directs her piano technique and gives her a
portrait of himself as a youth of nineteen. She experiences vibrations and
magnetism "from the Etheric Plane." Mesmer appears and advises her
regimen. More than six hundred pages of manuscript are automatically
written under spirit guidance, she declares. It is an amazing book,
wrought with intelligence and sincerity; but to accept it would be to
forfeit one's hold on reality and juggle the stars.

A few hours before his death Dickens was at work upon *The Mystery of Edwin Drood*. What was to have been the outcome of the plot, and what was John Jasper's secret are baffling moot-points that have vexed the curious. Three years after Dickens' passing, the first American attempt to finish the story was made through the mediumistic pen of Thomas P. James, of Brattleboro, Vermont, who published what Dickens had written "prior to the termination of the Author's Earth-Life" together with 284 pages (Part Second) of revealed elucidation. Dated 1873, this odd volume has a four-page "Medium's Preface," and another by "The Author." In the former, the medium in his own guise writes:

> By those who are acquainted with the principles of spiritualism (and those who are not can easily understand them by adopting Mr. Dickens' suggestions, as given in his Preface to this work), it will be easily understood that the first production of a spirit pen would be very liable to contain some imperfections; and more especially would that be the case, where both the medium and the spirit by whom he is controlled, are lacking in experience, and consequently development; but I believe future works, which are to come from the spirit-pen of Mr. Dickens, will be entirely free from imperfections, even if any such exist in the present volume.

But a callous world did not heed; in the minds of most the mystery of Edwin Drood remained unsolved. From the inspiration of the Brattleboro entrepreneur issued no other posthumous tokens of "the spirit-pen of Mr. Dickens."

A noted recruit was gained in the novelist Basil King, author of *The Inner Shrine, The Street Called Straight*, and *The Wild Olive*. He followed in the footsteps of Sir Arthur Conan Doyle (whose conversion cost him a peerage) and Sir Oliver Lodge by a public affirmation of his belief in spirit communication; he believed that his story *Earthbound*, the first of spiritism motion pictures, was so conveyed to him. A decade before his death in 1928, King published *The Abolishing of Death*,

containing messages received through the automatic medium of a girl
friend. In his foreword he maintains that "communication with the plane
next above us is as natural as speech." But it is significant that he had
read *Raymond* and *The Seven Purposes*. We are assured that he took
"absolutely no liberty with the text," which was received through
Jennifer, previously unfamiliar with automatic writing. With naïve
confidence he confides "That there was no conscious participation on her
own side she was sure."

The spirit messages came to King at first from several spokesmen,
then chiefly from one he calls "Henry Talbot, the great chemist, to avoid
the use of a name well known throughout America and Europe." In a
quiz of his spirit dictator, King refers to the description by "Raymond"
(son of Sir Oliver Lodge), of the plane in which the latter found himself.
King says:

> If I remember rightly, he speaks of factories.
> Nothing is manufactured here. The factories might
> easily be called up by his desire to see familiar things. There
> is much work done here, but no labor.
> I think he mentions tennis and tobacco.
> We sometimes play games; and the tobacco is quite
> natural, although the pleasure in it passes quickly, as it is
> not a thing of innate beauty.

Recounting the reception of the messages, King states: "The
nearest parallel I can find to these conversations between Henry Talbot
and myself is that of speaking through another person at a telephone,
with a third person at the end of the wire. Jennifer sits at my end, I put
my questions to her; they are heard and answered, while she writes the
replies on the scribbling-block, which, in most houses, lies near the
receiver. In the whole process there is nothing more mysterious than
that." But he admits "there are imperfections in transmission."

At one point in the discussions on spirituality the ethereal Henry
Talbot states: "The sexes continue, sex being a part of individuality."

But a year later another heavenly commentator propounded a somewhat different opinion. Influenced by their mediumistic friend Margaret Cameron, author of *The Seven Purposes*, a twain under the pen-name "Joan and Darby" tried their hands at the ouija board. The result, published in 1920, was *Our Unseen Guest* in which the spirit voice was "Stephen," who had "gone over the top of life to victory." "What of sex?" Stephen was asked. "In heaven," Stephen replied, "there is neither marriage nor giving in marriage. There is no sex here as you know it. There is in consciousness what an electrician might be tempted to call a negative and positive division. . . . But there is no birth here."

There are a few, but a very few, works of tender feeling and genuine inspirational impulse about which it would be unkind to say with dogmatic dismissal that their pretensions to having been communicated with by dear departed ones is sheer delusion. Who shall say that the spirit does not speak where such bonds exalt? One may have considerably more mental reservations concerning automatic authorship that conjures an imaginary personality, for instance Mrs. Pearl Curran and her *alter ego* Patience Worth, than one has when the dictating control is an historical personage. But there can be nothing but downright scorn for the ignorant and spurious concoction perpetrated in 1924 by Adelaide D. Kingsley in *Sky Lines*. A prefatory note declares: "These poems have been prepared on the Astral Plane especially for this book and given automatically by us to our inspired medium Adelaide D. Kingsley." The *us* is staggering, and betokens no other than the galaxy of the literary great who thus confide their after-death effusions to the mental telegraphy of Adelaide. The first poem in the thin volume is signed: "Goeffrey Chaucer—Given automatically to our inspired amanuensis Adelaide Kingsley"; its concluding lines are generally characteristic of the whole:

> *The English are not faultless yet they try,*
> *To keep a place in heart for God most high,*
> *And I find in this upper heavenly clime,*
> *Many from that dear land that once was mine.*

With this starter, Adelaide goes on to act as vehicle for the spirit voices of Homer, Hesiod, and Virgil, followed by Mary Jane Sigourney, J. G. Holland, and Ella Wheeler Wilcox. The medium is most receptive to the heavenly choir and as all-inclusive as the manufacture of her muse permits. Spelling and punctuation suffer in the round trip between Here and There; we find Milton and Felica Hermans (*sic*), Goldsmith and J. W. Von Geothe (*sic*), Freidrich (*sic*) Schiller and Scott, *Sir* Matthew (not Edwin) Arnold, Edgar Allen Poe, *Sir* Cecil Rhodes and Michael Muldoon, Robert Burns and Temperance Ted.

In her Foreword Adelaide discloses: "The author of this book, who received the remarkable messages from the psychic realm that it contains, was spending a winter in the leisure of a Southern resort, when she began to notice that every time she undertook to use a lead pencil some invisible power seemed to be making an effort to control her hand and the movement of the pencil, and soon this effort to control extended to her mind also. She has never shown, or felt, any psychic tendencies before; but during this winter, and the two or three years following, she received the charming, entertaining, and altogether interesting contents of this volume, by this method; that is, by taking a pencil in hand, and allowing the power that manifested on these occasions to guide the pencil over the paper, and to guide her own thought as well. . . ."

Some of the effusions in *Sky Lines* append intimate comment or footnote confessions by the departed famous. Homer confides *via* Adelaide's page that "Virgil and I have kept together through the centuries, by waiting for each other as we came back from incarnations. Then we would spend some heavenly years together before returning to earth life again." Schiller transmits from the Astral Plane a rhyme beginning:

> *It was June and frogs were croaking,*
> *In the ponds the boys were soaking;*

Poe is credited with these ethereal lines:

Our heavenly homes are beautiful,
And suited well to every life.
If to all worthy things you here are dutiful,
And have not entered into discords rife, . . .

Seriously intended, but as fantastic as Swift's *Gulliver* or Bulwer Lytton's *Coming Race*, is *Gone West: Three Narratives of After-Death Experiences* communicated through the mediumship of J. S. M. Ward in 1917. The medium, "a scholar and prizeman of Trinity Hall, Cambridge," received this material, partly through "coherent visions" and in part by automatic writing, while in a state of trance. Most of the data vouchsafed from the planes of the hereafter can be foregone, but the only direct information available concerning *libraria* there must be quoted. One of the ethereal narrators in *Gone West*, designated H.J.L., gave fuller details than could be printed: "The original plan of the work," says the Introduction, "was to have included 'The Realm of Belief,' but owing to the enhanced cost of production due to the War, it was found necessary to reduce the book to a manageable size. To do this we were reluctantly compelled to publish only the Astral Plane, Hell, and the Realm of Half-Belief." The omitted Realm of Belief, in addition to other matters, we are told, "gave a most striking account of a library in the Realm of Belief." A hint of the revelation is in these transmitted words:

These libraries are on so vast a scale that they look almost like cities; there are many of them, of course, but each is divided into three sections. The first contains the forms of books which have ceased to exist. I mean by this the actual volumes themselves. Of course all books do not come to us, many go to Hell . . .

The second section is very different, for in it the books are not the forms of books made on earth but those created here. The best way in which I can describe them is to compare them with picture books. In short, they contain

ideas in picture form, and can be read by us just as the
thought-pictures of our friends can be understood by us.
. . . Few books are written for the first time over here in
script.

The third type are difficult to describe as books at all,
for the picture idea has been carried out to its logical
conclusion. The nearest thing to it on earth is the modern
picture-palace. . . . An episode in History will be enacted in
all its detail before our eyes.

But, recall, there are three spirit narrators in this bounteous book. From
"The Officer's Narrative" come the following facts about "A Library in
Hell":

It was an enormous place, and was divided into three
sections: Book forms; Idea books; Living thought
visualizations. Among the "forms" were all books dealing
with cruelty and hate for their own sake. I saw there shelves
filled with the records of the Inquisition, books describing
methods of poisoning your foes, books relating hideous crimes
and savage tortures, histories of torture. . . . The "idea"
books contained pictures instead of writing, and were quite
diabolical. But the third section was the worst. In it torture
was enacted in the present tense.

Automatic writing, in which there is alleged communication with the
deceased, implies, of course, the continuity of personality after death.
With the bounds of psychic telepathy still virtually unexplored, it is
intended as no reflection on the sincere contentions of spiritualism (more
properly spiritism) to say that fakirs find easy refuge under the wing of
the occult. An example of this dubious esotericism is William Dudley
Pelley, whose defunct weekly sheet *Liberation* had forsaken clairvoyance
for anti-Semitism when it suspended publication in 1934, and whose
sponsor has since been properly in jail.

In its earlier incarnation, Pelley's paper contained articles in which
that decidedly pseudo-sage held the pen though the inspiration was

"received clairaudiently on a Master Wave-Length." He claimed to get messages "in Sanskrit, phonetically, a language which he has never studied or heard spoken." There were those who had "heard Mr. Pelley speak fluently in Lemurian and Atlantean, languages which have disappeared from the earth for nearly ten thousand years." How listeners could have judged the fluency of these hypothetical idioms of the primordial sunken continents is not vouchsafed! And the "nearly ten thousand years is a typical touch—as if there were absolute certainty that the assumed cataclysm could not have occurred eleven thousand years ago! But then Pelley's periods all came from "Sources Behind or Above Mortality" (much more impressive in the capitals in which he puts it).

On its earlier masthead *Liberation* carried these portentous words: "The Contents of This Magazine Were Designated, Were Received 'Clairaudiently' via the Psychic Radio, from Great Souls Who Have Graduated Out of This Three-Dimensional World into Other Areas of Time and Space."

The revelations were also in booklet and lecture form, and the extra-mundane wave-length projected, via Pelley, such titles as "How You Came Back Many Times to Earth-Life," "Seven Minutes in Eternity," "Were the Oceans Once in the Skies?" But suddenly the clairaudient messages developed a spiritual static and ceased.

So-called automatic writing, ascribed to such books of alleged astral authorship and presuming dictation by the dead, is not as extensive as the literature in commentary thereon. The shelf restricted to such books would include only those where the trance or mediumistic element is present. It would exclude such works as those of Richard Brothers, the erratic Englishman whose writings were "revealed" rather than dictated with himself as the passive recorder; he was not automaton but active agent. And there have been others like him, not embraced under the present heading, which is concerned solely with alleged spirit control.

The problem of dual personality is involved in those books in which an *alter ego* controls the writer; with the classic case of William Sharp and Fiona McLeod in mind, a final judgment must be withheld. But it would seem a psychic infirmity that confuses the gift of imagination, and outcroppings of the subliminal self, for an outer presence; and this verges on benign obsession when it nominates a departed personality for the actual author, or endows a fictive figure, such as Patience Worth, with the attributes of actual authorship.

Scanning the volumes that have been given the world through the medium of automatic authorship confirms the impression that, when the celebrated names of deceased authors are invoked as the other-world controls, the comparison with their works written in the flesh casts no credit on the posthumous abode as fostering good literature. Invariably the consignments through mediums seem to suffer deleterious effects.

However, when the medium is the automatic recorder of the authorship of an imaginary personality, there are no previous writings to be used as a basis for comparison. Such a phantom author was the phenomenon to which Mrs. Pearl Curran gave the name Patience Worth. Students of the stream of consciousness find this an absorbing case.

It is the province of this chapter to discuss books ascribed to deceased authorship, not to probe the alleged phenomena of automatic writing, nor plumb the question of continuity after death. The approach is literary, not occult. But, after reading all accessible volumes in this category and delving a bit in the available commentary, it may not be overventuresome to set down the following conclusion.

Excluding that portion of pretended automatism in literature which may be ascribed to charlatanry, a range of psychic phenomena does exist, due on the one hand to self-deception, on the other to those unexplained facts connected with dissociated personality. It is no more than an opinion to state that, with respect to dictation by the deceased or astral authorship, no credence can be placed in any evidential matter so far afforded. Spiritism, as manifested in books ostensibly written by the dead through mediumistic aid, is a delusion. There are, however, unaccounted psychic potentialities latent in clairvoyance, telepathy, and hypnotism, as well as in the normal dream state, and the facts will yield to rational approach. If the dead commune with favored mortals, it is not in the idiom of the ouija board, not through the figment of a fictitious personality conjured from the Beyond, nor in literal messages transmitted by the departed.

Such of the books described as may be deemed authentic in the sense that no conscious duplicity entered into their composition may be accounted for on the grounds of split personality (schizophrenia), or by reason of a hyperesthesia to which some persons are more inclined than others. Though one may admit with Hamlet, that there are more things in heaven and earth than are dreamt of, yet one is reluctant to grant that the dead could indulge in vapid moralizings and inane maunderings. Automatic writing, we suspect, is merely a sort of manual somnambulism on the part of literary aspirants of susceptible mentality.

From Plotinus, the Neo-Platonic seer of ecstatic visions, to Swedenborg, the mystic, is not a far cry, but from the gropings of old Dr. Dee to Sir Oliver Lodge is quite a leap. So far as telepathy and clairvoyance are concerned, wholly apart from the question of continuity after death and a spiritual wireless, the explanation of Sinel in his engaging book, *The Sixth Sense,* has at least the virtue of rational approach. Sinel says that in the brains of all vertebrates there is a little mass known as the "Pineal body" which in adult humans is the size of a cherrystone. He believes its function "is the reception of etheric rays that elude the ordinary sense organs and that at the same time pass them on to those portions of the brain that can render them manifest, and even resolve them into some form of consciousness." Within its province are, perhaps, instinct and intuition, sublimated in some as telepathy and clairvoyance. Awareness through vibration is still virtually an unexplored arcanum. Sub-human life has its counterparts in this mystery: the homing instinct in pigeons, the beeline to the apiary, are not less strange, as Sinel points out, than the impulse impelling that bog-plant, the sundew which nourishes on insects, to yearn toward a fixed fly.

In the face of these phenomena one withholds rejection of that facet of the hidden called automatic writing. In the words of the old historian,

Robertson, we have ventured to inquire without presuming to decide.

One would anticipate the noblest qualities—a transcendent *verve* leavening winged wisdom—in the word-waftings of those who bespeak their ethereal minds from the celebrated Beyond. But most of the messages, brief or diffuse, are commonplace when they are not trivial. Now and then occurs a purple passage, an exalted mood, a solacing reassurance, but, by and large, they are petty, vapid, and disappointing. The departed seem overly concerned with mundane matters; they lack the detachment somehow expected of the unfleshed.

The late Mrs. Marian Bush believed herself to be an instrument of spirits whom she called "They," which is the title of her book published in 1947, wherein exhortations are enhanced with spirit pictures reproduced from her automatic paintings. Manifest in her moralizing is the influence of her social background. So, too, Hélène Smith's Martian language is suspiciously like French in its syntax and grammar.

In recent years Mary Stephenson Barnes of California made "clairsentient" transcripts of disembodied Robert Browning's verse, transmitted from the fourth-dimensional plane. She confided: "It seems a little strange that Browning would choose me as a collaborator. . . . But that's the way it is."

An instance of mediation-writing palpably fantastic was the romance of Mars by Sarah Weiss, which appeared in 1906 under the title *Decimon Huydas*. It was transcribed "under the Editorial Direction of Spirit Carl De L'Ester," whose Martian style was not Olympian. More practiced was the authorship of Winifred Graham, who died in 1950 at Hampton-on-Thames at the age of seventy-six. She wrote eighty-eight volumes of which only one, *My Letters from Heaven*, was vouchsafed her obedient hand.

In 1950 the talented poet Percy Mackaye presented in *The Mystery of Hamlet* four poetic dramas portraying the life of the Danish court in the years preceding Shakespeare's *Hamlet*. Mackaye intimates that the composition was semi-automatic. He avows: "It was compelled by powers beyond this material scene." In 1953 another talented contemporary,

Mrs. Louis K. Anspacher, presented the public with *Enigma*, a collection of poems recorded from a oiuja board.

By no means are all these astral volumes alleged to have been recorded through the medium of automatic writing. It is sometimes impossible to determine the degree of passivity on the part of the living scribe for that is a matter between the Recording Angel and the recording agent. But, under the head of communication with those whom the rationalist designates as the dead, there are, in addition to avowed automatic writings, volumes that claim to transmit spirit voices or messages from the "astral plane," whether the scribe be tranced or aware as he acts as agent. In a word, the degree of automatism varies; the hand or the mind may preponderate as the controlled instrument.

In addition to the formidable array of books of this classification housed in the New York Public Library, there is the rather meager list of Bayley in his *The Undiscovered Country,* and the citations of Lowi in her modest survey of the *Best Books on Spirit Phenomena.* Those so inclined may browse among these astral volumes, but others may recall with relish the observation concerning Dante's immortal work, that with all his genius he could not redeem heaven from monotony.

AN ALCOVE FOR ALIENISTS

THE DERANGEMENT of mortals has occasionally taken on a literary guise. It is a pathetic subject; moreover, a rehearsal of such works has its difficulties. One need have no compunction about citing books that have been written by madmen, but how shall one regard the borderland types? There have been men, apparently rational, who have written volumes that verge on the irrational; and there have been books with a measure of cogency written by individuals the world branded as demented.

Most of the works that fall into this category of deranged literature are characterized by prolixity. Usually they lack form, are incoherent, sometimes to the point of being unintelligible. Many of the authors write on subjects on which they are woefully uninformed. Frequently the titles are long, pompous, and aberrant.

The alienist Dr. Arthur MacDonald, once known for his studies on the kinship of genius and insanity, in 1911 wrote a little article on "Eccentric Literature" in which he stated: "Many aberrated persons with literary claims and scientific associations produce volumes in which the steps from eccentricity to partial or complete insanity can be traced. There is enough of such curious and eccentric literature almost to make a library. There are at least 284 authors who have written eccentric literature." Theology heads the list of subjects, and the authors of eccentrica are "usually cranks or mattoids."

Delepierre in 1860 wrote that in his time the University of Cambridge had a separate shelf for deranged literature and the works of nitwits. The New York Public Library groups its catalogue cards of such volumes, to the number of about a hundred and fifty, under the classification "Eccentric Literature." Several other large libraries do likewise and actually segregate irrational works on their shelves. Thus, as in real life many of these authors are sequestered from rational society, so their books fare in the routine of the library.

The erratic is reflected in literature by books which range from mere crotchets to sheer lunacy, from what may be designated as milder crankiana to what Delepierre terms dementiana, like the essay written by an inmate of literary leanings to prove that Byron was a centipede. Pertinent is the old couplet of Dryden in "Absalom and Achitophel":

> *Great wits are sure to madness near allied,*
> *And thin partitions do their bounds divide.*

Between genius and twisted mentality the dividing line is often difficult to determine. Wilhelm Lange-Eichbaum, one of the foremost authorities to consider the relationship, was the author of a formidable German treatise on the subject containing the "pathographies," or clinical histories, of eight hundred individuals whom fame designates as geniuses. His studies appeared also in a condensed English volume, *The Problem of Genius*, in which he reached the unpalatable conclusion that nine-tenths of what the world has acclaimed as genius "is intimately associated with 'insanity,' with psychopathy, or psychosis." The further genius is distinguished from mere talent, the more it approaches abnormality of mind, was his contention. Though this may be too sweeping a dictum, it has a modicum of truth. After all, Aristotle declared: "No great genius was ever without some mixture of madness."

In the space of a few pages little more can be done than glance at this subject. A true book ferret, bent on corralling all such devious volumes in a single bibliography, could enumerate several hundred which, by their content or the circumstances of their publication, clearly indicate the obsessed state of the authors. This does not mean that such literary figures were raving madmen; they may have been mild, even companionable, yet the works of most reveal little or naught of the rational.

Religion has been a fertile field in this respect; for the human mind seems more easily unhinged in matters having to do with divinity and seeking to plumb the mysteries of life. Many writers have had their mentalities unseated in efforts to interpret the more mystical element of the Bible, to bring an early millennium to mankind, to redeem the souls of those said to have gone astray, to point the way to the Absolute. The assumed gift of prophecy led to febrile works such as that of Joanna Southcott.

In his credulous day William Postel believed himself to have been merely the copyist of the Latin work for which he was best known, and was firm in describing Jesus as the real author. At about the same time a German physician at Leipsic printed a book concerning a child born with a golden tooth which he attributed to the influence of the stars. There were not a few such early volumes midway between the old alchemical vagaries and the nascent striving after a scientific explanation of the world and the strange things that went on in it. So, too, in the realm of astrology, that illegitimate sister of astronomy.

Bluet d'Arbéres in the seventeenth century called himself an author, though he deigned neither to read nor to write. This amiable potential scribe was a vagabond who assumed the title *Comte de Permission*. In the year 1600 he published a list of his supposed works, citing 103 titles, none of which was ever written. He died in poverty at Paris in 1606. In a similar vein there is an instance of an erratic author who, at the end of his book, lists sixty or more projected volumes.

Adrien Hoverlant de Beauwelaere devoted himself to the chronicle of his native town Tournay in Belgium. In the years 1805–1834 he wrote and at his own expense published not less than 117 volumes, without order, plan or reason, an indigested mass of documents, full of calumnies, forgetting no one whom he did not like. A complete exemplar

of this history of a town of five thousand is in the Bibliothèque
Nationale.

Typical of pseudo-scientific literature is the *Glory or Gravity* of
John Hutchinson, which in all its 154 pages has nothing more lucid than
the baffling title page. The deeper one probes in works of this kind, the
more meaningless they become. For example, there is Gleizes who, before
his death in 1845, had written works on vegetarianism. Though he loved
his wife, he deserted her, so it is said, because she persisted in eating
meat. He held that meat was atheistic, that fruits contained the true
religion, and that vegetables were an antidote for all evils. He left an
indifferent world ten volumes.

Books on eccentric characters, of which there have been several, and
books on men of folly, yield occasional instances of individuals who were
authors. J. C. Adelung, as early as 1785–1789, in a pioneer German
work of seven volumes on *The History of Human Folly* (*Geschichte der
menschlichen Narrheit*), supplies biographies of "celebrated
necromancers, alchemists, exorcists, conjurers, astrologers, soothsayers,
prophets, fanatics, visionaries, fortune-tellers, prognosticators, and other
philosophical monsters."

Several of the early charlatans listed by Adelung set forth their
philosophic perversions in books more or less irrational and eccentric.
And others there are of the same brood who have written volumes on
alchemy, apparitions, astrology, cheiromancy, demonology, evil spirits,
hermetics, black magic, phrenology, prophecy, sorcery, divination,
vampires, lycanthropy, witchcraft, and what not.

A century later Gustave Brunet, under the pen-name Philomneste,
Jr., produced his little work *Les Fous Littéraires*, in which he has an
alphabetical listing of one hundred or more odd authors and their odder
works, most of which exhibit a religious psychosis. He is partial to
mystics, ascetics, and disciples of the occult; but he is too inclusive when
he couples, as erratic, names like Poe and Whitman with those of Blake
and Swedenborg. However, many of the queer books cited by him were

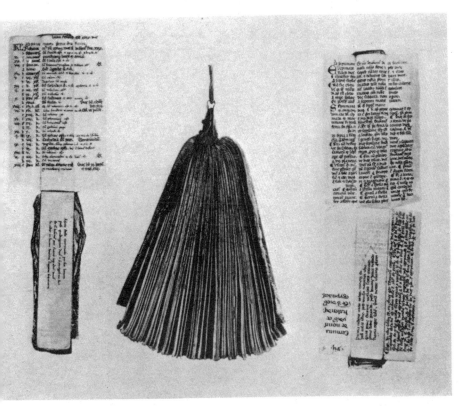

*A Latin breviary (1454) in manuscript on a
3" x 4" page; bound into a soft doeskin pouch to be
carried fastened to a belt or girdle; fewer than
fifteen of such rarities have survived.*

*This early almanac (Computers), dated 1294, is a
precious specimen of the folding girdle book. Of
Italian origin, this Latin manuscript, measuring
(closed) 5⅕" x 16⅙", was fastened to the belt.
(From the Staatsbibliothek of Berlin.)*

TWO EXAMPLES OF ELABORATE HANDICRAFT

*These seventeenth-century embroidered
needlework bindings for prized books
(usually devotional) employed colored silks,
sequins, and gold or silver bullion threads;
specimens in good condition are rarities.*

*Cut-leather binding. Early
fourteenth-century Egypto-
Arabic, Mamluck; center
medallion, corner sections, and
flap are decorated with a fine
design of arabesques in cutwork
on a green background.*

definitely the product of deranged minds, such as that one which seeks to end death among mortals, or that other devoted to the adoration of various parts of the Virgin Mary's body.

The noted bibliophile Charles Nodier, in two brief causeries in the *Bulletin du Bibliophile* of 1835 mentioned several early *écrivains aliénés*, among them François Colonna or Columna, whose *Hypnerotomachia Poliphili* is a conglomeration of pedantic, medieval nonsense, the babel of a delirious imagination; it remains, however, one of the most superbly illustrated works in all the world.

D'Israeli in his *Calamities of Authors* has a chapter on "Literary Disappointments Disordering the Intellect" in which he adverts to John Leland, who was appointed the King's Antiquary by Henry VIII and who, though he sought to write the whole of British antiquities, went mad before the achievement of the task.

Irresponsible literature cannot be said to invite the average collector. But as an alcove for alienists such books have appeal, and it is possible to classify the bedlam shelves, for the vagaries and aberrations of mankind do fall into erratic patterns, as Joseph Jastrow demonstrated in his *Wish and Wisdom* concerning cults and the credulous mind. This cursory survey is merely a bird's-eye view, for the vista of deranged authorship stretches through the centuries.

Les Controverses des Sexes masculin et feminin, written in meter by Gratian de Pont and published at Lyon in 1537, asserts that every man on the day of resurrection will come into bodily perfection, without deformity or blemish, that Adam will regain the rib from which Eve was formed and Eve lose her identity in Adam's side. And so will it be with all humankind—every man will be like unto Adam, and every woman incorporated in man like Eve—leading to his conclusion that what Kipling later called "a rag, a bone and a hank of hair" would cease to be.

The cabbala of numerology has its cloudy devotees. Thus an 1817 German work, *Deutung der Null*, on the significance of the algebraic naught has its anonymous preface signed "Ich die Zahl" (I, the Number) and professes to be "An Explanation of Zero or Fiery Rays in the Dawn of Truth!"

A five-hundred-page volume, *The Tempter of Eve* by Charles Carroll, which appeared in 1902 in St. Louis, assumes to take us from the antediluvian era to the author's own time in one of those pious but bigoted surveys of the cosmos that so many victims of biblical obsession have indulged in ever since—and even before—printing began. This author had no love for Negroes; he deprives them of souls, derives them from the apes (not so the whites), and assembles a mass of devout and pseudo-scientific balderdash to bolster his contention of the danger of extending political, religious and social equality to them. A page at the end announces many other works to appear—a common symptom.

It is a relief to mention that a quite rational book was composed, printed, and bound by lunatics at the asylum of Konradsdorf, Stockholm, in 1884. A small printing equipment was set up in the institution in the hope of benefitting an author who was one of the inmates. The author-inmate evinced an interest in the novelty and some took instruction in typography from him. The book so strangely produced dealt with madness and the psychology of the demented.

Many of the published projections of unseated mentality found few readers. There were others, however, that gained a following. Need one point to the *Protocols of the Elders of Zion*, fabricated by that half-mad and wholly mystic monk, Nilus? Typical of this group of fanatics was Richard Brothers.

Cecil Roth, in an aptly titled sketch *The Nephew of the Almighty* (London, 1933) gave the vitals of that febrile figure. Decorously born in Newfoundland, in 1771 young Brothers, then fourteen years old, was sent to England to become a midshipman. Though he went on to become a Lieutenant, by thirty-two he had scruples that he "could not conscientiously receive the wages of plunder, bloodshed and murder," and quit the Royal Navy. At this time celestial visions were manifested to him, and he predicted the downfall of London in fulfillment of apocalyptical prophecies contained in the seventh chapter of the Book of Daniel.

In 1794, after the Almighty had confided to Brothers "that I call you my nephew," that he was descended from King David through James, the *brother* of Jesus, he finished his tract, *The Nephew of the Almighty; a Revealed Knowledge of the Prophecies & Times. Wrote under the Direction of the Lord God & published by his sacred command. It being the First Sign of Warning.* The lower half of the title page modestly predicted the "Restoration of the Hebrews to Jerusalem by the year 1798 under their revealed Prince and Prophet Richard Brothers."

In this and in another tract appearing a few months after, disasters were predicted with precise chronology. Copies were sent to the King, ambassadors, bishops, and members of Parliament by the impecunious author. In 1795 the Minister of State for Home Affairs sent two King's Messengers to arrest the arrant sub-deity; subsequently a jury found him insane and committed him to an asylum.

Meanwhile the world at large was in political tumult, and in Britain the strange figure of Joanna Southcott was indulging in divagations. Cecil Roth writes: "Edition after edition of the two parts of the *Revealed Knowledge* followed one another from the press, and was eagerly bought up. The work was reprinted in Ireland and in America, where it attracted almost as much attention as in England. It appeared even in a French translation in the Fourth Year of the One and Indivisible Republic. Many persons throughout England began to make preparations for the immediate removal to the Holy Land."

Previously, in the very year of Brothers' incarceration, an Anglo-Indian scholar and member of the House of Commons, Nathaniel Brassey Halhed, wrote *A Testimony of the Authenticity of the Prophecies of Richard Brothers and of his Mission to Recall the Jews,* with a prefatory note by the prophet himself, and it quickly went through two editions.

Month after month in the asylum Brothers wrote pamphlet after pamphlet in pursuance of the divine mandate, while willing recruits grew eloquent on the outside. Within the institution the Nephew of the

Almighty set about drawing up a set of plans and regimentation for the
New Jerusalem. Outside, his views won a wealthy disciple, John
Finlayson, who now aided in getting the plans published. According to
the biographer, "the *opus* was issued, accompanied by ample
illustrations. These included the ground-plan of the New Jerusalem, with
its 56 squares, 20 colleges, 16 market-places and 320 streets, together
with the adjacent Garden of Eden, as a sort of glorified Hyde Park."
There were also abundant specimens of temples and private palaces.
Finlayson's outlay approximated £1,200, and a subscription set of the
plates cost ten guineas.

Finlayson, in addition to steadily impoverishing himself, agitated
for the release of Brothers and secured it after the prophet had been
eleven years in confinement. Lacking neither disciples nor persistence, the
prophet in 1822 published *A Correct Account of the Invasion and
Conquest of this Island by the Saxons, necessary to be known by the
English Nation, the Descendants of the Greater Part of the Ten Tribes.*
Not content, he wrote *The New Covenant between God and His People,*
with details of the to-be revived Hebrew state—judicial, fiscal,
administrative, and social—including robes to be worn. Finlayson in due
course published a lavish edition of this work, enhanced by colored plates
from his own hand.

Other exponents were also active in literary behalf of the movement,
even after Brothers died in 1824 and was buried in the same churchyard
as Joanna Southcott. Inveterate Finlayson continued writing for a new
generation in the spirit of Brothers, under such titles as *The Seven Seals
of Revelation* and *The Seven Metaphorical Angels.* In his eighty-fifth
year, destitute but still firm in the faith that Brothers had been a divine
messenger, the tenacious Scotchman died and was laid to apparent rest
beside the Prince of the Hebrews and Nephew of the Almighty.

The annals of authorship do not lack instances in which men
impoverished themselves to get their unsound books printed. Having
expended £32,000 on his *opus,* Lord Kingsborough went to a debtor's
gaol and died there, although he succeeded in giving posterity the nine

massive (imperial folio) volumes of his sumptuous *Mexican Antiquities*, with colored hieroglyphic plates and its labored thesis that the ancient Americans stemmed from Israel because they practiced circumcision, had flood traditions, and abstained from eating swine—a contention, by the way, that has a literature all its own.

Other names come to mind, but it must suffice to cite the case of Thomas Wirgman. He expended a small fortune of some thousands of pounds sterling for printing his books, which were published in London more than a century ago. It is said that no more than twenty copies were ever sold. The most pretentious is entitled *Divarication of the Sacred Volume, the New Testament, into Doctrine (The Word of God) and History (The Word of Man)*. First published in 1830, the second edition of 1834 has 552 pages with two blue title pages lettered in gold. It is dedicated to William IV and inscribed on another page to Lord Brougham. The first 410 pages are designated a preface! Yellow and blue panels bearing text matter are scattered throughout this prodigious preface. Then comes a lengthy introduction. The final hundred pages are in yellow and blue columns arranging the New Testament under "Soul, Doctrine, Thesis" (yellow), "Body, History, Antithesis" (blue). At the top of each yellow column is written: "Doctrine: The Word of God— Reason," and at the top of each blue column, "History: The Word of Man—Sense."

This work, like his smaller volumes, is unintelligible. His 1824 *Kantesian Philosophy* is a booklet of some thirty pages, in English and French, dedicated to George IV and containing "A Map of the Human Mind," a baffling tabulation of the qualities of the mind in time and space, and assorted axioms, definitions, and principles, all aiming to present Kant in pellet paragraphs.

The author, a former seller of snuff boxes, was convinced that when his ideas were universally adopted, they would bring peace and harmony on earth, and virtue would be enthroned among men. He applied for the chair of moral philosophy at the University of London, and wrote to George IV that only by adopting the principles of his books could either the monarch or his subjects be saved in the world to come. He lavished money in the curious coloring of the pages of his several works, discarding the printed forms that did not please him and having others differently made.

Well known to booklovers and students of Americana is the eccentric Timothy Dexter, whose title of Lord Dexter was self-conferred. In 1769, at the age of twenty-two, after a term of apprenticeship as a leather dresser, he arrived in Newburyport, Massachusetts, with, as he afterwards wrote, a "bondel" and "Eight Dolors & 20 sents" in cash. Throughout his life he disdained formal spelling.

With the little money he had accumulated he bought up depreciated Continental currency during and after the Revolution. When, in 1791, Hamilton's policy of "funding and assumption" went into effect, Dexter redeemed his holdings and became affluent. Joined to inordinate vanity and an eccentricity verging on insanity was a cunning in speculation. There seems some basis for his boasts that he had sent forty-two thousand warming pans to Cuba, where they were sold as cooking utensils; that he cornered the market in whalebone, selling 342 tons at a large profit; and that he made a further huge gain on twenty-one thousand Bibles which he sold in the "west inges." If he sent coals to Newcastle, they were anthracite and in demand. When he sent mittens to the tropics, a Norwegian sea captain bought them for a frigid clime.

Dexter retained as laureate one Jonathan Plummer, a former fish peddler, and had him write odes in honor of his patron. "Lord" Timothy kept his coffin ready in the parlor, and on one occasion held a mock funeral, beating his wife thereafter for her failure to weep at the rehearsal.

Timothy Dexter calls for inclusion here because of his pamphlet, *A Pickle for the Knowing Ones*, which appeared in 1802. It comprises a version of his exploits, recounted in the ludicrous spelling that attaches to his name, and minus punctuation. At least nine editions and reprints of this curious effort have appeared. The Peter Quince edition of 1838, published thirty-two years after "his lordship's" death, contained half a

page of assorted punctuation purporting to have been reprinted from the
second edition of Dexter's pamphlet, and bearing the caption:

(NOTE TO DEXTER'S SECOND EDITION)
fourder mister printer the Nowing ones complane of my
book the fust edition had no stops I put in A nuf here and
thay may peper and solt it as they plese

However, Edmund Pearson pointed out that the second edition does
not contain these rows of stops. It seems that Dexter, following the
issuance of his pamphlet, may have faced attacks with a fugitive
broadside that contained the wholesale punctuation; or perhaps it was a
loose leaf to be inserted in the pamphlet, or even a variant issue of the
same. It appeared in no edition printed in Dexter's lifetime.

The 1847 revised edition tampers with the text, and the overzealous
editor introduced punctuation in an effort to make the screed intelligible.
A subsequent edition in 1858 of Samuel L. Knapp's biography of
Dexter, including a reprint of *A Pickle for the Knowing Ones,* goes one
better than the Peter Quince edition by adding another whole page of
punctuation—asterisks, daggers, brackets, paragraph marks, and the like
—a good measure indeed.

Pertinent is the observation of the bookish essayist W. G. Clifford
who, flouting the grammarian's rules of punctuation as too stilted and
confining, says: "Punctuation is as personal as the use of pepper and
salt. An author sprinkles his work with stops to help the flavour he
desires to impart."

Augustus De Morgan, using the word paradox in the old sense as
"something which is apart from general opinion, either in subjectmatter,
method, or conclusion," gave us a delightful and erudite *A Budget of
Paradoxes* (London, 1872) which in its five hundred pages cites many an
odd treatise and tract that falls within the category of deranged
authorship. All of these are downright fantastical; some should be
designated as lunacy at large, others as crotchets, the quaintness of
which is tinged with the taint of mental malady. De Morgan, father of

the novelist, was a mathematician of explorative mind and had a partiality for those aberrant works that may be termed pseudo-scientific.

De Morgan cites that febrile work, the two volumes of the Reverend J. Dobson entitled *The Elements of Geometry* (Cambridge, 1815). It seems this clerical author's chief claim to distinction was the fact that he disdained punctuation though, unlike Lord Timothy Dexter, he did not lack literacy. His above-mentioned work and other mathematical tracts carried periods only at the end of paragraphs. All capitals were eschewed, save one to start each paragraph. Its theorems were on a par with its punctuation. The publishers managed to insert in their title-page imprint a comma, semicolon, colon, and period, as if to acquit themselves of the author's vagary. Few copies of the two-volume work were printed and fewer of the tracts. "It is doubtful whether any were sold," says De Morgan, who with delightful whimsicality prints his page-and-a-half description of the Dobson work minus stops and aping the comma-less, pointless style of the original. A third edition of De Morgan's *Budget of Paradoxes* appeared at London and Chicago in 1954, and in two volumes enticing to all those having a penchant for such collections of curiosa.

Perhaps the queerest character in the annals of the American stage was George Jones, who forsook England about 1828 and came to be known as Count Johannes. He had a vanity allied to madness, and his career was a strange one. Whatever talent or scholarship he had was offset by a growing mental disorder. His stage career began about 1833 and his favorite rôle was Hamlet. It is said that he was the original of the *Crushed Tragedian*, a play in which Sothern appeared. The Hamlet of George Jones was always the butt of audiences and led to much ridicule. He played Hamlet many times, until be became too mad to portray even the Mad Prince. He was admitted to the Bar of New York about 1862 as a sort of joke, and he always appeared in a velvet coat with many decorations. He is included here as the author of *The Original History of Ancient America, Anterior to Columbus*, which, with a grandiose dedication, had the distinction of simultaneous publication in

1843 in London, New York, Berlin, and Paris. In this work, with
amazing particularity, he conjures up hypothetical history, contending
that the Tyrians and Israelites had contributed to the peopling of
primitive America. He was also the author of a curious drama in blank
verse entitled *Tecumseh* which in 1844 was likewise published in four
countries, and in which the aborigines and the ancient Israelites were
assumed to have been of the same stock. Half a dozen other works were
announced by him but never appeared.

In 1886, Bloodgood Haviland Cutter, then nearly seventy, published
at his own cost *The Long Island Farmer's Poems*, which has been termed
"perhaps the bulkiest, certainly the most amazing *omnium-gatherum* of
one poet's defective poetry ever assembled." In 1867 he had been a fellow-
passenger of Mark Twain on the steamship *Quaker City*, bound on a
pleasure cruise, and Samuel Clemens pokes fun at him in *The Innocents
Abroad*, saying "the laureate of the ship is not popular," and telling how
Cutter wrote reams of trashy doggerel on every possible occasion, and
bestowed these ludicrous scribblings on anyone in sight. Twenty years
later, when Cutter's book appeared, the title page bore the line "Mark
Twain's 'Larriat' in 'Innocents Abroad.' "

His Long Island homestead, we are told, was a mammoth clutter of
books, antiques, and curiosities, including eight thousand volumes of
which some two hundred were Bibles, stuffed birds and animals, countless
of his manuscript effusions, assorted bells (one of which weighed a ton),
scores of waistcoats of all patterns, firearms galore, and oddments that
made a twenty-eight page inventory of his possessions when, after his
death, the lots were sold at auction. His whole estate amounted to
$900,662.95, two-thirds of which was bequeathed to the American Bible
Society. In addition to his fat volume of execrable verse, he had many
hundreds of absurd broadsides printed at his own expense.

There were other curious poetical effusions, like for instance *A
Genial Anecdote: forming an Episode illustrating the mysterious fracas
between Royal spouses and peace*, by Dr. Ram Kinoo Dutt, retired
medical officer on pension of Chittagong, India. It is impossible to tell

how much of this oddity in verse, published in 1884, must be ascribed to pidgin-English and how much to the derangement of the Hindu author.

And let us not overlook Nancy Luce who dwelt in Martha's Vineyard, eking out a living selling eggs and poetry. Each egg was not only dated but inscribed with the elegant name of the hen that laid it. Her feeble verses eulogized her animal pets in bad grammar and with lack of rhyme. She had her poems printed in 1860 and several times thereafter, and sold the slender sheaf at 25¢ a copy at her farm and at camp-meetings.

Windy titles are typical of this class of books. One by "Amicus Humani Generis" devotes the top half of the title page to *The Labor Question, or an exact science of equivalents; and also containing a new theory of cosmogony, showing the beginning and the ending of all things or individualities; and also showing that the story of the Creation in the Bible contains a true tradition.* The lower half of this title has much else, including *I am Alpha and Omega, the beginning and the ending.* It is a volume of 186 pages issued by the Chicago Legal News Company in 1881. This Utopian author, at least, does not announce a whole shelf of projected works.

A lady published in 1901 at her own expense *Sordid Amok!* and described it on the title page as being by "A Common Centurion" (Clairon de Bruyère), who elsewhere in the book has the alias Ivor Otho Star. The volume is a record of her thoughts during six months' incarceration in a Paris asylum. There are profuse quotations from Ecclesiasticus, Plato, Emerson, and others. She attempts suicide, and narrates her failure. "Human beings," she observes, "looking out over the entire expanse encompassing all the marvels of the science and the genius of Civilizations, Ancient and Modern, are still unable even to make an 'Eyelash,' which carries in itself its own inherent mystery of extension." It is a pathetic volume, choked with incoherence and formlessness. She devises a coat-of-arms for herself, and states that the motto it bears is "My Rights or I Bite."

Pretentious title pages abound in works of this character. The mystic number 666 led many minds astray, and a curious tract printed in Nova Scotia in 1883 applies this symbol to elucidation of the "Fisheries Commission Frauds," with the help of "masking numbers taken from the thirteenth chapter of Revelation."

The titles of most of these books beyond the norm betray the mental lapses of their authors. Moreover, these strange works are encountered almost as often in the twentieth century as in the seventeenth. Here is one that defies analysis: *The Discovery of Discoveries, Climaxingly collated in the Month of Una-and-her-lion (1908) inclusive of August, and Fulfilling "The Message of Ishtar."*

A privately printed item, dated 1911, purports to solve for the first time, among other things, "the ancient Hebrew Mystery of Aaron's Breastplate." Written by H. Emerson, it is entitled *Psychocraft, re Instinct using Human Organic Mechanisms with giant strength on aerial touch to avert disaster.* There are occult designs by the author and a "system of Answers for the Oracle of Ellu," with colored balls in a patent box at the end of the book.

In the realm of spiritualism, Liverpool in 1910 produced: *The First Judgment of the Christians by The Spirit, Alpha and Omega. An Authorized Revision of St. Matthew, and the History of this Planet from the First Strata to the End. Written for the Spirit at Command by F. W. Cunard.*

Many similar lucubrations might be cited, but to what purpose? Few gained any considerable circulation. And yet the lycanthropic novel by Herman Hesse entitled *Steppenwolf*, published and printed in Germany in 1929, sold more than fifty thousand copies and bears the subtitle "For Madmen Only." It is a neurotic story of a man who conceives his human form as possessed by a wolf of the steppes contending for the sinister conquest of his soul; and there is a touch of the maniacal to its abnormal telling.

There are other books of recent decades which one hesitates to classify, save among freaks, if nothing more, of literature. *The Book of the Damned, Lo!, New Lands,* and *Wild Talents*, by Charles Fort who died in 1932, present data of strange phenomena concerning showers of frogs, blizzards of snails, black and red rains, bleeding images, poisoned fogs, luminous beings, concussions in the sky, green moons, sea serpents, and cosmic dust. Each reader must decide for himself in what category works such as these belong. The critic must be cautious in the alcove for alienists. Marcel Proust in one of his maxims declared: "Everything great in the world comes from neurotics. They alone have founded our religions and composed our masterpieces."

A rather preposterous incantation of nonsense, *Geyserland: Empiricisms in Social Reform* was published in Washington in 1928 by Mark Stubble. This is a philosophical-fictional-Utopian hodgepodge describing (à la Donnelly's sunken Atlantis) the antediluvian Geyserlanders. The pages purport "to contrast their system with ours by relating the experiences of an English castaway who passed several years in Geyserland." The cataclysm is dated 9262 B.C.

Here, then, is a shelf of literature exhibiting various degrees of clouded mentality, having, so to speak, a dimension too much, or too little. There are many more unmentioned in this melancholy list.

A relevant word may be devoted to the book madness that has possessed certain collectors to the point of disequilibrium, as marked by Dibdin's designation, "Bibliomania." There have been more than a few of those who immure themselves among books to the exclusion of all other normal living, whose acquisitive frenzy verges on derangement. The obsession of such bookmen ranges from a mere amiable eccentricity to what is regarded, in the words of Edmund Pearson, as "a rather distinguished form of lunacy." There is a story about an Englishman who prized a volume he deemed unique; on discovering a second copy in the possession of a Frenchman, he induced the latter to sell him the duplicate and then promptly tossed it in the grate before the astonished eyes of its late possessor.

Chronic collectors relish the story respecting Don Vincente, a Spanish savant of the last century, who committed murder to indulge his unholy passion for books. Don Vincente is said to have slain a rival who,

in competing for an item deemed unique, outbid him at auction by
fourteen pesetas. Jules Janin gives the difference in bids which he reduces
to French currency as 1,334 francs and 44 centimes, as compared with
1,320 francs.

If compassion for those poor unfortunates who poured forth their
unintelligible maunderings in print were not dominant, we might, like
W. G. Clifford, invoke that old book of Wilkins, Bishop of Chester, which
in 1640 announced *The Discovery of a New World, or a Discourse
tending to prove that 'tis probable there may be another habitable World
in the Moone, and, concerning the possibility of a Passage thither.*
Clifford facetiously accepting the theory of Wilkins that a "vessell" filled
with heated or "aethereall aire" would be navigable in the firmament and
"remaine swimming there," suggests that a mixed contingent of "moon
migrants," comprising fanatics and other bothersome folk be packed off
on the first lunar trip. But without these vexers, or those of lunatic
propensity, this might become a too equable and tedious earth. And, when
all the deranged volumes are a-row, who shall answer that barbed query
of Flaubert: "What if the absurd be true?"

CHRONICLE OF FRUSTRATIONS

THOUGH ONE MAY SPECULATE on what the dénouement or delineation of the unfinished part might have been had the author completed his work, who is there who would augment Coleridge's "Kubla Khan"? or fill the two vacant niches of the Medici Chapel in Florence? or venture to add to Schubert's "Unfinished Symphony"? Not always wasted is such unconsummated effort. Stevenson, who quitted life at the crest and left two major manuscripts unended, once observed: "It is not only in finished undertaking that we ought to honor labor. A spirit goes out of the man who means execution, which outlives the most untimely end."

There is, nevertheless, peculiar pathos in the thought of unfinished books, cut short by time or contingency. One recalls a pleasant essay on "The Beginnings of Novels," treating of the variable technique of the opening paragraph as employed in masterpieces of fiction. The brave flourish with which a writer may open his work is not as influenced by sentiment as his closing paragraphs. He remembers, one surmises, the many times between the first and last pages when inspiration seemed to desert him, or the springs of energy flagged. Usually, however, the urge is such, the grit or the vanity so strong, most literary efforts are pressed onward to the designed conclusion. All the more cheerless, then, is the array of some fine adventures of the pen in which the final phrase fades into dots.

Endless discussion, conjecture, and assumption have sought to postulate the outcome of Dickens' *The Mystery of Edwin Drood*. This was to have been concluded in twelve monthly numbers, but only six parts had been written, and three published, when in 1870 "the magic pen dropped from the hand that would never again resume its wonted task." As a mystery story it gained added prestige from the circumstance of its incompletion, for there is a psychological let-down once a reader learns the author's solution. Of this last of a great gallery of Dickensian works, Chesterton said: "The only one of Dickens novels which he did not finish was the only one that really needed finishing. He never had but one thoroughly good plot to tell; and that he has only told in heaven."

Despite this note of critical condescension, the Dickens' plots smack of life as he knew it. As for the telling in heaven, one "medium" finished the novel as dictated to him by the alleged spirit pen of Dickens from the Beyond. And ever since Dickens' death ambitious writers have tried their skill at finishing the story; there are exactly a baker's dozen of these second-hand endings, and of the lot at least three quite different outcomes by as many ingenious pens.

It is curious that Dickens left no skeletal scheme of his plot, which would have spared Droodists their Droodian dilemma and relieved library shelves of sequels and second parts composed by others. But the Drood mystery has one virtue: as each such attempt appears in fiction guise, or an essay wrestles with the outcome of a plot Dickens himself may not have decided, confirmed Dickensians ponder the matter anew, and then, still baffled, they read *Drood* again!

The story, so far as it goes, describes Jasper, degenerate choir leader and opium addict, plotting the murder of Drood, his nephew, in drugged slumber, to obtain the latter's fiancée. He is overheard by an old hag, keeper of the opium den, who follows him on the night of the murder. She gives the clue to Datchery, the detective—and here the book ends.

There are those who have resented the hubbub in literary circles concerning the outcome of *Drood*. J. C. Squire, in comment, expresses satisfaction that no one has had the temerity to try to finish Stevenson's *Weir of Hermiston*, or the unended novels of Jane Austen. "But," he says, "I do wish that somebody, anybody, Mrs. Dickens, Miss Dickens, Master Dickens, or Wilkie Collins, had finished 'Edwin Drood,' for then we should have been spared this endless controversy. It breaks out yearly like prairie fires. . . . There seem to be tens of thousands of persons in this country who worry over the Drood problem as chess enthusiasts do over mates in five moves. And the extraordinary thing is that they have a way of talking about the mystery of Drood and his latter end as though they were talking about something that really happened."

He can tolerate attempts to solve real mysteries, but not *Drood:* "It is a comprehensible pastime to attempt to identify the Man in the Iron Mask or to try to demonstrate that Sir Philip Francis did or did not write the 'Letters of Junius.' Somebody wrote the 'Letters of Junius': they exist. . . . But it is a totally different thing to dispute about who did what and what happened to whom in an uncompleted story which is not a history but a fiction. The commonsense position is that nothing whatever happened to Edwin Drood, that he himself and all his confrères were the acme of inactivity; for the simple reason that there were (in the highly appropriate words of their own fabulist) no sich persons."

From what Dickens told his friend and biographer, John Forster, the novel was to have included the murderer's own view of his crime and the causes that led up to it; but those who have attempted to complete the novel do not adhere to this formula. One of the earliest sequels entitled *John Jasper's Secret*, by Henry Morford and his wife, was issued by T. B. Peterson & Brothers, Philadelphia publishers, from October, 1871, to March, 1872, and appeared in England anonymously in eight parts. A version of this same continuation was printed in 1901 by an unscrupulous publisher with the amazing and false announcement on the title page that the book was by Wilkie Collins and Charles Dickens the Younger. It was preceded only by Orpheus Kerr's *The Cloven Foot,* which was something of a burlesque, brought out in the year of Dickens' death and adapted to American scenes and customs.

The original Drood manuscript is now in the South Kensington Museum as one of the cherished items of the John Forster collection. Forster restored to the published text many passages the author had deleted in the script. Dickens was to have received the equivalent of £7,500 for the copyright, and one-half share of the profits after twenty-five thousand copies had been sold; in addition he was to receive five thousand dollars for advance sheets sent to America. It has been said that up to that time this was the largest sum ever contracted to be paid for a novel by a publisher. Curiously enough, the publisher had inserted a clause in the agreement covering the contingency of death.

As Dr. Rosenbach observed of *Drood*, Poe alone might have solved the mystery. In *Graham's Weekly* of May 1, 1841, Poe analyzed the plot of Dickens' *Barnaby Rudge*, though he had seen only the introductory chapter, and Dickens was so amazed he wrote to ask Poe if he were the Devil himself.

Some eighteen books, five plays, and more than eighty articles have been devoted to the subject since Dickens died in 1870—nor have the films overlooked it. One of the volumes attempting a fictional ending is that entitled *Epilogue* (1934), by Bruce Graeme, in which a modern Scotland Yard detective conducts the investigation which leads to a solution of the problem posed by Dickens—and then awakes with a copy of *Drood* beside his bed.

Walter Scott's *The Siege of Malta*, which he intended as the last of the Waverley Novels, was about half completed when he died in 1832. Although the existence of the manuscript had long been known from notations in Scott's journal, it remained locked up in his old home in Abbotsford for nearly a century before the story was sold to a noted dealer having the unfulfilled intention to publish it on the occasion of the centenary of Scott's death in 1932. The manuscript, now in the New York Public Library's Berg Collection, consists of 150 sheets, containing some sixty-five thousand words, and deals with the great attack on the

island of Malta by the Turks in 1565, in which the Knights of St. John
eventually triumphed. The handwriting shows Scott's failing strength
and the manuscript ends in the middle of a sentence—"Thus a line of
princes"—possibly the last words he ever wrote.

Thackeray's *Denis Duval* is another half-told story, the last serial
installment in the *Cornhill Magazine* of June, 1864, ending with an
editorial benediction. Like Dickens, Thackeray had embarked upon the
serial publication of his novel before he had wrought its conclusion.
Strangely enough, although repeated efforts were made to piece out
Dickens' broken narrative, no one was rash enough to venture
terminating *Denis Duval*, in which it is likely that Marie Antoinette
would have figured.

Pater's *Gaston de Latour: An Unfinished Romance* and Meredith's
Celt and Saxon are known to few. And prolific Alexandre Dumas in his
half-finished *Isaac Laquedem* attempted to depict the Wandering Jew.

Stevenson's romance *St. Ives* was brought to a conclusion by Sir
Arthur Quiller-Couch; but no one has done the like for *Weir of
Hermiston*, with which the author struggled in his last hours at Samoa.
With the words "a wilful convulsion of brute nature," the latter tale
breaks off. According to Sir Sidney Colvin, "they were dictated, I
believe, on the very morning of the writer's sudden seizure and death."
Critical opinion has contended that *Weir of Hermiston* gave promise of
being the best work of its author. Included in the sale of the Henry A.
Colgate collection in 1928 was the manuscript of *St. Ives* (in the
handwriting of Mrs. Isobel Strong at Stevenson's dictation), and the
unpublished manuscript of *The Go-Between: A Boy's Romance*, as well
as some pages of original autograph notes for a projected
autobiography, and memoranda for another chapter of *Weir of
Hermiston*.

An odd slant in this connection is the fact that Arthur D. Howden
Smith undertook, in the nature of sequels, the pursuance of stories
Stevenson wrote or might have written had he been granted a longer lease
of life. In *Porto Bello Gold* Smith narrated how the treasure came to

Treasure Island, and in *Alan Breck Again* he took a character that appears in *Kidnapped* and in *David Balfour* and ensconced him in a story about a character out of the past who was limned in Andrew Lang's monograph, *Pickles the Spy*. Lang had once suggested to Stevenson the use of this figure in a novel, but the book was never written.

Many American authors suffered this frustration of work unconcluded. In poetic comment on Hawthorne's unfinished novel, *The Dolliver Romance*, Longfellow wrote:

> *Ah, who shall lift that wand of magic power,*
> *And the lost clue regain!*
> *The unfinished window in Aladdin's tower*
> *Unfinished must remain.*

Another of Hawthorne's works, *Doctor Grimshawe's Secret*, was also unconcluded. And *Septimus Felton*, which concerned the elixir of life was, ironically, relinquished in an effort to conclude *The Dolliver Romance* at a time the author was aware of his approaching end. He had begun to write it for magazine publication; three times he vainly sought to bring this strange tale of the bloody footstep to a conclusion, but the tale half-told was abruptly terminated by death. Speaking of Hawthorne, Brander Matthews says: "The sudden death of Dickens and Thackeray was his also, and his instalment of life in this world was sharply cut off—to be continued in our next."

Jane Austen's *Sandition* is a fragment; likewise *The Watsons*, both of which were printed and, indeed, reprinted. Among Disraeli's papers was discovered an unfinished novel which had his rival Gladstone as its main character. It was begun after Lord Beaconsfield's retirement from the Prime Ministry in 1880. The fragment, consisting of nine skeletonized chapters, was published in 1905 in the London *Times*, and, even though no more than sketched, reveals the deft hand that wrote *Coningsby* and *Lothair*. Among the manuscripts of Carlyle in the Morgan Memorial Library, Hartford, is a short unfinished article "An Excursion to Paris" and, more important, an incomplete novel, *Wotten*

Reinfred, which was never printed and concerning which little is known.

In a mélange of prose and verse, Swinburne attempted a disjointed romance, *Lesbier Brandon*. To Richard Burton he wrote in 1867: "I have in hand a scheme of mixed verse and prose—a sort of *étude à la Balzac* plus the poetry—which I flatter myself will be more offensive and objectionable to Britannia than anything I have yet done. You see I have now a character to keep up." According to Edmund Gosse the script was set up in type in 1877 after having been ten years in manuscript. It is now lost, and only one galley proof, lacking both beginning and ending, is extant.

George Gissing's *Veranilda*, a story of Roman life in the sixth century, was left incomplete by a few chapters. Admirers of Henry James doubtless wish *The Ivory Tower* with its international background had been finished.

The last novel, *Helianthus*, by Ouida (Louise de la Ramée) was published in its incomplete form as she left it. Prolific Anthony Trollope's story *Mr. Scarborough's Family* was running in *All the Year Round* when he passed away; his *An Old Man's Love* had been completed in manuscript, and *The Land-Leaguers* was virtually complete. Gogol's *Dead Soul* was also unconcluded, and Dostoieffsky's *Brothers Karamazoff*, although lengthy, was unterminated—a fact realized by few of its readers.

The widow of Joseph Conrad emphatically declined to permit *Suspense* to be brought to a vicarious close. In its serial publication, a magazine printing the story offered a contest prize for the best ending submitted by any reader. This romance of the Mediterranean in the stirring days of Napoleon's downfall is not a fragment like many half-told tales, for it runs to ninety thousand words, as long as many finished novels. "A fragment—yes," says the author's friend Richard Curle, "but a fragment full of power and fire; a fragment that will take its place among the recognized masterpieces of this remarkable man." *Suspense* has the proportions of a novel, yet lacks conclusion. In 1926 it evoked a long critical article in the *Revue des Deux Mondes* in which Louis Gillet, the French critic, regarded this novel as the most entrancing story Conrad had to tell and mourns the fact that the novelist took with him the secret of its ending. Conrad's *The Sisters* was also cut short of completion.

Notable among fictional works completed by another hand was Sterne's *Sentimental Journey*, brought to finality by a friend when the licentious Reverend died. William Wilkie Collins' story *Blind Love* was running serially when he passed on in 1889, and it was completed by Sir Walter Besant. Sir Arthur Conan Doyle finished Grant Allen's *Hilda Wade* when the latter was on his death-bed in Surrey with two unwritten installments still to appear in the *Strand Magazine*. Charles Kingsley's *The Tutor's Story* was completed by Lucas Malet, his daughter. The novel *Enoch Crane*, begun by F. Hopkinson Smith, was finished by his son F. Berkeley Smith. And a brother of Thomas Nelson Page added the last few pages to *The Red Riders* from notes left by the author.

William de Morgan's last two books were finished by his widow along lines she knew he had intended. This author became a novelist of distinction when most men would have been dissuaded from taxing their mentalities in the writing of creative fiction. Of the two novels, *The Old Madhouse* and *The Old Man's Youth*, one lacked only the last chapter; the other was more fragmentary. His widow was aided by notes for the missing parts which William de Morgan had left, and no sooner had her task been completed than she, too, died.

The Huntington Library has manuscripts of two unfinished Jack London novels, *Assassination Bureau* and *Cherry*. Arnold Bennett's *Stroke of Luck* and *Dream of Destiny* appeared as one volume in 1932, the latter an unfinished novel. The manuscript of Frank Norris's incomplete *Vandover and the Brute* was discovered long after it had been believed lost in the San Francisco fire, and was completed by his younger brother, Charles G. Norris, twelve years after the author's death. Terminated without being ended was Edith Wharton's *The Buccaneers*, depicting the social climbing of American expatriates in London. And several of Sherwood Anderson's incomplete works are in manuscript at Chicago's Newberry Library.

In passing, mention should be made of unsolved endings in fiction as distinguished from unfinished works, as in Frank Stockton's *Lady and the Tiger*, concerning which an extant letter of the author confesses he himself did not know the answer.

A curious instance, in the nature of a bibliographical sport, is presented by Theodore Dreiser's partially published novel issued in the form of an advertising dummy in 1916 with several pages of text set up. Thirty years ago a want-ad in *The Saturday Review*, sought a copy of *The Bulwark*, stating that "Several copies are known to exist in good state." One copy only, however, was known to Vrest Orton, who states in his *Dreiserana* (1929) that its possessor was of the opinion this single copy had been made up simply to show to Dreiser.

In the field of poetry, also, there are notable instances of unfinished efforts. Chaucer undertook to translate the *Romance of the Rose*, but left the rendition unfinished. As to the *Canterbury Tales* we know of but twenty-four; there might have been many more, and perhaps others were actually written and then lost. Six books of Spenser's *Faerie Queene* were lost, if ever they were written, for tradition has it they were destroyed in the fire that burned Kilcolman Castle. Marlowe's "Hero and Leander," praised by one critic as "perhaps the loveliest poem in couplets in the language," was continued by Chapman, with results that did not justify the attempt. Oliver Goldsmith in his series of mock epitaphs on contemporaries entitled "Retaliation," had half finished the sketch on Sir Joshua Reynolds when in the middle of a line he laid down his quill forever.

A brief essay entitled "The Great Unfinished" in J. C. Squire's *Life and Letters* points out that Virgil did not bring the *Æneid* to the conclusion he is believed to have desired. Byron's *Don Juan* leaves off "at a situation as teasing to the reader as it was certainly awkward for the characters; and his 'Childe Harold' was never completed by him, though there exists a French continuation by the versatile Lamartine. Keats' 'Hyperion,' his greatest poem, is no more than the torso of a Titan, and we lost something very great in the missing part of Shelley's 'Triumph of Life.' "

Ben Jonson's *The Sad Shepherd, or a Tale of Robin Hood* is also a fragment, first printed four years after the poet's death. Of Samuel Butler's *Hudibras* three parts appeared in the space of fifteen years, and more was intended, for it ends abruptly, hung in the air.

There is a presumption that Shakespeare's *Poems* never achieved the completion he would have wrought had the hidden plot of his life permitted. The intentions, like the frustrations, of this peerless depictor of human nature remain shrouded in inference and supposition.

Molière's renditions of *Lucretius* were cast into the fireplace in a passion when he learned his valet had used several leaves for curlpapers; and the widow of Sir Richard Burton burned his all but complete *Scented Garden* soon after her husband's death. Cowley in his *Maid of Aragon* and the poet Gray both left unfinished works. Wordsworth's *Excursion*, too, is incomplete.

A notable instance of afflatus flown is that of Coleridge with his "Kubla Khan," of which he had composed some three hundred lines in a dream. But only this fragment had been imperishably committed to paper when an inopportune visitor interrupted the trance-like transcription. When the intruder had gone, the poet found he had forgotten the rest.

Keats left his "Hyperion" incomplete because he deemed it too Miltonian in treatment, and he detested the imitative. Considering the brevity of his life span, it is not surprising that "King Stephen," "Cap and Bells," and the "Eve of Saint Mark" should also be fragments only.

Occasionally savants have knowingly undertaken a pretentious opus so formidable in scope they could not hope to finish it in a lifetime. Thus Sir Walter Raleigh's intended *History of the World*, to which he devoted all the years of his imprisonment in the Tower, brought the narrative, which began with the Creation, little further than the beginning of the

Christian era. It was to have been in three volumes, of which only the first appeared in 1614.

Buckle's grandiose scheme of a *History of Civilization* comes to mind. The three volumes that were published as the result of twenty years' research comprise only the introduction of the colossal work he had planned. When his health failed he sought a change of climate and died at Damascus, his last words lamenting, "My book, my book! I shall never finish my book!"

It is well known to admirers of Napoleon that in his youth he had an ambition to write. About 1789 he began a romance, possibly autobiographical, but only the first sheaf of folio pages in his closely written illegible hand survive. That it was composed before his twentieth year, perhaps begun when he was little more than sixteen, is the opinion of experts. Written when he was sixteen, a manuscript fragment of his unfinished *Clisson and Eugénie* sold for £2,300 ($6,440) in London in 1955. The hero was a young officer.

Calmet's long-since-unread *Antiquities Sacred and Profane*, which was rendered from the French into English in 1727 to edify the curates of Albion, was unfinished. Thomas Campbell, the passable poet, anonymously hacked two volumes of his *History of Our Own Times* in the 1840's, the second volume appearing after his death, and unterminated.

Though Charles Dodgson in his *alter ego* brought Alice safely back from Wonderland, his demise cut short three mathematical works, part one only of each having been published before Lewis Carroll bade adieu to a stranger world than any he had fancied through the Looking Glass of his imagination.

John Forster died as he was correcting the proof of the first volume of his life of Swift, for which he had collected abundant materials.

Macaulay when past middle life undertook his never completed *History of England*. In his forty-ninth year the first two volumes appeared, after unsparing research. The second two followed after the lapse of seven arduous years. In his diary, under a date in 1849, he outlined a plan of study and composition that would bring the work to finality "in the Autumn of 1853." But in October, 1856, he wrote: "God knows whether I shall ever finish this part. . . . I find it difficult to settle to my work. . . . The chief reason, I believe, is the great doubt I feel whether I shall live long enough to finish another volume." And so it proved, for death confirmed his forebodings.

Other histories have been well begun but sadly unended. Freeman's pretentious *Sicily* was one such. Four volumes appeared, the last posthumously; and his *Western Europe in the Fifth Century* was likewise lopped by the scythe. *Jewish Contributions to Civilization*, a work of pioneer scholarship by Joseph Jacobs, was in its early stages at the author's death and was printed subsequently in that form. Joseph Sabin's *Dictionary of Books Relating to America* remained in some twenty volumes (as far as the letter S) for several decades, until that doyen among Americanists, Wilberforce Eames, undertook the final editorial labors, in turn consummated by Robert W. G. Vail, the bibliographer.

The facets of a literary theme such as this are many. For instance, one might digress on the question of sequels written by other hands to books or plays in themselves complete. Many an author in the old days was subjected to virtual piracy by seeing unauthorized continuations published without redress. *Pilgrim's Progress, Don Quixote, Robinson Crusoe* were so treated. Richardson's *Pamela* was published in 1740. A bookseller commissioned a Grub Street writer to write a sequel; in self-defense Richardson himself wrote a continuation, but the interloper's *Pamela's Conduct in High Life* came out three months before Richardson's authentic *Second Part*. There was such an impudent sequel to Fielding's *Tom Jones*. Dickens was likewise a victim of the sequel writer. Under the title *The Pickwicks Abroad*, by G. W. M. Reynolds, twenty parts were published in 1839. Even *The Merchant of Venice* has its sequel by St. John Ervine.

In a consideration of unfinished books, one is tempted to cite those not even begun. One critic of yore in a cynical moment suggested that a revealing and cathartic story of mankind might be written under the title *A History of Human Imbecility*, embracing "the narrative of our

adventures since we mortals were first foolish enough to leave records."
Actually, in 1932, the public was given *A Short Introduction to the History of Human Stupidity* (in a mere 574 pages), by Walter B. Pitkin, a commendable inkling of this vast topic in respect to its brevity and rewarding reading.

Finally, in the chronicle of books lacking completion, one recalls with zest the tradition concerning a Chinese savant who began writing a prodigious romance at its conclusion, and throughout his lifetime wrote steadily toward the outset of the touching events—which he never reached. This may well be deemed unique among unfinished books!

How much more might be recited under this head. Many years ago in England was published an annotated bibliography of unended literary works, embracing some twenty-five hundred titles. The list begins with this first entry:

> Abbot (John), Iesus præfigured; or, A poëme of the holy name of Iesus. In five bookes. The first, and second booke. Pp. 110. Antwerp, 1623, 4°. No more published.

And ends with this last one:

> Zuriel, *pseud.* A series of lectures on the science of celestial philosophy . . . Part I, containing the fundamental principles. London, 1835, 8°. No more published.

The cruel truth is that scrutiny of the titles between this first and last brings conviction of no great loss to literature with regard to the incompletion of most of these works. Garnered from the catalogues, this listing is a register of miscellanea without regard to intrinsic merit (sometimes one regrets only the unended work of those who excel). Thus Mazzuchelli began *Gli Scrittori d'Italia*, but was enabled to finish only the first two letters of the alphabet.

It is a "melancholy muster," in the phrase of Vincent Starrett, that includes among half-told tales the unfulfilled fictions of Flaubert and Maupassant, of Balzac and Daudet, of Mark Twain and D. H. Lawrence, of Charlotte Brontë, Mary Webb, and Kate Douglas Wiggin—of all those who now know the end of the great story to be told only in the Hereafter.

For the most part we are content with the fragments of noted works that have come down to us. Luckily some are virtually complete. The soul is there though the perfection is halted. Seldom if ever can that first fine rapture of inspiration be captured by a substitute, or the form of creative artistry be fulfilled by another hand. The greater the work, in that degree is a broken ending preferable to a tinkered finis.

Several decades ago a monthly magazine in England launched a symposium with illustrations by various well-known artists seeking to picture the aspect in which the missing arms of the Venus de Milo might have been originally disposed. Some showed the classic figure gazing into a hand-mirror; others, arranging her hair or holding a fold of drapery. None, however, made us regret that the ancient statue comes to us armless!

CHILDREN'S BOOKS

IN 1640 Governor John Winthrop, in writing about a deranged young matron, explained that the loss of her reason "had been growing upon her divers years by occasion of giving herself wholly to reading and writing. . . . For if she had attended to her household affairs, and such things as belong to women, and not gone out of her way and calling to meddle in such things as are proper for men whose minds are stronger, she had kept her Wits. . . ."

Strange times! Until the close of the seventeenth century girls had little or no schooling, and in New England not until after the Revolution was there a free public school which girls might attend. To the end of the seventeenth century, in New England and Virginia, a majority of women's signatures on extant deeds and depositions were the marks that indicate illiteracy. Nor were the boys much better off, for then the three D's—Duty, Devotions, Deportment—were of more concern than the R's. In 1671, crusty Governor William Berkeley of Virginia wrote: "I thank God there are no free schools, nor printing; and I hope we shall not have them these hundred years. . . ."

Well past the year 1700 the reading regimen of little Puritans ran the gamut of hornbook, primer, psalter, Testament and Bible. American children of colonial days were made to read for piety, rather than diversion; early American children's books were doleful rather than delightful.

The infant scholar of two centuries or more back, having conned the hornbook (or its cardboard replica, the battledore), was given a *New-England Primer*, of which scores of editions were issued from about 1685 with varying sober content from rules of conduct to selections from Watts' *Divine Hymns*, and with such fine things as "Now I lay me down to sleep, I pray the Lord my soul to keep. . . ." The pervasive tone of these Primers was that of behavior and blessedness—or brimstone. Thus a 1749 imprint had an Alphabet for Youth which warned:

*F*oolishness is bound up in the Heart of a Child,
But the Rod of Correction shall drive it from him.

The Quakers from their first coming led the way in enlightened views. A Philadelphia Quaker, George Fox, proffered children his *Instructions for Right Spelling* as early as 1702. But the good Friend himself now and then nodded. Thus, in describing a comma he discloses that a "Comma is a little stop or breathing; as Behold O Lord"—but we note he failed to breathe after Behold!

More than a century later, in 1831, anonymous Mr. Stops evidenced early western culture with his *Punctuation Personified; or Pointing Made Easy*. Mr. Stops, with exclamation points for legs, parentheses for stomach, and other punctuated anatomy, is depicted telling little Robert and sister:

> *Ev'ry lady in this land*
> *Has twenty nails upon each hand*
> *Five and twenty on hands and feet*
> *And this is true without deceit.*
> But when the stops were placed aright,
> The real sense was brought to light.

Robert and sister are instructed by Mr. Stops concerning the period —an Important Person:

This fullfaced gentelman here shown,
To all my friends, no doubt, is known:
He always ends a perfect sentence,
As Crime is followed by Repentance.

In that sawbuck and rail-splitting era of the 1830's and 1840's when a cabin and a crib spelt domestic comfort for westering America, spelling-bees for the young came into vogue to compete with husking-bees and quilting-bees for the elders. In a quaint Vermont schoolbook of 1830, Peter Good's *Exercises, Designed to Assist Young Persons to Pronounce and Spell Correctly*, nearly all the words are misspelled, a rear index giving the correct spelling for the learner to consult and be set aright.

There also appeared in the 1830's, with colored embellishment, the unforgotten *Peter Piper's Practical Principles of Perfect Pronunciation*, with precocious puckerings from that day to this of the tongue-twisting peck of pickled peppers that is still being persistently picked by picayunes. The author: "prays Parents to Purchase this Playful Performance, Partly to Pay him for his Patience and Pains; Partly to Provide for the Printers and Publishers; but Principally to Prevent the Pernicious Prevalence of Perverse Pronunciation."

Various types of early books for children may be merely alluded to here, for the concern of these few pages is chiefly with the odd juvenile bookshelf, such as the so-called hieroglyphic Bibles of a century ago.

It is a curious fact that an "ABC Book" was possibly printed by Gutenberg before he printed the Bible. A single copy of this earliest known abecedarian, printed in English about 1538 in swart Gothic type, is located in the library of Cambridge University.

The hornbook was really not a book at all, but a small board plaque shaped like a hand-mirror on which a card bearing the alphabet, the Lord's Prayer, and the like, was tacked and then covered with a transparent sheet of horn. Sometimes the handle had a hole for a cord. Sprats of the gentry often had silver or ivory or needlework specimens. One of silver, dated 1682, was sold at auction in London in 1929 for

£475. In teaching the alphabet, hornbooks were used in lieu of and long prior to schoolbooks. In the early eighteenth century the colony of Georgia ordered two hundred, at a few pence each, from abroad.

One of the rarest of pietistic minims for tots is called *Agnus Dei* (Lamb of God) by John Weever, with the earliest edition dated 1601. Not much larger than a postage stamp and with not many pages, the only extant copy of this precious bijou is valued in the thousands. It was long in the possession of the late Dr. Rosenbach, who gave his extensive collection of early American children's books to the public library of his home city. Dr. Rosenbach similarly treasured the only known copy of the 1606 edition of this English tractate, as well as a black letter "Tom Thumb" of 1630 that is smaller than the palm of a child old enough to read it.

As early as 1614 John Taylor, a Thames waterman, made a versified version of Bible passages to which he gave the clumsy Latin title, *Verbum Sempiternum*, but which became "Thumb Bible" in the vernacular. A pudgy volume which a child could put in a diminutive pocket, it appeared in many editions during the following two centuries. Only one example of the original 1614 edition of this extinct variety of juvenile literature survives, treasured by the Library of Aberdeen University. Of Thumb-Bible printings between 1614 and 1693, Wilbur Macey Stone listed seventeen known extant copies, mostly imperfect.

In 1727 Wilkin in London issued a miniature Bible, really a prose synopsis, intended for old as well as young, which was reprinted in later editions. But the first "Children's Bible" (1763) to be printed in America is extant in only one copy.

There were also diminutive Bibles which were really excerpts or paraphrases of Biblical passages. Several editions of these midget volumes were less than two inches tall. One of them was called *The History of the Bible, Compiled for the Use of the Emperor of Lilliputia, Lilliput, 1775* (Lilliput was London in such juvenilia).

One moral miniature bore the odd title *A Wedding Ring Fit for the Finger; or the Salve of Divinity on the Sore of Humanity*. Written by

William Secker, an English cleric and published in Boston in 1705, only one perfect copy is known of this first miniature book published in America.

It was preceded by another quaint title: *Spiritual Milk for Boston Babes: Drawn out of the Breast of Both Testaments.* No copies are extant of the earliest edition of this first book written and printed in America for children. Curdled by John Cotton, grandfather of Cotton Mather, it may have been first printed by Stephen Day at Cambridge about 1646. Only one copy of the Boston edition of 1684 is known. This peculiar suckling juvenile with its Scriptural nipple was popular, although its purpose was to teach the little ones to die with unction. It has been said: "The ecstasy over the departure of a pure young child is one of the most remarkable manifestations of the Puritan spirit." This was exemplified by the Rev. James Janeway in his *A Token for Children, being an Exact Account of the Conversion, Holy and Exemplary Lives and Joyous Deaths of Several Young Children* (Philadelphia, 1749). Dowered on childhood in England, the good sale abroad led Benjamin Franklin to reprint the Janeway book. To the original English edition Cotton Mather added *Token for the Children of New England*, anent joyous dirges in his diocese.

Under the spell of the early puritanical clergy, children were brands to be plucked from the burning. The childish mind was regaled with sentiments such as this:

> *My days will quickly end, and I must lie*
> *Broyling in flames to all Eternity.*

Or this tender token from a little book published in Boston in 1714:

> Oh, Children of New England, Poor Hearts You are
> going to hell, indeed: But will it not be a dreadful thing to
> go to hell from New England?

Let it not be thought these hell or heaven evocations were the exception and not the rule. They persisted for more than a century.

There was *A Legacy for Children, Being Some of the Last Expressions and Dying Sayings of Hannah Hill . . . Aged Eleven and near Three Months* (Philadelphia, 1717), and *Christian Character Exemplified, in the Life of Adeline Marble, Corresponding Secretary of the Female Juvenile Mite Society, of New Haven; Who Died May the 3d, 1822* (New Haven, 1822). There was George Headley's *A Memorial for Children, Being an Authentic Account of the Conversion, Experience, and Happy Deaths of Eighteen Children* (New Haven, 1806). Even American Indian small-fry were fed missionary renditions such as the Choctaw version of *Triumphant Deaths of Pious Children* (Boston, 1835).

During all this span of years Isaac Watts' pious poems for children, embraced in his *Divine Songs,* were conned by young and old. First published in 1715, there were more than six hundred English and American editions, totaling possibly seven million copies. But their vogue passed, and Watts' familiar "How doth the little busy bee" was parodied by Lewis Carroll in "How doth the little crocodile."

If the period to about 1800 was permeated with moralistic tone that persisted in subsequent *Cautionary Verses,* there was, nevertheless, occasional juvenile rejoicing at less somber reading, thanks to John Newberry of London, who in 1744 began publishing the gay little books for boys and girls which Franklin in Philadelphia and Hugh Gaines in New York imported. Gaines gave American children an abridged *Robinson Crusoe* in 1774, of which only one copy survives; and by 1837 *Sindbad the Sailor* had arrived on one of his surprising voyages. By the latter year there had been thirteen American curtailed editions of the Defoe classic, "canonized by childhood delight." With the first of the young folks' magazines, the *Juvenile Olio* (1802), and its successors, to *The Children's Magazine* (1829), the new era had begun.

Yet the sad note of young death was not altogether over. For Julia A. Moore, the "Sweet Singer of Michigan," was still to perpetrate her atrocious verses. Her second book, *A Few Choice Words to the Public, with New and Original Poems* (Grand Rapids, 1878), was every bit as horrendous as her first. Therein we may read the lament on Little Libbie and learn that

> *While eating dinner, this dear little child*
> *Was choked on a piece of beef.*

Still another variety of early children's books, in addition to catechisms, were certain of those curious little screeds called chapbooks, sold by itinerant book agents called chapmen. Most of these specimens were intended for adults, but not all, and many are now exceedingly scarce.

John Mein, of Boston, came to America in 1764 and was the foremost American publisher until he returned to England in 1769 because of his political views. Mein reprinted four of the Newbery chapbooks so popular in Britain. One, *The Renowned History of Giles Gingerbroad*, told how young Giles learned to read so that he might grow up to have a fine coach like Sir Toby Wilson, who was once a poor man's son. Like other Newbery titles it was widely sold, and was pirated or imported by other American publishers. Yet of Giles, few of the copies printed at Newport in 1771 or at Worcester in 1787 are extant.

In contrast to most present-day books for young children which make a virtue of their size, the juveniles of an elder day were almost always small, and in the case of miniature books so tiny the French called them *microbes du livre*. Hieroglyphic Bibles were relatively large, though they seldom exceeded five inches in height. It was early recognized that, to the childish mind, piety could be conveyed through pictures. Hence, it was an inspiration to devise the Hieroglyphic Bibles, which were really mere excerpts of selected texts interspersed with spot illustrations. In a sense they were puzzle-books, so that the childish mind was inveigled to this devout reading.

The earliest Old World picture-book for children, designated *Orbis Pictus*, was written by Comenius in 1658 in German and Latin, and translated the next year into English as *The Visible World Displayed*. Under each picture therein was a little description in German and Latin

in parallel columns. Translated into various languages, it was so popular
that twelve English editions had been published by 1777. The success of
this little work led to the compilation of a somewhat similar Latin-
English schoolbook entitled *Youth's Visible Bible*, written by Elisha
Coles. It was, according to its title page, "An alphabetical collection
from the whole Bible of such General Heads as were judged most capable
of Hieroglyphics." Moreover, childish readers are told on the title page:
"You shall make Latin Whether you Will or No." The copperplates are
divided into squares, in each of which is an image of some beast, bird,
tree, or the like.

In 1780 an allied picture-book for children made its appearance in
England under the title, *A Curious Hieroglyphic Bible*. Printed and sold
by the bookseller T. Hodgson, it enjoyed at least twenty editions to the
year 1812, besides four unauthorized reprints published at Dublin.
During the thirty years following, similar Hieroglyphic Bibles were
issued by different printers or booksellers throughout Britain. Most of
these, sewed in paper covers, were literally thumbed out of existence. The
earliest of the brood contained woodcuts by the famous Bewick. Its final
comforting statement on the last page reads: "They are cast into Hell,
there to be tormented with the devil and his angels."

By the time the so-called 25th edition in English appeared, foisted
on the public as a replica of Hodgson's book but in reality having
nothing of the original work except the title page, there was a surfeit of
this curious picture puzzle known as the rebus, by which a term or name
is phonetically pictured. Thus, for the pronoun "I" there is a figure of
an eye; for "all" a shoemaker's awl; for the verb "arose" the letter A and
the figure of a rose; for "not" a ribbon tied into a bow-knot.

Such was the havoc wrought on the first Hieroglyphic edition by
childish hands that the British Museum does not possess a copy, and
holds its specimen of the second edition, 1784, as a prime rarity. No
perfect copies are known of the first five editions, up to 1787. Bassam's
London edition of 1796 is the thirteenth.

Naturally the Hieroglyphic Bibles subsequently appeared in various

European languages, but the last recorded English one was printed at London in 1863, entitled *One Hundred Hieroglyphic Bible Readings for the Young*. In America the earliest of this variety of youthful reading was printed by Isaiah Thomas at Worcester in 1788. Another well-known edition was published at Charleston, Massachusetts, in 1820. Apparently the last American reprint is dated 1857, "with nearly 500 cuts," though there may have been subsequent editions.

Some of the crude pictures in the range of Hieroglyphic Bibles are quite mirth-provoking, as the one showing the prodigal son's return, the father embracing a mere whippet such as the reader is supposed to be; or Jonah escaping from the yawning mouth of the whale while the clipper ship is still in sight; or one of the Wise Men of the East wearing a hat suspiciously like a derby. One of the risible rebuses is the outline of a hand for the conjunction "and"—a Cockney slip! Also, in one of these little volumes, Biblical shepherds with their crooks and flocks are pictured in the raiment of the period when the book was published. But probably the children noted no incongruity.

Isaiah Thomas began to print children's books in 1785. His first title was *The Beauty and the Monster*, from the French of the Countess de Genlis. The following year appeared the first American *Mother Goose*. His publications for the moppets of that generation varied in size and retailed at from four cents to twenty. In 1787 nineteen titles appeared with his imprint. His juvenile list comprised in all about sixty-six titles in 119 editions.

Early editions of *Little Goody Two-Shoes*, attributed to Oliver Goldsmith, are extremely rare. Not more than three or four copies of the first four editions of this nursery classic appear to be known, even in imperfect state. No copy of the first or second London edition of 1765 has survived, and only one, apparently, of the third. Even a fifth edition specimen is a prize. The first American edition was printed by Hugh Gaine of New York in 1775. Of this imprint four copies are extant, three imperfect, and the fourth worm-holed and soiled but otherwise sound.

In the formative years of the struggling young Republic the first faint traces of Americanism found their way into children's books. These emendations varied from mere change of place names to patriotic touches; but the Revolution was too close for the heroic proportions of Bunker Hill or Valley Forge or the stature of the Founding Fathers to be limned as they are now.

No perfect copy of the first American imprint of *Mother Goose's Melody* is known; but in the second edition, in two extant copies, "Se saw, sacaradown, Which is the way to London town" becomes "Boston town."

Even the *New England Primer*, which in 1749 carried the couplet:

> *Whales in the Sea*
> *God's voice obey.*

in 1800 had substituted:

> *By Washington*
> *Great deeds were done.*

The first American printing of *The History of Little Goody Two-Shoes* was content to follow the British original, but Peter Brynberg of Wilmington in his 1796 edition, quaintly bound in the figured wallpaper style that was his innovation, ends the tale with this note: "Such is the state of things in Britain. *Americans* prize your liberty, guard over your rights and be happy."

There was even the beginning of pictorial patriotism in schoolbooks, with the first American woodcuts in which Independence Hall supplanted Parliament, the Indian tomahawk replaced the pike, and the gathering of tobacco was depicted in preference to primroses. The American spirit vigorously manifested itself in elementary schoolbooks with Noah Webster's blue-backed *Speller* (1783), buttressed by a *Grammar* (1784), and a *Reader* (1785). The compiler of this phenomenally popular and constantly reprinted trio injected perfervid patriotism, contended for American pronunciation and American spelling to grace a native literature, and with his first *Dictionary* in 1806 not only standardized speech and writing but rendered American education nationalistic.

The next generation had its Americanism cemented with McGuffey's

Readers (1836–1844), which in text and pictures were native to the core and imbued with frontier appeal, molding character by a presentation that was captivating. For wellnigh a century the Webster *Spellers* and the McGuffey *Readers* were the foundations of primary education in America, and more than a hundred million copies of each were the first approach to literacy by young Americans.

Those who recall *Slovenly Peter* may have forgotten it was a rendition from the German *Struwwelpeter* of Dr. Hoffman-Donner, who wrote it in 1834 and drew whimsical crayon pictures for his young offspring with no thought that it would appear in print, much less that it would enjoy numerous editions (without reward to him) in English. Only two copies are known of the first English edition, which appeared at Leipsic in 1848. The only known copy of the first American edition of 1849 was found in September, 1954.

So, too, and even rarer in good condition is the first English edition of *The Swiss Family Robinson* by David Wyss. In 1935 a worn 1814 copy of the first part of the thrilling but moral adventures of the family brought $1,100 at book auction. It was bound in "contemporary sheep." But the following year an exemplar of both parts in original boards sold for $2,350 under the hammer.

This work, one of the most widely read and appreciated juveniles of the nineteenth century, if not also the twentieth, was first published in German at Zurich in 1812–1813. The author was a Swiss military chaplain, who founded his story on the reported discovery of a Swiss clergyman who had been shipwrecked on an island of New Guinea. Appearing in English as *The Family Robinson Crusoe*, the narrative came to be more generally known as *The Swiss Family Robinson*. It is the journal of a father cast away with his wife and children on an uninhabited island. The 1814 edition exists in two forms. The original plan was probably to publish the entire translation in two volumes, but when the rendition of the second part was delayed (the second part was not published in English until 1816), the first part was split into two volumes. The original manuscript with illustrations by the author's son, Johann, is in the possession of a descendant in Berne.

From Peter Piper to Newell's *Hole Book* there have been quaint
conceits of format and contents. In recent years there has been *Telltime
the Rabbit,* an octagonal little item having a dial with movable hands.
Likewise the Book Piano with a diminutive keyboard and eighteen Mother
Goose tunes, with notes, verse, and playing chart. There was the Jingle
Bell book of a decade ago, with six two-tone bells that start a merry
medley at the slightest touch. The three-dimensional jumpups fascinate
as each page is turned. The squeekum book of 1940 was important: with
colored illustrations of farmyard animals; as the pages are pressed by
means of a simple device concealed between the book's pages, the cow says
"Moo," the sheep "Baa," the kitten "Meow."

But collectors of children's books revert to an earlier curiosity that
appears for sale in a dealer's catalogue perhaps once in a decade.
Published in London about 1860, *The Speaking Picture Book: With
Characteristical Voices,* has nine chromo lithographs of birds and animals,
with a voice for each. Since the sounds are operated by strings with bone
grips which the child gently pulls, a perfect example is hardly to be
hoped for.

This recalls *The Musical Geography,* by Miss Sarah M. Lyon of
Troy, which was accouched in that city in 1848. It arrays the rivers,
mountains, lakes, cities, and other features of the globe in rhyme to be
chanted as a mnemonic aid—"in a manner so as to be speedily learned and
long remembered."

The author of this novelty of a century ago is unlikely to have
known of a precedent volume. One of the many rarities in the John
Carter Brown Library at Providence is a first edition of the versified
cosmography of John Honter, dated 1542 and several times republished
thereafter.

The first American geography came after the Revolution in 1784.
Jedidiah Morse called his work *Geography Made Easy,* and its
popularity led to enlargement five years later. But as Alice Morse Earle
says, "It had a mean little map of the United States, only a few inches
square." Stilted dialogues for birchrod teacher and priggish pupil
consumed many pages. The child is made to respond to lessons thus:

> I am very thankful, sir, for your entertaining
> instruction, and I shall never forget what you have been
> telling me.
>
> I long, sir, for tomorrow to come that I may hear more
> of your information.

Nineteen editions of *Geography Made Easy* were printed by Isaiah Thomas, and after 1790 almost as many more of Morse's *American Geography* and *American Universal Geography*, with the compiler receiving 5 per cent of the profits.

Few American children's rhymes over a century old have endured in popularity. Other than Sarah J. Hale's "Mary had a little lamb" and Clement C. Moore's "The Night Before Christmas" such verse for young readers is mostly forgotten. Indeed, all American children's books prior to Hawthorne's *Wonder-Book for Girls and Boys* of 1852 are rather in the nature of collector's items, many at prohibitive prices.

Only six recorded copies are extant of the volume in which "Mary had a little lamb" first appeared. One of these copies, in original printed wrappers, of Mrs. Hale's *Poems for Our Children: Written to inculcate Moral Truth and Virtuous Sentiments* (Boston, 1830) sold for $725 at the dispersal of the Frank J. Hogan library in 1945. The Rev. Clement Moore's "Visit from St. Nicholas," which he esteemed less than his neglected compilation of a Hebrew grammar, first appeared in book form in 1837 in an anthology, *The New-York Book of Poetry*, and then in 1844 in a volume of Moore's *Poems*.

Fifteen years before the *Wonder-Book*, Hawthorne and his sister had wrought, as anonymous hackwork, *Peter Parley's Universal History*, which proved unexpectedly popular and a first edition of which is now a prime rarity. Hawthorne gained confidence with his "Grandfather's Chair," "Liberty Tree," and other tales for the young, and then, before the "elegant melancholy" of his later days, transmuted the classical fables of antiquity into his *Wonder-Book*, followed by *Tanglewood Tales*. The first of this twain was written in one spell of six weeks in the summer of 1852. Concerning the linked titles his biographer, George E. Woodberry, exclaims "nor are there any children's books so dipped in morning dews."

Overseas two score years before, Charles and Mary Lamb, despite the blight that harassed their lives, had written the *Tales from Shakespeare*. The greater number were Mary's; the more robust his. He exulted at the sixty guineas he was to receive for this childhood enchantment, but the brother and sister received little or nothing for the first American edition of *Poetry for Children* in 1812 or for the *Tales* in 1813.

Illustrations in American toy books were crude and smudgy (with faces looking like so many cranberries) before Alexander Anderson, born the year of the Boston Tea Party, began to make his adept woodcuts for several publishers of juveniles from 1805 onward. In earlier miniature books the same primitive cuts were used over and over with little reference to the text.

Thus, *The History of the Holy Jesus* (Boston, 1749) picturing the "Wise Men Come from the East" displays a trio of Puritans gazing through a spyglass at a comet. Another cut in this curiosity depicts Jesus teaching the multitude in the vesture of a Puritan divine speaking from a pulpit before which stand three Puritan men on one side and three Salem-garbed women on the other. Many times reprinted, the earlier editions of this rarity in rhyme show the soldiers of Herod armed with guns and displaying the Union Jack.

Nearly half a century later came *The History of America* (Philadelphia, 1795), the first little work of its kind, abridged for American children from a larger retrospect of that year. Pervaded by the new spirit of the stripling Republic, this toy tome, 2½" by 4", portrayed discoverers, noted figures, and governors with crude woodcuts interspersing the text. These portrayals were much alike except that some notables wore a tricorn hat sporting a cockade, while others gazed stonily from beneath a braided periwig. Americus Vespucius and Governor John Sullivan of New Hampshire appear to be identical twins! Christopher Columbus in continental regalia, and decked in a tricorn, closely resembles Patrick Henry, Governor Samuel Adams, and several other worthies. Washington, still living, is neglected in the text but portrayed in a periwig, with more chin than brow, an illustration that would have served as well for Paul Revere or Yankee Doodle.

It was Weems's little *Life of Washington* that exalted the Father of His Country in 1800, with eighty-four subsequent editions to 1927. However, Parson Weems's fifth edition of 1806 was the first to include the hatchet and cherry tree story. In one of the later New England Primers, a century after the presumed first, there is a libellous crude woodcut of Washington, as a framed bust, which so far as likeness is concerned could have been captioned Bluebeard or John Bunyan. So, too, in a German edition of Weems's chapbook life of the first President, printed in Maryland in 1809, the frontispiece might just as well be Sindbad or St. Memin.

The one memorable illustration, aside from the later engravings of Anderson, Doolittle, and Revere, that became familiar to American children and lingered in their minds was of British origin. It depicted Sir Walter Raleigh having his pipe quenched by a basin of water thrown at the presumed blaze by his serving man, who thought the master was afire. It appears as a copperplate in William Darton's *Little Truths Better Than Great Fables* (Philadelphia, 1800).

From these crude pictorial beginnings, children's books here and abroad have been graced by consummate artistry in the procession of the years: Abbey, Artzybasheff, Bewick, Blake, Caldecott, Cattermole, Crane, Cruikshank, Dulac, Frost, Greenaway, and so through the alphabet, not forgetting Howard Pyle, Arthur Rackham, and John Tenniel.

If the image of Sir Walter Raleigh's smoke-rings being drenched by an alarmed valet was unforgettable to young readers, no less vivid in their minds was the pipe-smoking terrier Tray, pictured in *Old Mother Hubbard and Her Dog*, which reached these shores after 1810. And though the cupboard is still bare, it is worthwhile recording that the manuscript and original illustrations of this immortal nursery rhyme, together with one of few known copies of the first printing (London, 1805), sold for $3,250 at a New York book-auction in 1945.

The authoress was Sarah Catherine Martin, who wrote the Mother
Hubbard verses in 1804 at the home of her father, Sir Henry Martin,
Bart., in Devon, where Mother Hubbard is believed to have been the
housekeeper at that time. The original manuscript was written in a small
notebook bound in marbled wrappers. With it were Miss Martin's fifteen
drawings in pencil and pen-and-ink wash. Verses and sketches had
disappeared for more than a century and were presumed lost. In 1936
these were discovered by Miss Mary E. A. May, great-great-niece of the
authoress, among a clutter of old family pictures and letters long
untouched in a chest.

Soon after the notebook and drawings came to light they were
exhibited by the Bodleian Library at Oxford. Miss May declined to part
with the manuscript and the Oxford University Press made a facsimile
illustrated reproduction in collotype of a thousand copies; the first
edition is so rare that even the British Museum does not possess a copy.
The earliest American imprints are also unprocurable, with subsequent
editions such as ᵗhat of Cooperstown, 1839, exceedingly scarce. Upon the
return of the manuscript by Oxford University to Miss May she
consistently refused offers for its purchase. However, when German
bombers threatened to destroy so much that Britain held dear, she agreed
to part with verses and sketches provided they be sold to safety in
America. The proceeds are believed to have been devoted by Miss May to
British war relief.

Over a span of thirty-seven years from 1835 the Danish poet and
fabulist, Hans Christian Andersen, wrote and published five volumes of
fairy tales, but it was not until 1870 that an authorized American edition
appeared. Yet the Brothers Grimm, his virtual contemporaries, were
introduced to English readers a decade after the first Berlin appearance
of their *Kinder-und Haus-Märchen*. A flawless copy of the two-volume
first edition of Jacob and Wilhelm Grimm's *German Popular Stories*
(London, 1823–1826), as issued with illustrations by George Cruikshank
and all the required "points," sold at a New York auction in 1919 for
$1,725.

The only known manuscript of the *Märchen*, consisting of forty-seven stories and fragments, was brought to New York in 1953 by the Father Abbot of the Cistercian Monastery at Oelenberg in Alsace-Lorraine, in order to raise money to repair the monastery, bombed during World War II. The manuscript on 113 closely written sheets had been given to the order in the 1840's. In 1954 it was bought from an American dealer, with whom it had been left for sale, by Dr. Martin Bodmer, a banker of Geneva, Switzerland, who has the finest privately owned rare book and manuscript collection in present-day Europe. The price paid was approximately twenty-five thousand dollars. In this original manuscript version are "Snow White and the Seven Dwarfs," "The Golden Goose," "The Sleeping Beauty" and those other tales now so intrinsic to childhood literature.

All values in juvenilia are dwarfed by the manuscript of *Alice's Adventures Underground*, subsequently published as *Alice's Adventures in Wonderland*. When first sold at auction in London in 1928 it brought £15,400. Resold in New York in 1946, it was relinquished by the buyer in 1948 and presented to the British Museum as a gift from the American people, whose voluntary contributions equalled the purchase price of fifty thousand dollars. A copy of the printed first edition (London, 1865), with original pencil drawings by Sir John Tenniel and autograph emendations of the author, sold for twenty-three thousand dollars at the dispersal of the Eldridge R. Johnson collection in 1946.

"Cinderella," "Little Red Riding-Hood," "Sleeping Beauty," and those other enchanting tales which Charles Perrault gathered from oral folklore in 1697 and entitled *Les Contes de ma Mère l'Oye* did not appear with American imprint as *Tales of Mother Goose* for almost a century, although John Newbery in London had published a translation about 1760. From Perrault to Hans Christian Andersen, from Goldsmith to Lewis Carroll, the childhood of America had reveled in Jacks and Jills, giants and blackamoors, goblins and goops, fairies and genii, harlequins and Simple Simons. From Jack and the Beanstalk to Alice in Wonderland, from Aladdin to Zobeide, there was relief from the earlier dread-and-damnation fodder and from the vapid cautionary school of Mrs. Anna Barbauld and her sedate sister moralists. And American youngsters made reading chums from Peter Parley to Penrod, with Huckleberry Finn and Tom Sawyer supreme as the greatest boys in American fiction.

Strangely enough, four of the most widely read of all volumes on the shelves were not intended by their authors as juvenile literature. *Pilgrim's Progress* which held generations of young readers spellbound, *Robinson Crusoe, Gulliver's Travels,* and *Munchausen* were not originally written for youngsters, but their narratives have captured the imagination of centuries of childhood in all climes.

From Weems to Webster marked an era. The appearance of *Alice in Wonderland* abroad and *Wonder-Tales* over here ushered in the deluge of printed color and confection. The variations seem never to be exhausted. A few years ago Margaret Wise Brown was declared to be a child's best seller. This American lady used three pseudonyms and in 1947 had written fifty-three books, forty-seven then in print and sold by seven different publishers. The *Little Fur Family* by this authoress is a small volume bound in New Zealand rabbit fur. There was a limited edition of two copies each in mink. Her *Cottontails,* designed for younger children, was a tactile book, meant to be handled rather than read: the appletree had red-glass buttons, the bunny had a tuft of cotton for a tail, and a bell on the cat's collar really tinkled.

An anecdote was related in *While Rome Burns* by Alexander Woollcott concerning an American woman visiting Paris, who saw a juvenile on a book-stall and desired to read it again as in her childhood. Picking it up she found that the name inscribed in it was her own, written many years before in her own childish scrawl. Which leads to the observation that two kinds of people are reliably pleasant folks: those who smoke pipes and those who collect juvenilia. As for those who do both, they might well be chosen for a companionable rendezvous in the hereafter.

THE BOUQUET OF OLD BOOKS

CONCERNING THE ENGAGING THEME of the subtle aroma given
forth by books singly or in great congregation, as well as those
artificially scented to enhance their appeal, virtually nothing beyond the
most trifling allusions has been written.

The East has long stressed the delights of scent, and as with so
much else, the Western world might well take tutelage from the older
Orient. The pleasant, faint aroma of sandalwood is occasionally
associated by the Japanese with their libraries; more frequently in their
books one finds the scent of musk. When it is not in use it is customary to
burn high-grade incense in the study to impart a favorite allure to the
room's books and prints. This is also done as a mark of honor before the
expected visit of a guest, in which case the incense used is of a kind
thought likely to please the visitor. In South China it is customary to
place boxes of camphorwood or insecticides of various odors near books to
keep them from being destroyed.

Some years ago a literary journal carried a paragraph stating that
in the Bodleian was preserved a manuscript copy of the poems of Jâmi
four centuries old and still fragrant with attar of roses. Although inquiry
brought no confirmation, the following pertinent statement was
vouchsafed:

The only scented book known to the writer is one which
came from Monte Cassino, and which, in transit, had been
partly saturated with some essential oil. There are, however,
distinctive perfumes in various parts of the Library. No one
can fail to note the rather earthy smell of Diocesan Records
in the Gough Room, the aromatic scent of russia-bound
books in the Mason Room, and the mellow odour emanating
from the library of Francis Douce. The importance of
perfume as an essential amenity of a library was not
overlooked by our Founder, who, when the Library was to be
visited by James I, gave orders that the floor should be
rubbed with rosemary, 'for a stronger scent I should not
like.' At the Tercentenary in 1902 no thought was given to
such a detail, and the *Times* correspondent specially
mentioned the reek of the linseed oil which had been used to
clean and freshen the ancient woodwork.

If you are familiar with a circulating library located in congested
city precincts where ventilation is none too good, you must have noticed
the somewhat fetid odor that is transferred to these popular books from
their visits in many homes. But the true essence of this neglected topic of
book odors is encountered in those sequestered collections with which the
quiet custodians become so intimate. Thus Philip Hofer of the Harvard
Houghton Library, who formerly had in charge the sumptuous Spencer
collection at the New York Public Library, confesses he might be able to
detect quite a few of the rarities by smell alone, for there are peculiar
identities to books in this respect.

Do you doubt that Esquemeling's buccaneer tales smell of pirates by
some esoteric conveyance of their rum-soaked corsair emanation, and that
many a tome is pungent with associations of place and time as well as in
its physical anatomy?

Hazlitt in his essay "On Reading New Books" remarks the delight
he felt "to inhale the fragrancy of the scarcely dried paper," and many
others have commented on the bouquet of old books. A single volume has,

for the susceptible, its olfactory individuality; and libraries differ from one another in what Southey called the "atmospheric odour of antiquity." Eugene Field in his *Love Affairs of a Bibliomaniac* exclaims: "Sweeter than thy unguents and cosmetics and Sabean perfumes is the smell of those old books of mine." Indeed, to the confirmed bookman the fragrances of books are as various as the sense of delight that runs its gamut in perceiving the beauties of their binding. The odor of leather, even the mustiness of old paper, pleases the inveterate bookman; and he who likes to haunt those booksellers' shops where shelves range with mellowed volumes well knows the gratified whiff with which he enters the portals and lingers to breathe in the allure of faint levant amid the aromatic medley of books touched by time. George Gissing tells us he knew every one of his books by its scent, and Charles Lamb spoke of inhaling learning as he roamed about the Bodleian.

As Holbrook Jackson all too briefly points out, there is another sense also in which smell pertains to books: that conveyed by the purport of their contents rather than by their physical selves. Thus Lafcadio Hearn declares that reading Arnold's *Light of Asia* veritably "perfumed his mind as with the incense of a strangely new and beautiful worship." There are volumes that by their bigotries and hellish poison are a foulness in the nostrils. If one can actually smell the spick ship in a clipper logbook that was long at sea, one can be no less aware of the offense that clings to an old New England tract, credulous of witchcraft. There is the antimacassar staleness of the window-closed drawingroom pervading the pages of the Brontë sisters, the sickly cloy of gardenia in the effusions of Verlaine, the reek of blood in the memoirs of headsman Sanson of the guillotine, the tang of brine in a Tomlinson sea yarn, the odor of sanctity hallowing a missal.

Naturally, this elusive matter of scent has led to somewhat futile efforts to give books a restorative aroma. The feeling collector whose *Lavender and Old Lace* has a sentimental association in that it belonged to his mother may be pardoned for regarding with tenderness the tiny packet of that shrub pressed between the covers. Perfumed copies of *The*

Technique of the Love Affair, which a temporarily esthetic publisher issued a few years back, were saturated with *Orchidée Bleu* essence. This recalls in preciosity the French volume of verse with tinted pages and appropriate hues of ink—a nature poem on apple-green paper, a love lyric on sanguine or tender rose-pink, a cheerful carol on sky-blue leaves. Certainly a volume on the conquest of the affections might well be atomized with *Rêve d'Amour* or *Une Nuit de Cléopâtre*.

The time may come when a whole series of volumes will be issued variously aromatic. As for the old books, most carry their own redolence and need no enhancement; others, benighted or wicked, could not be made pleasant by all the perfumes of Araby. Such are mephitic beyond all salvation.

Harking back to the days of Queen Elizabeth we find a curious custom in bookbinding which prevailed during her period. In *Queen Elizabeth's Progresses* we read: "After one or two removes, she reached Audley End on the twenty-sixth of July, where by arrangement a deputation from the University of Cambridge waited on her. They had previously announced to Lord Burghley, their chancellor, their desire of doing so, wishing to hold a deputation before her and to present her with a book; to which he assented, but added, 'that they must have regard that the book do not savour of spyke, which commonly bookbinders did seek to add to make their books savour well; for that Her Majesty could not abide such a strong scent.' "

A later commentator observes: "Her Majesty may well have disliked the smell of spyke, for in odour it is but little better than turpentine. There is much paste used in bookbinding and it was a common practice to put into it a few drops of the otto of spike; the best thing, however, would be otto of birchbark, as this fragrance resembles Russia leather."

And yet perfumes were never richer, more costly, nor more delicate than in the reign of Elizabeth. There is ample evidence that she had rather a penchant for perfumery, for she found much pleasure when first presented with perfumed gloves, which were brought into England by the Earl of Oxford, Edward de Vere, and which were known as "sweet gloves." Indeed, many receipts were devised for the perfuming of gloves.

A proper disquisition on the bibliophile's sensibility to the scents of books remains to be written. Lafcadio Hearn, who once wrote a now scarce little treatise on perfume, lamented the fact that the olfactory sense of human beings had been allowed to diminish. But the booklover still enjoys the esoteric delights of bookish inhalation.

Bookbinders of distinction have sought to eliminate from the processes of their craft unwanted essences such as those "Her Majesty could not abide." The exquisite lacquered bindings of the East subdue the acid; and towards the close of the eighteenth century there existed in Paris a bookbindery using *vernis sans odeur,* otherwise *Vernis Martin.*

As certain words have a spell and potency beyond their rigid meaning and are woven into sequences of imperishable appeal, so have certain books attributes other than their grosser form and context, and the shelves of a fine library more than a mere range of leather and print. The sense of smell, most ethereal of the five-fold gifts, as the ancients held, has a delectation all its own in any assemblage of fine books. In the pleasant aisles of a venerable library one "breathes the fragrance of aging leather, a musty incense proper to an ancient ritual." One is aware of the waft of vellum, faint as the almond flavor in certain Calabrian wine, and of russia, sending from its scented pores the birchbark infusion in which it was steeped.

Perfume is the harbinger of the starry destiny of man—the poets have always held it so. Read, in Andrew Bradley's *A Miscellany* (London, 1929), the essay on "Odours and Flowers in the Poetry of Shelley." Of reclining Cleopatra in her barge of state, Shakespeare writes:

> *Purple the sails, and so perfumed that*
> *The winds were love-sick with them. . . .*

In *Marius, the Epicurean,* Pater tells how Marius and Flavian read a scroll perfumed with oil of sandalwood. Ancient scrolls were sometimes protected against injury from insects by being steeped in cedar oil, which, however, marred their whiteness with a yellowish tinge. A group of such rolls were placed together in a wooden box or canister (in Egypt jars were used), especially when they represented the several volumes of a larger work.

Sixty miles from Cairo, in the Province of Fayum, some fellaheen or peasants working in a field more than a century ago dug up an earthenware pot containing about fifty rolls of papyri. This was before archeology made such finds valuable, and, we are told, "all the rolls save one were burnt by the fellaheen for the sake of the aromatic smell they gave out when ignited."

The Orient affords other such literary associations with scent. Jametel speaks of Buddhist liturgies in boxes of perfumed woods. In the annals of Chinese literature the poems and prose of Han Yü have been esteemed for more than a thousand years; indeed, his works were so revered by his friend and contemporary, Liu Tsung-yüan, that the latter never ventured to open them "without first washing his hands in rose-water."

There is a metaphysic to this matter; it may well be that an occult aura pervades certain tomes that enshrine the quintessence of man's glory; or that a malific and impalpable miasma clings to those base and diabolic treatises and tracts that have denigrated the spirit of humans. But this is apart from the physical attributes of those curious spoors of the soul men call books.

Only the initiated can appreciate how the pervasive fragrances of libraries differ in symphonies of smell. The natural scent of books is as intrinsic a quality as the mellow and contemplative serenity that haunts a proper library. As there are individuals who are color-blind or tone-deaf, so some cannot authentically smell. Among bibliophiles perhaps there may be here and there an unfortunate anosmic, as the medicos call it, but it is doubtful.

It was, naturally, a Frenchman, the romantic André Theuriet, who in *La Chanoinesse* declared that an indiscreet (how much more a lascivious) volume exhaled "*une odeur de volupté perverse, quelque chose comme de parfum aphrodisiac des seringes et des tubereuses dans une chambre close.*" If the sticky scent of the tuberose pervades the macabre pages of Verlaine, does not a vellum-bound recital of the amours of the Chevalier de Faublas conjure the heavy cloy of a nosegay of beribboned but bedraggled gardenia?

There are wizard bookmen whose familiarity with "the bibliothecal aisles" is such that, blindfolded and handed a volume, through the sense of smell, of touch, and of hearing, can tell the approximate literary vintage of the tome. A thousand subtle clues enter into this feat. The heft and bulk, the tactile and aromatic hints of the binding, the texture, crackle, and gauge of the paper, all help to identify the century, often the decade, and sometimes the country of publication as well. But this playful stunt should not be too hard pressed. It is a mere overtone of the theme that the ardent booklover indulges in nasal esthetics in conjunction with his browsing much as the seasoned vintner inhales with delectation before he quaffs with delight.

The scent of books comes naturally, with aging. New works have an upstart air in the nose of the connoisseur, a sort of commercial sachet. Even the indifferent bookman, who may use Foxe's *Book of Martyrs* for a doorstop and sever the pages of an anguished "first" with a careless forefinger, knows that a shopful of new books smells unlike a dealer's secondhand collection. A true devotee of the shelves knows the redolence of rarities, the mellow pungencies of books with a past. In the outer world there are repellent odors, but among the secluded tiers of reading all is agreeable save for those few evil relics of the mind that by reason of their foul contents or depraved association are like psychic *fleurs de mal.*

How Cyrano with his prodigious advantage must have loved to browse and sniff amid the musty annals and romances of chivalry stacked in the attics of old Gascony

In the pages of Dan McKenzie's *Aromatics and the Soul* (London, 1923), the sum and substance of the bouquet of old books is set forth thus eloquently:

THE BOUQUET OF OLD BOOKS

Of all the odours in life none surely is so rich both in retrospect and in prospect as the smell of books to him who loves them. The cosy invitation of a library! Not a public library, needless to say, where the intimate appeal is lost in a jumble of smells—dust, paste, ink, and clammy overcoats. Such public mixtures the bookworm, that solitary self-centered individual, must, by reason of his shyness, ever consistently shun. But usher him into the private room of a private house where books, many books, have reposed for many years. Then go away and leave him to it.

The smell of a room full of books is slow to form. Like the bouquet of wine, it must ripen. You have to wait. But if you are able to wait, then one fine day you will be welcomed there by the snuggest smell in all the world, which, when once it comes, will for ever remain, like rooks in a clump of elms. I know a few houses where this most seductive of all perfumes has resided for untold years, and whence it will never depart as long as our immemorial England endures. But alas! like most people, I have been only a fleeting visitor to those nooks of enchantment, and have had to wait myself not once, but many times, as often indeed as I have shifted my roof-tree, for that ancient fusty atmosphere. There is, I fear, no way of hastening the appearance of this beckoning finger to oblivion. We need not linger over the analysis of this particular odour. Book-lovers know it. Others don't care.

CATALOGITIS
COLLECTORS' MALADY

A CHOICE STORY, no less amusing because true, was told by Augustine Birrell—a story he was well qualified to tell as the author of *In the Name of the Bodleian*. Speaking at the National Liberal Club about 1916, he related the "tragic story" of the librarian of the Bodley Library, who, being a man of small build, "found it necessary to raise the height of his chair by sitting on a volume from the library. He sat upon the book for thirty years, while he was completing his catalogue, and when his *magnum opus* was finished he had forgotten to include in that catalogue the vellum volume upon which he sat." That this is a fact is confirmed by a note in the second edition of Macray's *Annals of the Bodleian*, wherein the sitter is disclosed to have been the Reverend Alfred Hackman, who departed from vicarage and vexations in 1874, after being in the employ of the Library for thirty-six years, eleven as assistant librarian.

But the story would not be complete for those of bookish bent without the name of the book, unmentioned by Macray, that had been so elevating to a man of religion. A column of anonymous chitchat in the *Bodleian Quarterly Record* for 1917 discloses that the title of the hefty folio was *Chronicon Gotwicense* (Tegernsee, 1732), now duly catalogued as Folio BS. 513. And finally, to clinch the anecdote we are told: "It is

true that in the New Catalogue prepared under his and Macray's
superintendence, between 1859 and 1878, it was not catalogued at all."

Perhaps no more dainty bit has ever been inspired by an item sold at
auction than Christopher Morley's sonnet in which he commemorates the
sale of a letter of John Keats to Fanny Brawne, at the Anderson
Galleries, in 1920. Here it is:

IN AN AUCTION ROOM

How about this lot? *said the auctioneer;*
One hundred, may I say, just for a start
Between the plum-red curtains, drawn apart,
A written sheet was held . . . And strange to hear
(Dealer, would I were steadfast as thou art)
The cold quick bids. (Against you in the rear!)
The crimson salon, in a glow more clear
Burned bloodlike purple as the poet's heart.
Song that outgrew the singer! Bitter Love
That broke the proud hot heart it held in thrall—
Poor script, where still those tragic passions move—
Eight hundred bid: fair warning: the last call:
The soul of Adonais, like a star . . .
Sold for eight hundred dollars—Doctor R.!

Time being an illusion, there is no more pleasant way of wasting it
than in reading book catalogues. Fie on him who doubts it. There are
those who hold that dealers' catalogues, auction sale catalogues, and
library catalogues are a trio of offenders cheating the bibliophile's
leisure of its opportunity to read the books he reads about. Whatever his
favorite author, period, or field, too often, instead of the plain
unvarnished scroll, he reads "about it and about." And catalogues are the
chief seduction—or diversion—whether one be devoted to Americana or
Alchemy. Some bookmen who love, say, Shakespeare or Shaw, Spinoza or
Santayana, Robert Sherwood or Carl Sandburg, are content to read the
author and let the commentator go hang. Many get lost in the

commentary and never fully embrace the original. As with tobacco, some
like Byron, while allured by disguises of the weed, yet give not a sneeze
for snuff, and quote:

> *Divine in hookas, glorious in a pipe*
> *When tipped with amber, mellow, rich, and ripe;*
> *Like other charmers, wooing the caress*
> *More dazzlingly when daring in full dress;*
> *Yet thy true lovers more admire by far*
> *Thy naked beauties—give me a cigar!*

Dr. Rosenbach, the inveterate collector and dispenser, used as a
motto on his catalogues a text from Proverbs: "It is naught, sayeth the
buyer; but when he is gone his way, then he boasteth."

Only the initiated know the zest of getting the better of a catalogue.
At a sale in London, Dr. R. bought Philip Paine's *Dailey Meditations*,
which was catalogued as printed in Cambridge by Marmaduke Johnson
in 1668. He recognized that it was Marmaduke Johnson of Cambridge,
Massachusetts, who printed the Eliot Indian Bible, the first Holy
Scriptures for the North American Indians; the others present, however,
assumed it was Cambridge, England. He bought the book for £51—the
only known copy of the first volume of verse printed in North America.
Gladly, he tells us, and told the auctioneer, he would have paid one
hundred times as much. The following year the only known copy of
another tract came up on the same block, Baxter's *Call to the
Unconverted*, translated by the Apostle Eliot into the idiom of the
Massachusetts Indians of pioneer days. This item, properly catalogued as
Cambridge, Massachusetts, brought £6,800, or about $34,000.

This merry gentleman several decades ago put a collection of
Shakespeare folios and quartos in his Quaker City show window with a
small card stating that the price of the lot was $985,000. As Chris
Morley observed: "He would have been very unhappy if anyone had
walked in, paid the price, and taken away the books." Indeed, he might as

readily have put his shelf of Caxtons on window display at a no less
fabulous figure.

In *Books and Bidders* Dr. Rosenbach observed: "A deadly malady
which attacks all collectors at one stage or another is catalogitis. Here is
a disease which will defy science as long as books and their ilk remain to
be collected. In the beginning, the symptoms are not grave. You will
quietly open your mail one morning to find a pamphlet enumerating
certain books offered for sale. From time to time other sales lists will be
sent you, and one day, when you have started to arrange your desk
neatly, you will be surprised that there are catalogues in nearly every
drawer. You quickly decide to throw them out. But something, the most
insidious germ of the disease, stays your hand. You have fallen a victim,
merely in keeping them."

Indeed, won over by the doctor, we are inclined to reverse ourselves
and agree with him that "catalogitis is never a waste of time." There are
experts like the late Seymour de Ricci, who gathered Continental
catalogues from the seventeenth century onward and compiled *a
catalogue of catalogues*, embracing more than forty thousand entries.

In modern catalogue making, treasures are described in great detail.
Says Andrews, "The compilation of one of these bibliopolistic menus has
as its fundamental principle the familiar couplet of Matthew Prior:

> *Be to her virtues very kind*
> *Be to her faults a little blind.*

Nor are these lists all drab. For the connoisseur, pencil in hand, they
conjure up all sorts of associations and occasional oddities. Hollings of
London sent out an unusual little catalogue, half of it old books and half
modern books. Opened at one end, the old books were arranged by title;
reversed, the modern books were listed.

Another odd specimen came from Hamrun, Malta. It includes
several hundred items, the novelty consisting in the fact that these are
not priced and that the "prospective buyer is requested to submit an offer
for selected items which will receive careful consideration." The word

catalogue covers a wide compass. Thus the new British Museum Library catalogue when achieving completion will fill one hundred sixty-five tall volumes.

Let it not be thought that those who devote themselves to such tasks are mere drudges. Moritz Steinschneider spent thirteen years in cataloguing the Hebrew books of the Oxford Bodleian Library. This was not drudgery for him, but constituted the happiest years of his life.

Yet there are those who make light of mortal man's passion for perpetuation "not only of the past but of evidence of the present for the benefit of generations to come . . . infected with the desire to hoard all the evidences of his own existence," which culminates, says one crabbed critic, in "the collecting craze." He adds that "libraries, too, are in a sense museums." And with ironic alarm he asks: "Will the last man die over an unfinished catalogue in the airless clutter of a monstrous museum?"

For the collector, condition is a prime consideration. It becomes second nature in reading dealers' catalogues to observe such descriptive points. This led the present scribe in the 1920's to a facetious listing which we venture to include here under the title:

CULLED FROM AN AUCTION CATALOGUE

1. Holmes (Oliver Wendell). "Autocrat of the Breakfast Table." *Plates Missing.*
2. Williams (Talcott). "Turkey a World Problem." *Half crushed levant.*
3. Peacock (Virginia). "Famous American Belles." *In original wrappers.*
4. Witwer (H. C.). "There Is No Plate Like Home." *Boards.*
5. Van Loon (H. W.). "Story of Mankind." *Half sheep.*
6. Browne (Walter). "Everywoman." *Curious.*
7. Shelley (P. B.). "Prometheus." *Unbound.*
8. Markham (Edwin). "Man with the Hoe." *Hand tooled.*
9. Donnelly (Ignatius). "Atlantis." *Damaged by Water.*
10. Steinmetz (Andrew). "History of Duelling." *Hundreds of Cuts.*
11. Canfield (Dorothy). "The Bent Twig." *Several leaves missing.*
12. Norris (Wm.). "A Legal Separation." *Half bound.*
13. Cervantes (Miguel de). "Don Quixote." *Cracked.*
14. Swinburne (A. C.). "Atlanta in Calydon." *Imitation antique.*

15. Wilcox (Ella Wheeler). "Poems of Passion." *Limp ooze.*
16. Lytton (Bulwer). "Last Days of Pompeii." *Shaken.*
17. Weyl (Dr. Walter). "Tired Radicals." *Imitation russia.*
18. Dumas (Alex.). "Queen's Lace Handkerchief." *Somewhat soiled.*
19. Jordan (Kate). "Trouble-The-House." *New kid.*
20. Stopes (Dr. Marie P.). "Married Love." *Rare in this state.*
21. Thomson (James). "The Seasons." *Divinity circuit.*
22. Omar Khayyam. "Rubaiyat." *Persian yapp.*
23. Wharton (Edith). "Age of Innocence." *Half calf.*
24. Hay (John). "Little Breeches." *Cloth, worn.*
25. Surtees (Robt. S.). "Hunting Hounds." *Foxed.*
26. Harvey (Wm.). "The Human Blood System." *For private circulation.*
27. Hogarth (William). "The Harlot's Progress." *In sheets. Patrons laid in.*
28. Shaw (S.). "William of Germany." *Trimmed.*
29. Mackenzie (Compton). "Rich Relatives." *Scarce in this condition.*
30. House (Colonel Edward M.). "Intimate Papers." *Padded rep.*
31. Moret (C. de). "Old Bourbon Days." *Square quarto.*
32. Chambers (Robt. W.). "The Eleventh Commandment." *Broken.*
33. Shaw (Bernard). "Mrs. Warren's Profession." *Loose.*
34. Hogarth (William). "The Rake's Progress." *Strained in the joints.*
35. Josephson (Matthew). "Robber Barons." *Title stained.*
36. Milton (John). "Paradise Lost." *With errata leaf.*
37. Riley (James Whitcomb). "The Old Swimming Hole." *Undressed kid.*
38. Mackinstry (E.). "Aladdin and the Wonderful Lamp." *Rubbed.*

Some day some one will write an enchanting book about book auctions; not a drab and spiritless rehearsal, but a recital worthy of those hours when collectors and dealers sitting under the tense spell of the auctioneer's monotone feel the quiver of excitement as a precious lot finds a new possessor. The points, the provenance, the price! The bidding and the bated breath! An heirloom, a literary landmark, a uniquity! The triumph of the victor and the chagrin of the underbidder! Theme for a new Dibdin gifted with the style of a Chris Morley. Indeed, America alone would afford ample annals of public book sales to tease the right pen into unthought-of immortality. The dire refrain of the Poeian raven was not more of a portent to make men quail than the final warning of old Stan Henkels—gavel suspended in destiny over a topnotch item—

"Lost to you and your heirs forevermore!" How many a maximum resolve of the soaring contenders was shattered under the impulse of that last-second intimation of defeat. The poised hammer, the inner struggle, the first ecstasy of ownership, the jounce to one's cultural ego, the magic indwelling to kindle the aura of rarity—all are compounded within the auctioneer's subtle crescendo, to our undoing and our delight.

Amid the maximum of mannered furore which the Briton of station will permit himself, the Duke of Roxburghe's books were sold in 1812. The *réclame* of the auction, and the notable contest between Lord Spencer and the Duke of Marlborough to acquire Boccaccio's *Il Decamerone*, printed at Venice by Valdarfer in 1471, resulted in the formation of the famous Roxburghe Club. When the Duke of Marlborough's library was sold in 1819, the Boccaccio which he had won at the price of £2,260 was gained by Earl Spencer for 875 guineas. Eighty years later it came, through the gift of Mrs. Rylands, to the John Rylands Library at Manchester.

The account of the 1819 sale of this work as set forth in an anonymous little volume entitled *Curiosities for the Ingenious* (London, 1821) has a contemporary flavor and echoes Dibdin. The sum involved, then impressive, has since dwindled, in comparison, to a minor figure, But let that old timer speak:

> This book had been purchased by the Duke of Marlborough for the enormous sum of £2,260! Notwithstanding the publicity of this fact, all researches throughout Europe to procure another copy of the same edition had proved entirely fruitless; this volume continued to be the only known perfect copy of that edition. Besides its merits as an unique, it contains many important readings which have not been followed in any subsequent edition.
>
> Never, perhaps, in this country or any other, was so great an interest excited about the fate of a book. Its extreme rarity, the enormous price it had realized at the Roxburghe sale, and the anxiety to see who would be the

fortunate purchaser on this occasion, were irresistible
attractions; and at a very early hour of the day, although
the book was to be the last article sold, the auction room
began to fill, and the company kept increasing until four
o'clock, when it became crowded to suffocation, and
admission was no longer to be obtained to hear or see what
was going on. A number of gentlemen then made their way to
the roof, which is a flat one with a dome skylight, and were
contented to snatch a sight from that situation, through the
glass, at this wonderful book! All those more fortunately
situated near the table, eagerly got hold of it; others, at a
greater distance, glutted their curiosity with a peep at it;
and others, at a still greater distance, were obliged to be
content with hearing the biddings.

Immediately after the last lot preceding the *Decameron*,
all became eager anxiety; and as soon as the clerk had, with
difficulty, brought the book to the table, every one pressed
forward to obtain a sight. The cry then became general for
"hats off," which was complied with. Silence being obtained,
Mr. Evans addressed the company in a most elaborate and
eloquent speech, which he delivered with great effect, and
concluded amid loud plaudits. The bidding then commenced.

Book auctions were introduced into England from Holland in 1676.
Curious variations of auction technique prevailed. Thus in a Dutch
auction items were (and are) offered at a top starting price, and then
successively at lower prices until one is accepted. A similar practice still
prevails in the sale of rugs in the Near East. It was the quaint custom in
early England to set up an inch of lighted candle, the last bidder before
the fall of the wick becoming the buyer. If the seller wished to stipulate a
minimum price, it was placed under the candlestick, and no lower bid
availed.

When certain of these private English libraries were dispersed, the
auction sales extended for lengthy periods. The immense accumulations of
Thomas Rawlinson provided materials for a series of auctions after his

death in 1725. The library of the Reverend Richard Farmer required thirty-six days' sale in 1798. The collection of the antiquarian John Brand occupied thirty-seven days in its sale in 1807, that of James Bindley forty-one days in 1818–1820. After the death of Richard Heber, who had accumulated hoards of heterogeneous volumes, sometimes buying whole libraries sight unseen, his vast gatherings which had been stored in eight houses were auctioned in 202 sales during 1834–1837. De Ricci estimates the total accumulations to have comprised between two and three hundred thousand books, but the sales catalogue in six portly volumes includes 119,613 volumes which brought £56,774.

The library of Dean Swift was sold at Dublin in 1746, and the only known copy of the catalogue was supposed to be that which had belonged to Sir Walter Scott, and which is still in the library at Abbotsford. But the discovery of a second copy led the Cambridge University Press to publish a volume, *Dean Swift's Library*, in 1932. Similarly, in 1930 appeared a reproduction in facsimile from a unique copy of the catalogue of Laurence Sterne's books which in 1768 were offered by a firm of booksellers in York with prices affixed. That Sterne took heavy toll from these volumes, notably from Burton and Rabelais, is pointed out in the introduction, where his system of appropriation is exposed as skillful but scandalous.

Among such mementos, who would not con with relish a replica of the twenty-eight-page catalogue of Samuel Johnson's shelves? Of the greatest rarity, only three or four copies are known. A copy was sold at Sotheby's in 1926 for £76, said to be the record price for an auction catalogue. This Great Cham's books, consisting of 662 lots, including a first folio Shakespeare, realized £242 9s. 9d. Sold "by Mr. Christie, at his Great Room in Pall Mall, on Wednesday, February 16, 1785, and three following days," these volumes are literally worth their weight in gold today if they bear the crabbed Johnsonian scrawl. But next to none are known, and all received rough usage at the hands of the most conspicuous of eighteenth-century literary figures.

The Isham copy of this catalogue, sold in 1933, is unique in that it is priced, with the buyers' names in a contemporary hand. The facsimile issued by A. Edward Newton in 1925 was made from this copy and dedicated to Colonel Isham. The Johnsonian books, sold two months after their owner's demise, ranged from *Mudge on the Small Pox* to a French Bible. Johnson's own copy of his dictionary brought thirteen shillings. The first-folio Shakespeare went for one pound two shillings to a gentleman named Ireland.

Samuel Johnson himself had a hand in a famous catalogue. When the Harleian Library was to be dispersed, he wrote an "Account" of its merits which appeared as an essay in the *Gentleman's Magazine* of December, 1742, and was reprinted the following year at the beginning of the five-volume *Catalogus Bibliotheca Harleiana*. It had first accompanied the proposals for printing the catalogue by subscription. Here is a taste of the swinging style:

> That our catalogue will excite any other man to emulate the collectors of this library, to prefer books and manuscripts to equipage and luxury, and to forsake noise and diversion for the conversation of the learned, and the satisfaction of extensive knowledge, we are very far from presuming to hope; but shall make no scruple to assert, that, if any man should happen to be seized with such laudable ambition, he may find in this catalogue hints and informations which are not easily to be met with; he will discover, that the boasted Bodleian library is very far from a perfect model. . . .
>
> But the collectors of libraries cannot be numerous, and, therefore, catalogues could not very properly be recommended to the public, if they had not a more general and frequent use, an use which every student has experienced, or neglected to his loss. By the means of catalogues only can it be known, what has been written on every part of learning, and the hazard avoided of encountering difficulties which have already been cleared, discussing questions which have already been decided, and

digging in mines of literature which former ages have exhausted.

No wonder Johnson raved about this great collection, a large part of which came to the British Museum by purchase in 1753; no wonder he endeavored in his own words "To shew that this collection deserves a particular degree of regard from the learned and the studious, that it excels any library that was ever yet offered to public sale, in the value as well as number of the volumes which it contains. . . ."

According to Boswell, many or all of the Latin descriptions of the books were written by Johnson for this catalogue, as well as the prefaces to one or more of the five volumes comprising it.

Impressive as are the card catalogues of the Library of Congress, or the all-inclusive printed listing of the British Museum, valuable as may be the massive sesames to Continental collections or the proud enumeration of noted private shelves, the books themselves bear witness to the fallacies that infest learning and to the oblivion that overtakes most authorship. In the sense that books are hoarded as relics, to that degree is a library akin to a mausoleum. The indwelling spirit of the masterpieces may be ageless, but most of the burden of the serried shelves is a clutter of stale stuff kept to satisfy our curiosity concerning the past. If pearls were as common as pebbles they would not be prized; and Shelley's *Fragments of Margaret Nicholson* fetches £1,350 because of no intrinsic worth. Men collect books from many motives, ignoble as well as laudable, but chiefly as a subtle effort to defeat the remorseless flow of time by clinging to vestiges of dead days, and to console themselves against the ineluctable by cherishing choice specimens of inspiration they choose to deem immortal.

If catalogues are the register of our present achievements, they are even more a guide to the repositories of the past. Crude, indeed, were the beginnings of such listings, primitive the early classifications of that printed residue of the generations called books, in reality a sort of precipitation of the soul of man.

It will be new to many to hear that the Oxford method of

cataloguing in the fifteenth century was "according to the last word on
the first leaf or the first word over the page." Concerning the fourteenth-
century library of Duke Humphrey of Gloucester, whose donations to
Oxford began the present Bodleian, "the first librarian was Gilles Malet,
who prepared a catalogue in 1373, which is still in existence." Also
extant is the catalogue of the books which he presented to Oxford on
several occasions, though most of the books themselves were destroyed in
the Reformation, or dispersed. The first general catalogue of any
European library is said to have been the 1605 printed list of the
Bodleian. An alphabetical manuscript catalogue compiled in 1611–1612
is still in that library.

But in 1620 appeared the first printed alphabetical catalogue of any
library, prepared by Dr. Thomas James, the first scientific English
bibliographer and keeper of the Bodleian during the first twenty years of
its existence. His remarks on cataloguing, in the introduction, are
important in the history of the subject. Only three perfect copies are
known of this *Catalogus universalis librorum Bibliotheca Bodleiana*. In
the enlarged 1635 edition the titles of English works are printed in black
letter, and many works of the Elizabethan poets and dramatists are
included, among them the first folio of Shakespeare.

The British Museum Library began humbly two centuries ago as the
National Library, and after thirty-four years the first printed catalogue
was issued in 1787 in two folio volumes. At that time there were fewer
than a score visitors daily. For decades the loss of time in locating a
desired book was proverbial. When several notable collections had been
bequeathed, together with other accessions, a new catalogue was issued in
seven octavo volumes, the publication of which extended from 1813 to
1819. Another appeared in 1881–1899. At present, there are more than
five million printed books, about 70,000 manuscripts, 100,000 charters
and rolls, and several thousand papyri. The present catalogue under way
since 1931 had reached its fiftieth massive volume by 1954, but only
achieved midway of *D* in the alphabet! Over here the Library of Congress
printed catalogue comprises 167 smaller volumes, but reaches finality.

Avaunt the thought that the theme of catalogues is a dreary one! Charles Lamb in his list of books that are not books cited directories, almanacs, pocketbooks, and statutes-at-large—as well as the works of Gibbon and Hume—but he was too good a bookman to include catalogues in his gentle jibes.

Indeed, the subject has its humorous aspects. Edmund L. Pearson had in mind the sometimes extravagant conditions attached to gifts of books to institutions when, in resigning from the New York Public Library, he sent this facetious note with a parcel of volumes:

> I have given to the Library some twenty or thirty books. I expect no special recognition of the gift. I only stipulated that they should be catalogued on gold-edged catalogue cards; have a special bookplate with my picture and name; be known henceforth as the Edmund Lester Pearson collection; be kept in a room by themselves, and issued to readers by somebody in full evening dress.

BIBLIOGRAPHY

CAVE, CRYPT AND COFFIN

BREASTED, J. H.: *Coffin Texts,* The Oriental Institute, Chicago, 1933, pp. 149 ff.

BRINTON, DANIEL G.: *The Lenâpe and Their Legends,* Philadelphia, 1885. A rendition of the Walam Olum, or buried bark record of the Delaware tribe.

BUCK, JANET CAMP: "Charles Howell and the Exhumation of Rossetti's Poems," *The Colophon,* pt. 15 (12 pp.), New York, 1933.

CARTER, THOMAS FRANCIS: *The Invention of Printing in China,* New York, 1931, pp. 39–46.

GOTTHEIL, RICHARD: "Tidbits from the Genizah," *Jewish Studies in Memory of Israel Abrahams,* Press of the Jewish Institute of Religion, New York, 1927, pp. 149–69.

HALPER, B.: *Descriptive Catalogue of Genizah Fragments in Philadelphia,* Philadelphia, 1924, 235 pp.

JACKSON, HOLBROOK: *The Anatomy of Bibliomania,* London, 1931, vol. 2, pp. 261–65.

STEIN, AUREL: *Serindia,* Oxford, 1921, vol. 2, pp. 791–937. On the caves of the thousand Buddhas.

———: *On Ancient Central-Asian Tracks,* London, 1933, pp. 203–16. On the Diamond Sutra of 868 C.E., the world's oldest printed book.

ECCENTRICA

BAUMGARTNER, LEONA; and FULTON, JOHN F.: *A Bibliography of the Poem Syphilis Sive Morbus Gallicus, by Girolamo Fracastoro of Verona,* New Haven, 1935.

BRIDGES, WILLIAM: "Freaks in the World of Books," *New York Evening Sun,*
October 31, 1931. Concerning the collection of Walter Hart Blumenthal.

FITZGERALD, PERCY: *The Book Fancier,* London, 1887, pp. 99–167.

JACKSON, HOLBROOK: *The Anatomy of Bibliomania,* London, 1931, vol. 2,
pp. 54–88.

MAGGS BROTHERS CATALOGUE, No. 574: *Strange Books and Curious Titles,*
London, 1932.

MATTHEWS, BRANDER: *Bookbindings Old and New,* New York, 1895, pp. 154–67,
209–12.

THOMPSON, LAWRENCE S.: "Bibliopegia Fantastica," *Bulletin of the New York
Public Library,* 1947, 22 pp.

UZANNE, OCTAVE: *Caprices d'un bibliophile,* Paris, 1878, 146 pp.; limited to 572
copies.

———: *Les zigzags d'un curieux,* Paris, 1888, 300 pp.; limited to 1,000 copies.

THE BOOKMAN SETS SAIL

ANON.: "The Pitcairn Bible," *Bulletin of the New York Public Library,* June,
1924, September, 1924; reprinted separately (12 pp.), July, 1924.

BARTHOLD, ALLEN J.: "Gazette françoise," Newport, R. I., 1780–1781; *Papers of
the Bibliographical Society of America,* vol. 28 (1934), pp. 64–79. Concerns
the seven issues and one supplement of the paper discovered in 1925;
comprising thirty pages in all, these papers were printed on shore by the
"sea-press" of the French fleet during 1780–1781.

BARWICK, G. F.: "Books Printed at Sea," *The Library,* London, n.s., vol. 1
(1900), pp. 163–66.

BLUMENTHAL, WALTER HART: "Printing Presses on the High Seas," *Valentine's
Book Notes,* Hartford, Conn., January, 1927.

CHAPIN, HOWARD M.: *Contributions to Rhode Island Bibliography,* No. 2, 1914.
Concerns the press of Rochambeau's French fleet in American waters
during the American Revolution.

———: "Early Sea-Presses," *Ars Typographica,* New York, vol. 2 (1925),
pp. 39–52; separate offprint (18 pp.), 1925.

———: *Gazette Françoise,* facsimile reprint, Grolier Club, New York, 1896;
seven numbers and supplement, with Introduction.

————: "More About Sea-Presses," *American Collector,* vol. 3 (1926), pp 86–88.

CUNDALL, JOSEPH: *Bookbinding, Ancient and Modern,* London, 1881, p. 17. On the loss and recovery of the Gospels of St. Cuthbert (see also Jackson, Holbrook, *infra*).

FABER, REGINALD S.: *The Library,* London, 1889, vol. 1, pp. 229–32.

FORBES-LEITH, WILLIAM: *Life of St. Margaret,* Edinburgh, 1884, pp. 66–68 (see also Madan, Falconer, *infra*).

JACKSON, HOLBROOK: *The Anatomy of Bibliomania,* London, 1931, vol. 2, pp. 100–101.

MADAN, FALCONER: *Books in Manuscript,* London, 1893, pp. 107–10.

MADERUS, JOACHIMUS JOHANNES: *De Bibliothecis atque Archivis virorum clarissimorum . . . libelli et commentationes. Cum præfactione de scriptis et bibliothecis antediluvianis,* Helmestadii, 1666; 2nd edition, 1702.

Notes and Queries, 4th Series, vol. 2 (1868), pp. 106–107. On the book found in a codfish (see also Jackson, Holbrook, *supra*).

PARÈS, A.-JACQUES: "Imprimeries d'escadre," *Extrait du Bulletin de la section de géographie, Comité des travaux historiques et scientifiques,* 1927, Académie du Var (Paris: Imprimerie Nationale).

THOMPSON, LAWRENCE S.: *Bulletin of the New York Public Library,* February, 1947; reprint (pp. 14–17). On fishskin bindings.

A BLOCKHEAD'S BOOKSHELF

BLUMENTHAL, WALTER HART: "A Shelf for Blockhead Bibliophiles," *Reading and Collecting,* February, 1938; reprinted, *Carrousel for Bibliophiles* (Wm. Targ, editor), New York, 1947, pp. 155–60.

BRINTON, DANIEL G.: *The Lenâpe and Their Legends,* Philadelphia, 1885. On record sticks, pp. 59–62; on Walam Olum, pp. 148–68.

CARTER, THOMAS FRANCIS: *The Invention of Printing in China and Its Spread Westward,* Columbia University Press, New York, 1931 (revision of 1925 edition). On Diamond Sutra, pp. 39–46; on Chinese wooden type of early fourteenth century, pp. 161–68; and *passim.*

CORNELL, HENRIK: *Biblia Pauperum,* Stockholm, 1925. A privately printed and exhaustive German work on block books.

Hodgkin, John Eliot: *Rariora*, London, vol. 2 (1900), pp. 37–46. On feasibility of separate letters in wood.

Joseph, Gerald A.: *"Ola MSS. and the Government Oriental Library of Ceylon,"* *The Library*, London, vol. 7 (1895), pp. 269–75.

Hunter, Dard: *Primitive Papermaking*, with thirty-four original specimens of barks used in the Pacific Islands in papermaking, Chillicothe, 1927; limited to 200 copies.

Riegl, Alois: *Die Holzkalender des Mittel-Alters*, Berlin, 1897.

Sotheby, S. Leigh: *Principia Typographica: Block Books Issued . . . during the Fifteenth Century*, London, 1858, 3 vols., folio, in limited edition.

Timperley, C. H.: *Encyclopedia of Typography*, London, 1842, pp. 18–20, 65. On ancient inscribed slabs, runic wooden almanacs, and bark writing.

NOT FOR THE THIN-SKINNED

American Notes and Queries, New York, vol. 4 (1944), p. 106.

Anon.: *Bibliofilia*, Florence, 1926, vol. 4, p. 332; vol. 14, p. 116.

Anon.: *The New York Sunday World*, August 21, 1927. On the Flammarion volume.

Anon.: "Vellum Carnis," *Current Literature* (Maggs Brothers), London, December, 1933, pp. 413–15.

Blumenthal, Walter Hart: *American Book Collector*, 1932, vol. 2, pp. 119–24.

Jackson, Holbrook: *Anatomy of Bibliomania*, London, 1931, vol. 2, pp. 88–93; reprinted, *Carrousel for Bibliophiles* (Wm. Targ, editor), New York, 1947, pp. 13–19.

Kersten, Paul: *Zeitschrift für Bücherfreunde*, Leipsic, 1911, vol. 2, pp. 263–64.

———: *Archiv für Buchbinderei*, 1909, p. 90.

Kirby, H. T.: *The Bookman*, London, March, 1932, pp. 334–36.

Rich, Stuart L.: *Boston Evening Transcript*, May 31, 1924. On George Walton, highwayman, whose skin adorns a book in the Athenaeum, Boston.

Thompson, Lawrence S.: *Book Collector's Packet*, vol. 4 (October, 1945), pp. 15–17; *Bulletin of the American Library Association*, vol. 34 (1946), pp. 93–102; *Hide and Leather*, vol. 101 (1946), pp. 20, 23, 34, 36.

Werner, N. J.: *Books Bound in Human Skin*, Inland Printer, July, 1922, p. 512; reprinted, *Boston Evening Transcript*, August 31, 1922.

BIBLIOGRAPHY

GOLIATHS OF BOOKDOM

> Scant allusion only has been accorded literary gigantica. No collective description of these titans of the library has hitherto appeared, so far as known to the present scrivener.

ANDREWS, MATTHEW PAGE: *The Story of the South,* Baltimore, 1925, 27 pp. A miniature replica of "The Biggest Book in the World," in octavo size, with an introduction by the author of the monster tome.

BRASSINGTON, W. S.: *The Art of Bookbinding,* London, 1894, p. 93.

FITZGERALD, PERCY: *The Book Fancier,* London, 1887, pp. 142–43.

JACKSON, HOLBROOK: *The Anatomy of Bibliomania,* London, 1930, vol. 1, pp. 41–44.

KOHNERT, WILHELM: "Der Reisenatlas des Grossen Kurfürsten und seine Restaurierung 1931," *Archiv für Buchbinderei,* Halle, 1931, pp. 102–105.

MUSCHAMP, EDWARD A.: *Audacious Audubon,* New York, 1929, 312 pp.

LILLIPUTS OR MIDGET BOOKS

ANDREWS, WILLIAM LORING: *Sextodecimos et Infra,* New York, 1899, 117 pp.; 150 copies printed. A superbly written essay on tiny books, illustrating early specimens.

BEIJERS, J. L.: "Editions de Format Microscopique," in *Collections Beijers,* La Haye, 1900, pt. 1, pp. 54–87.

BENSON, A. C., and WEAVER, SIR LAWRENCE: *The Book of the Queen's Doll House,* London, 1924. Volume II (398 pp.), edited by E. V. Lucas, describes the books.

BLUMENTHAL, WALTER HART: "Midgets of the Book World," *Avocations,* New York, vol. 1 (1937), pp. 136–40.

BROCKHAUS, ALBERT: *Verzeichniss einer Sammlung Mikroskopischer Drucke,* Leipsic, 1888, 42 pp.

GROLIER CLUB: *List of Microscopic Books in the Library of the Grolier Club,* New York, 1911, 36 pp.

HENDERSON, JAMES D. (ed.): *News-Letters of the LXIVMOS;* 21 folders issued from 1927 to 1929, printed at Brookline and elsewhere for literary microphiles. Nos. 3 and 4 contain bibliographies of midget books.

LÜTHI, KARL J.: Bücher kleinsten Formates, Berne, 1924, 45 pp.; 250 copies printed. Includes ten plates and eight title-page reproductions.

BIBLIOGRAPHY

Mikrobiblion: Das Buch von den kleinen Büchern, Berlin, 1928, 32 mo.

NAUROY, C.: *Bibliographie des impressions microscopiques,* Paris, 1881. The earliest approximation of the literature found in tiny format.

STONE, WILBUR MACEY: *A Snuff-Boxful of Bibles,* Carteret Book Club, Newark, N. J., 1926, 110 pp.

————: *The Gigantick Histories of Thomas Boreman,* Portland, Me., 1933, 41 pp.

————: *The Holy Bible in Verse,* 1698, 7 pp.; reprinted from the *Proceedings of the American Antiquarian Society,* Worcester, Mass., 1935.

————: *The Thumb Bible of John Taylor,* Brookline, 1928, 79 pp.

THOMPSON, EBEN FRANCIS: *A Thimbleful of Books,* Worcester, Mass., 1933, 36 pp., privately printed.

TISSANDIER, GASTON: *Livres minuscules: La plus grande bibliothèque des plus petits livres du monde. Collection de M. George Salomon. (Extrait de La Nature.)* G. Masson, (ed.), Paris, 1894 (Imprimerie Lahure). Includes illustrations (actual size) of bindings and title pages from the famous collection of M. Salomon, celebrated once upon a time for its "microbes du livre."

TUNEEWA, MADAM A.: *Zentralblat für Bibliothekswesen,* Leipsic, November, 1926, 21 pp. On the collection of miniature books in the State Library in Odessa.

OLIO OF ODDITIES

Eccentric Formats, Cut Hymn-Books, and Volvelles:

The subject of books of odd shape as a bypath for the literary commentator has been a neglected topic; not one citation is available in the nature of a covering article, and only a single brief description of an example—a circular book. As for cut hymn-books and volvelles, research has yielded only one article concerning each.

METCALF, FRANK J.: "Cut Hymn-Books," *The American Collector,* January, 1927, pp. 159–61.

REDGRAVE, GILBERT R.: "Books Containing Volvelles," *Booklover's Magazine,* London, vol. 6 (1905), pp. 209–13.

SCHMIDT, CHRISTEL: "Kreisrunder Renaissanceband der Caspar Meuser," *Festschrift Loubier: Buch und Bucheinband,* Leipsic, 1923, pp. 194–98.

BIBLIOGRAPHY

CURIOUSER AND CURIOUSER

BROWN, KARL, and HASKELL, DANIEL C. (compilers): "Shorthand Books in the New York Public Library," *Bulletin of the New York Public Library,* September, 1934. Editions of the Bible and of literary works in shorthand listed, pp. 761–95.

CAREY, JOHN B.: *The Oddities of Shorthand,* New York, 1891, 270 pp. Fictional sketches on shorthand as an aid to crime and its detection.

GREGG, J. R.: "Julius Caesar's Stenographer," *Century Magazine,* May, 1921.

LONCHAMP, F. C.: *Manuel de Bibliophile Français,* Paris, 1927, vol. 2, p. 518. Lists sixteen early French works engraved throughout.

LONG, JOSEPH SCHUYLER: *Sign Language,* Washington, 1910, 164 pp. About fifteen hundred signs used by the deaf in the United States and Canada.

PEIGNOT, GABRIEL: *Répertoire de bibliographies spéciales,* Dijon, 1810, pp. 185–210. Lists volumes engraved throughout.

SETON, ERNEST THOMPSON: *Sign Talk,* New York, 1919, 237 pp. Gesture language of the Cheyenne Indians, augmented to 1,725 signs.

UPDIKE, DANIEL B.: *Printing Types,* Harvard University Press, Cambridge, Mass., 1922, vol. 1, pp. 125–32. On the Aldine italic.

ZEH, LILLIAN E.: "Indian Shortland Writers of British Columbia," *Pacific Monthly,* December, 1906, pp. 692–96.

HOT STAKE OR COLD CHOP

ANDREWS, WILLIAM: *Old-Time Punishments,* Hull, 1890, pp. 90–104.

D'ISRAELI, ISAAC: *Calamities of Authors,* London, 1812. Two erudite but fascinating volumes by the father of literary anecdotes and of Benjamin Disraeli; see also *Curiosities of Literature* and Mitchell, *infra.*

——: *Curiosities of Literature* (collected edition), London, 1866, 3 vols.

DITCHFIELD, P. H.: *Books Fatal to Their Authors,* London, 1903, 244 pp. A precise chronicle of the dismal rewards of authorship.

KLOTZIUS, JOH. CHRIST: *De Libris Auctoribus suis Fatalibus liber singularis,* Lipsiae, 1761. Lives of one hundred forgotten authors whose books were responsible for their persecution or ostracism in an age of strangled opinion.

MITCHELL, EDWIN VALENTINE: *Curiosities* (selected and edited one-volume edition), New York, 1932. Chapters on imprisonment of the learned, and condemned poets.

VICKERS, ROBERT H.: *Martyrdoms of Literature*, Chicago, [1891], 451 pp. A little-known but learned work, anti-Catholic in bias, and ranging from China to Chili through the ages in narrating the destruction of literature and persecution of authors.

SIGHTLESS AUTHORS OF INNER VISION

BIRD, JOHN: *Essay on the Life, Character, and Writings of Blind James Wilson*, London, 1856, 300 pp.

BROWN, ELEANOR GERTRUDE: *Milton's Blindness*, Columbia University Press, New York, 1934, 167 pp. The author, herself blind, probes the influence of blindness on Milton.

FRENCH, RICHARD S.: *From Homer to Helen Keller*, New York, 1932, 298 pp., with bibliography, pp. 287–94. Pertinent on blind authors, pp. 64–74.

KLENZ, HEINRICH: *Zeitschrift für Bücherfreunde*, 1917, n.s., vol. 9, pp. 121–24. Concerns sightless authors from ancient days to close of the seventeenth century not covered in other accessible sources.

MANNIX, JOHN B.: *Heroes of Darkness*, London, 1911, 322 pp. An excellent work on eleven noted figures from John Milton to Helen Keller.

Perkins Institution Special Reference Library of Books Relating to the Blind. Pt. 1, compiled by Michael Anagnos, Boston, 1907, 192 pp.; First Supplement to pt. 1, compiled by Edward E. Allen, Boston (1916), 128 pp.; Special Reference Supplement 3 (1944), prepared by Mary E. Sawyer. In pt. 1: "Books by Blind Authors," pp. 40–72, "Blind in Literature," pp. 73–89; in Supplement, "Books by Blind Authors," pp. 27–39, "Blind in Literature," pp. 40–62; in Special Reference Supplement, pp. 26–63.

WILSON, JAMES: *Biography of the Blind: Poets, Philosophers, Artists, etc.*, Birmingham, 1820. Augmented in editions of 1833 and 1835, including an autobiography of the author.

ASTRAL AUTHORSHIP AND AUTOMATIC WRITING

AUSTIN, MARY: "Automatism in Writing," *Unpartisan Review*, New York, vol. 14 (1920), pp. 336–47. A lucid analysis of the psychism of Mrs. Pearl Curran and her "spirit communicant, Patience Worth."

BAYLEY, HAROLD: *The Undiscovered Country*, London, 1918, 270 pp. An
anthology of automatic writings, selected from published and unpublished
sources, with an Introduction by Sir Arthur Conan Doyle.

BIRD, JAMES M.: *"Margery," the Medium*, Boston, 1925, 518 pp.

BOND, FREDERICK BLIGH: *The Gate of Remembrance*, London, 1918, New York,
1934, 215 pp. Automatic psychic guidance as an aid in archæology.

BUTT, G. BASEDEN: *Occult Review*, London, vol. 41 (1925), pp. 92–99.
Concerning the strange career of Andrew Jackson Davis, American
clairvoyant.

DAVIS, ANDREW JACKSON: *Starnos: Quotations from the Inspired Writings of*,
Boston, 1891, 210 pp. Selected and edited by Della E. Davis.

————: *The Magic Staff: An Autobiography*, New York, 1857, 552 pp.; eighth
edition, Boston, 1867.

HAINES, HELEN E.: "Philosophy," *The Bookman*, New York, March, 1928,
pp. 43–47. On the "amazing flock of books of psychic vagary"; a succinct
and skeptical survey.

LOVI, HENRIETTA: *Best Books on Spirit Phenomena, 1847–1925*, Boston, 1925,
94 pp. Contains readable chapter on "Automatic Writings, Spirit Letters,
Planchette and Oiuja Board Messages," pp. 45–57.

MONTEITH, MARY E.: *The Nineteenth Century and After*, New York, vol. 83
(1918), pp. 779–89. A self-analysis of a medium.

MOORE, JAMES LOWELL: *Introduction to the Writings of Andrew Jackson Davis*,
Boston, 1930, 190 pp.

PRINCE, WALTER FRANKLIN: *The Case of Patience Worth*, Boston, 1927, 509 pp.
Extracts of the works of "Patience Worth," through the mediumship of
Mrs. Pearl Curran, with attempted explanation by Dr. Prince, of the Boston
Society for Psychic Research; reprints of Mrs. Curran's own interpretation
of her automatism, and comments of others, including Charles E. Cory's
analysis of this mediumship, from *The Psychological Review*, 1919,
pp. 397–407.

RICHET, CHARLES: "Xénoglossie: l'Ecriture automatique en Langues Etrangères,"
Proceedings of the Society for Psychical Research, Glasgow, 1907, pp. 195–
266; see also vol. 20, pp. 1–432; vol. 21, pp. 166–391. Includes discussion
by Sir Oliver Lodge and others.

SINEL, JOSEPH: *The Sixth Sense*, London, 1927, 180 pp. Contends that the pineal body in the brain of higher animals is the active agent in clairvoyance and telepathy.

SMITH, HESTER TRAVERS: *Voices from the Void: Six Years' Experience in Automatic Communications*, New York, 1919, 164 pp. By the eldest daughter of Professor Edward Dowden, with Introduction by Sir William F. Barrett.

TAYLOR, SARAH E. L.: *Fox-Taylor Automatic Writing, 1869–1892*, Minneapolis, 1932, 400 pp. Record and text of mirror-writing of Katie Fox.

TRETHEWY, A. W.: *The "Controls" of Stainton Moses*, London, 1923, 292 pp. On automatic writing in unknown characters, and communications from forty-nine spirits, ranging from Plato to Swedenborg.

AN ALCOVE FOR ALIENISTS

BLUMENTHAL, WALTER HART: "An Alcove for Alienists," *The Colophon*, pt. X, New York, 1932.

CLARE, JOHN: *The Asylum Poems of John Clare, Including his Life*, London and Northampton, 1872.

DELEPIERRE, JOSEPH OCTAVE: "Démentiana," *Philobiblon Society Miscellanies*, London, vol. 8 (1862–1863), 42 pp. On unbalanced authors.

————: "Démentiana. Des Hallucinations dans la Republique des Lettres," *Philobiblon Society Miscellanies*, London, vol. 9 (1865–1866), 29 pp. Hallucinations and monomanias of literary men.

————: "Essai biographique sur l'histoire littéraire des fous," *Philobiblon Society Miscellanies*, London, vol. 4 (1857–1858), 135 pp. The fullest treatment of the subject by this author:

————: "Études Bio-bibliographiques sur les fous littéraires," *Philobiblon Society Miscellanies*, London, vol. 3 (1856–1857), 79 pp. Entirely on Bluet d'Arbères.

DE MORGAN, AUGUSTUS: *A Budget of Paradoxes*, London, 1872, 500 pp.; revised edition (2 vols.), London and Chicago, 1915, Chicago, 1953.

LANGE-EICHBAUM, WILHELM: *The Problem of Genius*, New York, 1932, 187 pp.

MACDONALD, ARTHUR: *Eccentric Literature*, reprinted from *The Monist*, July, 1911, 12 pp.

MARQUAND, JOHN PHILLIPS: *Lord Timothy Dexter of Newburyport, Mass.*, New York, 1925, 384 pp. A biography of an eighteenth-century eccentric who shocked conventional Newburyport by his vagaries.

NODIER, CHARLES: "Bibliographie de fous; de quelques livres excentriques," *Bulletin du Bibliophile*, nos. 21 and 23, Paris, 1835.

PEARSON, EDMUND L.: "Timothy Dexter and his 'Pickle for the Knowing Ones,'" *Bulletin of the New York Public Library*, 1922, 13 pp.; reprinted, with revisions, in his *Books in Black or Red*, New York, 1923, pp. 157–73.

————: *Queer Books*, New York, 1928. "Crotchets," pp. 145–62, is apparently the same as his article on "Crank Literature" in *The Bookman*, November, 1928, pp. 300–304.

PHILOMNESTE, JUNIOR (GUSTAVE BRUNET): *Les Fous Littéraires. Essai bibliographique sur la littérature excentrique, les illuminés, visionnaires, etc.*, Brussels, 1880, 227 pp.; limited to 500 numbered copies. Alphabetical list of some one hundred odd authors and their odder works, mostly exhibiting religious psychosis.

ROTH, CECIL: *Nephew of the Almighty*, London, 1933, 110 pp. A life of Richard Brothers.

TIMBS, JOHN: *English Eccentrics and Eccentricities*, London, 1875, pp. 417–524, and particularly pp. 508–13.

WINTERICH, JOHN T.: "Life and Works of Bloodgood Haviland Cutter," *The Colophon*, 1930, pt. 2.

CHRONICLE OF FRUSTRATIONS

CORNS, A. R., and SPARKE, ARCHIBALD: *A Bibliography of Unfinished Books in the English Language, with Annotations*, London, 1915, 255 pp.; 2,500 citations with an Introduction; 300 copies privately printed.

MILNE, J.: *Some Unfinished English Novels, Pages in Waiting*, New York, 1927, pp. 79–89.

NICOLL, W. ROBERTSON: *The Problem of Edwin Drood: A Study in the Methods of Dickens*, London, 1912, 212 pp; includes a bibliography by B. W. Matz (pp. 203–209) comprising 98 items.

SPARKE, ARCHIBALD: *Manchester Quarterly*, vol. 35 (1916), pp. 49–56; reprinted, *British Library Association Record*, vol. 18 (1916), pp. 150–56. Originally the Introduction to his privately printed volume in collaboration with A. R. Corns, *supra*.

SQUIRE, J. C.: *Great Unfinished, in Life and Letters*, London, 1921, pp. 189–95.

STARRETT, VINCENT: *Books Alive,* New York, 1940, pp. 228–43.

WALBRIDGE, EARLE F.: "Unfinished Novels in English Literature," *Publishers' Weekly,* August 1, 1925; "Unfinished Novels Here and Abroad," *ibid.,* June 22, 1929.

CHILDREN'S BOOKS

BLANCK, JACOB: *Peter Parley to Penrod,* New York, 1938, 153 pp.

BLUMENTHAL, WALTER HART: "A Forgotten Oddity in Children's Books," *The American Hebrew,* April 4, 1930, p. 750.

CLOUSTON, W. A.: *Hieroglyphic Bibles: Their Origin and History,* Glasgow, 1894, 316 pp.

HALSEY, ROSALIE V.: *Forgotten Books of the American Nursery,* Boston, 1911, 230 pp.

KIEFER, MONICA: *American Children through Their Books, 1700–1835,* Philadelphia, 1948, 248 pp.

McGUIRE, JAMES C.: "The Hornbook," *Bulletin of the New York Public Library,* 1927, 10 pp.

PLYMPTON, GEORGE A.: "The Hornbook in America," *American Antiquarian Society Proceedings,* n.s., vol. 26 (1916), pp. 264–72.

ROSENBACH, A. S. W.: *Early American Children's Books,* Portland, Me., 1933, 254 pp.

————: *Books and Bidders,* Boston, 1927, pp. 179–209.

STONE, WILBUR MACEY: *A Snuff-Boxful of Bibles,* Cartaret Book Club, Newark, N. J., 1926, 110 pp.

————: *The Thumb Bible of John Taylor,* Brookline, 1928, 79 pp., privately printed.

TUER, ANDREW: *History of the Hornbook,* London, 1896, 2 vols.

WEISS, HARRY B.: *American Chapbooks,* Trenton, 1938, 32 pp., privately printed. *Bulletin of the New York Public Library,* vol. 49 (1945), pp. 491–98, 587–96.

THE BOUQUET OF OLD BOOKS

Books in this category appear never to have elicited more than casual allusion.

BLUMENTHAL, WALTER HART: "Bouquet of Old Books," *The Colophon,* New York, vol. 2 (1937), n.s., no. 4, pp. 594–601.

GRUEL, LÉON: *Reliures en vernis sans odeur,* Paris, 1900, 12 pp.; offprint from the *Bullein du Bibliophile,* 100 copies.

CATALOGITIS—COLLECTOR'S MALADY

ALLINGHAM, E. G.: *A Romance of the Rostrum,* with a preface by Lord Rothschild, London, 1924. On British sales during the last century.

ARNOLD, WILLIAM HARRIS: *First Report of A Book-Collector,* New York, 1898, 148 pp.

BRIGHAM, CLARENCE S.: "History of Book Auctions in America," *Bulletin of the New York Public Library,* February, 1935. Introductory essay.

COWTAN, ROBERT: *Memories of the British Museum,* London, 1872, pp. 275–302.

LAWLER, JOHN: *Book Auctions in England in the Seventeenth Century (1676–1700),* London, 1898, 241 pp.

NEWTON, A. EDWARD: *This Book-Collecting Game,* Boston, 1928, pp. 175–206.

POLLARD, ALFRED W.: "English Book Sales," *Bibliographica,* London, 1895–1896; vol. 1, pp. 373–84; vol. 2, pp. 112–26. On sales from 1676 to 1686.

ROSENBACH, A. S. W.: *Books and Bidders,* Boston, 1927, pp. 68–97.

SLATER, J. H.: *How to Collect Books,* London, 1905, pp. 166–79.

TURNBULL, J. M.: "The Romance of Old Catalogues," *Bookman's Journal,* London, vol. 3 (1921), p. 352.